Israel, Rapture, Tribulation

How to Sort Biblical Fact from Theological Fiction

Michael Earl Riemer

authorHOUSE®

AuthorHouse™
1663 Liberty Drive
Bloomington, IN 47403
www.authorhouse.com
Phone: 833-262-8899

Permission is hereby granted to any church, mission, magazine, newsletter, book, or periodical to reprint or quote from any portion of this book on condition the passage is quoted in context; and due acknowledgment of source be given. Any portion of this book may be freely distributed, if it is without charge or obligation. The only requirement and qualification for the above permission is the name of the author and his email address must be given, and all references from the quoted portion (s) must be stated in full.

Published by AuthorHouse 05/21/2021

ISBN: 978-1-6655-2551-0 (sc)
ISBN: 978-1-6655-2549-7 (hc)
ISBN: 978-1-6655-2550-3 (e)

Library of Congress Control Number: 2021909696

Print information available on the last page.

Any people depicted in stock imagery provided by Getty Images are models, and such images are being used for illustrative purposes only. Certain stock imagery © Getty Images.

This book is printed on acid-free paper.

Unless otherwise indicated, Bible quotations are taken from the King James Version.

"For yet a little while, and he that shall come
will come, and will not tarry."

Hebrews 10:37

CONTENTS

ACKNOWLEDGMENTS

The original book could not have been written without the help of some very special people. Jeff Searing from Wisconsin spent much time reading the manuscript and provided needed suggestions and corrections. Geri Kiltinen, Michael Dosie, and others helped with proofreading and corrections. A special thanks to author and evangelist Ralph Woodrow who read the original manuscript and offered good suggestions for improving the content. A special thank you to English Professor Peter J. Fraser who did most of the editing of the original manuscript.

This revision could not have been completed without assistance. Bill Dougherty, J. Michael Collins, and others proofread. I would like to extend my special gratitude to Journalist Alex Alexander from the UK for his much-needed help in the revision of this manuscript. Bruce Zatkow was a deeply appreciated and much-needed help with the editing, structuring, and preparation of the manuscript.

I offer my gratitude to "sharp as a tack" researcher Michelle Smallback, who reviewed the manuscript and made important contributions in the form of pertinent questions, needed corrections, observations, and sound suggestions.

I would like to thank author, reformer, and missionary Bojidar Marinov for permission to use his well-written article, "A Tale of Two Eschatologies." I would also like to extend my appreciation to Frontline Ministries and missionary, reformer, and author Dr. Peter Hammond, for allowing me to reprint his inspiring article, "What Difference Can One Person Make?"

In addition, I would like to thank John Noē from the Prophecy Reformation Institute and Edward E. Stevens from the International Preterist Association for permission to use their well-stated "9.5 Theses for the Next Reformation," and their timeline at the beginning of Chapter 6.

FOREWORD TO FIRST EDITION

In his provocative new book, Michael Riemer uncovers the contradictions of dispensational "end times" theology. Riemer argues that the false emphases that Dispensationalists have placed on the "imminent second coming" and the "Rapture" have led many Christians to a life of unfruitful speculation, rather than service and love. Instead of finding new ways to spread the Gospel and to bring blessings to the world, Dispensationalists have inclined Christians toward a bunker mentality— live separately and wait to be spirited away.

In plain and engaging language Riemer traces many of the excesses of the Dispensationalists, including their wildly contradictory dating of the end of the world and their wrenching of the context of Daniel's Seventy Weeks. Riemer also provides an insightful discussion of Jesus's Olivet Discourse, in which he argues convincingly that the original listeners and the First-century Church would have understood Jesus's words of warning in the context of the destruction of Jerusalem by the Romans in AD 70, not some tribulation to occur two thousand years later.

All in all, Riemer chastens many modern American Christians for the arrogance that has led to the notion that we are the special ones, the ones privy to the secret knowledge of the latter dispensation. He calls for humility and a return to the great theological traditions of the Church that have been passed down through the centuries.

Professor Peter J. Fraser
January 2002

PREFACE TO FIRST EDITION

If preaching the imminent coming of the Lord brings people to Christ, wouldn't it be a worthy doctrine? In 2001 I received literature from Grason Home Video, a ministry of the Billy Graham Evangelistic Association, about the book series *Left Behind* (over 20 million copies sold). They state "Tens of thousands have come to Christ. And hundreds of thousands have had their faith challenged and strengthened by these spellbinding stories of the last days." I wonder where these "tens of thousands" of new converts are today. Some people may have come to trust the Lord through these books, but it has also given them a large dose of error—the false hope of soon being taken off the earth via the "Rapture." Like poison, however, the smallest portion is enough to corrupt. Who knows what damage these books have done to God's kingdom and the souls Christ died for?

The 2014 movie *Left Behind*, based on the book series of the same name, may have impressed some people with the possibility of millions of humans suddenly vanishing worldwide. But it will be the same as it was after Edgar C. Whisenant Jr. published his two-part book, *88 Reasons Why The Rapture Will Be In 1988–On Borrowed Time.* For a while, there was considerable excitement in the air because 300,000 copies were mailed free of charge to ministers across America, while 4.5 million copies were sold in bookstores and elsewhere. Once all the excitement had died down, many of the faithful stopped going to church when they realized they were sorely deceived: Jesus's coming was not quite as "soon" as they had been led to believe.

In the short term it seemed a wonderful thing had happened, many souls entered the kingdom of God. But the long-term effect would prove devastating. How many are now cynical of the Church and all the hype surrounding Jesus's supposed return? Fostering and spreading such a seminal lie is not good doctrine. The end does not justify the means. Much of the world mocks Christians already. Why give the naysayers yet more ammunition?

We need to use truth to draw people to the Lord, not gimmicks. The end times books by LaHaye and Jenkins may be spellbinding stories, but they are just fictional accounts of events that will never happen, which misrepresent Scripture, and which in no way portray *"the faith which was once delivered unto the saints"* (Jude 3). A well-written book of fiction presented as fact can be very harmful to the unwary.

This book is not meant to downplay all the good the preachers and teachers I take issue with may have done. Some of these men have wonderful ministries which have helped thousands of people. However, their teachings on the "last days" have caused, and continue to cause, considerable harm for the advancement of the kingdom of Christ. I pray that when they read this book, they will liken it to a discourse from Apollos, who was *"fervent in the spirit,"* and listened to and believed Aquila and Priscilla when they *"expounded unto him the way of God more perfectly"* (Acts 18:26).

Michael Earl Riemer
January 2002

PREFACE TO FIRST REVISION

The first thing the reader will notice is the book's new title, *Israel, Rapture, Tribulation: How to Sort Biblical Fact from Theological Fiction*. It was formerly named, *It Was at Hand: A Biblical Response to Dispensationalism*. The new title better reflects the context and theme of the book.

There has been a slight overhaul of the text. The language has been updated, and there are some minor corrections in spelling, grammar, and punctuation. I have added much text to Chapters 4, 7, and 8, with some bits and pieces spliced here and there into the other chapters.

Three new chapters (numbers 10, 11, and 12) and an epilogue have been added. The original appendix has been updated; one new illustration, three new articles, and information about the author have been added.

Articles by missionaries and reformers Dr. Peter Hammond and Bojidar Marinov (Appendices C and D) articulate so well some main points and arguments I have tried so hard to relate. Both scholars understand firsthand the power a positive eschatology* can have on the work of the kingdom. Their articles illustrate in profound and insightful ways how our beliefs and thoughts influence our actions. Thus, without total belief and impassioned commitment, we will never achieve our objectives.

Dr. Hammond's account of William Carey's missionary exploits—with its trials, temptations, heartaches, never-ending series of obstacles, opposition, and failures—clearly demonstrates Carey's victorious eschatology. William Carey was building a sure foundation that would buttress future generations of Christians, whom he believed would come

---

* "A theological term used to designate the doctrine of last things, particularly those dealing with the second coming of Christ and the events preceding and following this great event." Unger's Bible Dictionary

after him and continue the cultural reforms he started. Carey envisioned a Christian nation, a "City set on a Hill"—a civilization built upon God's Law, where evil could not gain a foothold. He began to transform the fabric of the nation of India into a disciple of Jesus, just as our Lord told His disciples to do (Matt. 28:19).

The "9.5 Theses for the Next Reformation" by Dr. John Noē of the Prophecy Reformation Institute has been appended to this revision. It represents a clear call to the Church of Christ and is in perfect harmony with the theme and premise of this book.

Someone has said after reading my book that it was "dripping with sarcasm." That is a harsh statement. There may be some instances of irony to reinforce a point, but I intend no malice. While my writing at times may seem somewhat caustic, I consider my prose to be a form of "tough love" when responding to views with which I disagree. I hope the love of God is primarily seen throughout my work.

I wrote this book out of concern for my family, my friends, my country, and those who will be born in the coming years. Those who come after us, our children and grandchildren, will have to live with the consequences of the mistakes we have made. Our misjudgments, misguided efforts, and failings may come back to haunt our progeny.

Do our actions and our work for the kingdom of God harm or advance the kingdom? Did William Carey's belief in postmillennialism harm or help the kingdom? Did his belief produce good fruit or rotten fruit? Does your belief in end-time events promote victorious living? Would a victorious faith produce hope for the future? In comparing the results of your beliefs with the results of the historic Church of Jesus Christ, you may not like what you find. May this book help you evaluate and strengthen your faith.

Michael Earl Riemer
San Francisco,
Agusan Del Sur, Philippines
April 7, 2021

ABOUT THE AUTHOR

Michael Earl Riemer is a skilled machinist, home Bible study teacher, Sunday School teacher, and author. Born and raised in Milwaukee, Wisconsin, he now makes his home in the Philippines, on its southern-most island, Mindanao. He resides there with his wife and son.

He enjoys writing and has authored gospel tracts and articles on various subjects and issues. He has written several books, including *The Path Life Takes*, a collection of poems and short stories. His book *Reindeer Don't Fly, Exploring the Evidence-Lacking Realm of Evolutionary Philosophy* is filled with scientific and logical reasons why the belief in evolution is ill-conceived; and *It Was at Hand, A Biblical Response to Dispensationalism*, explores the monumental importance of eschatology.

He is fascinated by nature and the wonders of creation. For much of his life, he has enjoyed reading about those subjects in books and magazines. However, after reading the Creation story in Genesis and the encapsulated history of the earth it presents, and contrasting it against the backdrop of billions of years of evolutionary history demanded by evolutionists and many other so-called scientists, the author began to perceive that hotly contested subject with greater clarity. Realizing that evolution is a thinly disguised religion hiding behind the veil of science, he has crafted numerous articles that unmask and expose this dangerous and destructive belief system.

The author is also very concerned about God's Kingdom, our Father's World. He beautifies His Kingdom by picking up trash, pulling out weeds, and planting bushes and flowers. He teaches those who attend his speaking engagements and Sunday school classes to take dominion over each square inch of ground their feet tread upon, for God is interested in everything—each and every activity done under the sun on His planet, throughout every culture and nation.

CHAPTER ONE

DISPENSATIONS: WHAT ARE THEY?

―⟨∞⟩―

ISSUES COVERED

There is a mountain of Scriptural evidence supporting the views this book advocates. But unless you, the reader, are able to entertain the idea that your end times doctrine may be wrong, your eyes will be closed tightly to the truth. Sometimes, a paradigm shift is needed in our thinking. If that does not happen, we may reinterpret, misconstrue, or even wrest the Scriptures to the preconceived beliefs many bring to the Bible, instead of using Scripture to interpret Scripture. Those unwilling to rethink and reanalyze the Scriptural issues that deal with modern Dispensational doctrine and its interpretation of the *end times* and *last days* need not read any further.

This book advocates the preterist view of the Scriptures, although its author does not hold to every finite nuance of that view. Futurists believe most end-time prophecies (especially the major ones) are yet to be fulfilled. Preterists believe all Bible prophecy has already been fulfilled in Christ and continues through the ongoing expansion of His Church. Most Futurists do not believe Christ has been successful in fully establishing His kingdom.[1] All Dispensationalists are Futurists.

Even though my view of future and past events from a Biblical perspective differs vastly from a Dispensational believer, neither I nor the millions of Christians who hold to the preterist view, am the enemy. *"Am I therefore become your enemy, because I tell you the truth"* (Gal. 4:16)? We

1

have ever been fellow brothers to all who trust in Jesus. Yet many pastors refuse to even consider the preterist view, adamantly ignoring the Bible's admonition: *"He that answereth a matter before he heareth it, it is folly and shame unto him"* (Prov. 18:13). Many sincere believers have been ostracized, excommunicated, and given the "left boot of disfellowship" from various churches for holding to and teaching the preterist view. Nevertheless, we share with Dispensationalists some of the same goals: spreading the Gospel of Jesus, teaching the love of God, sharing the good news of Jesus's death, burial, and resurrection; and advancing the kingdom of Christ through the power of the Holy Spirit.

For many years I taught home Bible studies. As I continued to teach and study God's Word, I noticed there was a discrepancy between the teacher's manual I was using and what the Word of God taught. The error became glaringly obvious. I had no desire to go against the flow of the doctrines of the Church I attended; but a long time ago, I had determined to walk in the truth, no matter where it led. As Emerson said, "The greatest homage we can pay to truth is to use it. This has been one of mankind's greatest failings because so much truth goes unused and unwanted. When truth comes marching by, too many let it march on without falling into step and following truth to its heaven-crowned destination." Stopfard A. Brooke reinforced this point when he said: "If a thousand old beliefs were ruined in our march to truth, we must still march on."[2] As I continued to study and ponder the Scriptures, I decided to put down on paper what I believe the Bible teaches about the end times, last days, and the Dispensational doctrine.

This book is not a scathing attack on Christians who hold to and teach Dispensationalism. It is not meant to demonize or denounce their beliefs as heresy. Nor is it a personal assault on the integrity or the character of the many pastors who would disagree with me. If I condemn them, I also have to chastise myself because I taught home Bible studies for years using the Dispensational framework. A false teacher, which is what I was when I taught Dispensational doctrine, does not even know the error he is teaching. Thus, it is unfortunately easy and common to teach false doctrine, for it is not obvious. They say there is nothing worse than a reformed smoker, who points out all the faults of those who still indulge. My goal is to encourage a deeper understanding of the Scriptures.

The teachings in this book result from many years of Bible study. Some of these teachings may seem strange to many contemporary Christians, but what is written here is as "old as the hills," and has been believed and taught by many men of God for generations. I just ask you to hear me out—you will be glad you did.

Among the important issues we will deal with are these:

1. It is a deceptive and spurious doctrine that teaches we will be raptured off the earth prior to a great tribulation.
2. The Dispensational doctrine distorts Bible verbiage and changes the meaning of Scripture.
3. The Seventieth Week of Daniel is not a future event, as it has already occurred.
4. The kingdom of God is a present reality.
5. The Olivet Discourse in Matthew 24 has been fulfilled.
6. The pessimistic outlook Dispensationalists have for the future is *not* based on Scripture. Christ's Church will overcome the world.
7. The Book of Revelation was written before AD 68.
8. Any so-called "signs of the times" after AD 70 do not, and will never again have anything to do with a second coming of Jesus.
9. We are not living in the last days or end times, for the last days took place over nineteen hundred years ago.
10. The "Great Tribulation" was a past historical event.
11. The Bible never mentions a period of seven years for any tribulation.
12. The so-called "Antichrist" spoken of by many Christians is not found in Scripture.
13. The Jews are not God's people so long as they reject Jesus. When they are converted and become Christians, they then become part of the Church, the Bride of Christ.

OVERVIEW OF DISPENSATIONS

Since this book deals with the Dispensational concept of the end times, an overview is in order. Charles C. Ryrie is probably the leading

Dispensational theologian of our time. He defines Dispensationalism in the following manner:

> Premillennialists [sc., Dispensationalists] believe theirs is the historic faith of the Church. Holding to a literal interpretation of the Scripture, they believe the promises made to Abraham and David are unconditional and have had, or will have, a literal fulfillment. In no sense have these promises made to Israel been abrogated or fulfilled by the Church, which is a distinct body in this age having promises and a destiny different from Israel's. At the close of this age, premillennialists believe Christ will return for His Church, meeting Her in the air (this is not the Second Coming of Christ), which event, called the rapture or translation, will usher in a seven-year period of tribulation on the earth. After this, the Lord will return to the earth (this is the Second Coming of Christ) to establish His Kingdom on the earth for a thousand years, during which time the promise to Israel will be fulfilled.[3]

The Dispensational view teaches there are seven dispensations: Innocence, Conscience, Human Government, Promise, Law, Grace, and the Millennial Kingdom of Christ. Each dispensation is a period of Biblical history. We are now supposedly living at the very end of the sixth dispensation of time, just before the Rapture and the second coming of Jesus.

Some teach that no signs will occur before the Rapture. John F. MacArthur declares, "there are no signs whatsoever that will precede the Rapture."[4] Others teach that signs will appear when the battle of Armageddon is about to happen. This battle is set to take place after the Church is raptured; thus, if we see signs of the battle, we will know that the Rapture is near. Other factions point to signs such as earthquakes, famines, pestilences, and wars, which mean Jesus is coming soon. W. Herschel Ford, writing in *Decision Magazine* declares: "But there are signs that point toward that great day ... Ye shall hear of wars and rumors of wars ... famines, and pestilences ..."[5] The regathering of the Jews to Israel is seen as yet another sign of the end of the Church age. Thomas Ice, the executive director of the Pre-Trib Research Center in Washington, D.C.

and a staunch Dispensationalist, recently stated, "... and the fact that ethnic Israel has been re-established as a nation and now controls Jerusalem is a strong indicator that we are near the end of the church 'age'."[6]

After the Rapture, when Jesus takes us (the saints, His Church) to heaven and the Marriage Supper of the Lamb, the world will go through the tribulation, lasting three and one-half or seven years. During the tribulation, the Antichrist and the Beast will be revealed and will persecute the Jews. Then, at the end of the tribulation, following whatever amount of time Dispensationalists think it will be, Jesus comes back again (for the third time, with his saints) in what is called the Revelation, or the Second Coming. He will then set up his kingdom and be physically present to rule the world "with a rod of iron" via the Church, from Jerusalem, for a thousand years (the Millennium). After the thousand years, Satan will be loosed from his prison (he was bound before the Millennium) and cause all the nations to rebel. (Even when Christ was physically present and ruling, He still failed to conquer most men's hearts, as this view implies.) The rebellious nations will then be wiped out by God with fire from heaven, enabling the New Heavens and New Earth to come into existence.

Of course, many differ on the details of the tribulation and other Biblical prophecies. A few years ago, I attended a prophecy conference where each preacher gave his view of the tribulation. One preacher thought it would last seven years. The next believed three and one-half years. One taught 14 years, and another averred the tribulation period would continue for 21 years. Therefore, I can only give you a general overview—at least until all the "experts" agree.

One minister of the Gospel said something recently I believe everyone should adhere to with all their heart. He said, "If the Bible does not teach it, we do not preach it." As this book will show, there are some doctrines ministers preach the Bible does not teach. I pray, after they read this book, they may rethink their sermons.

Please understand, what we present here is not new. It is not something I came up with through a vision after eating too much pizza, or from a small voice that came down in the wee hours of the morning. It is based on solid logic, hermeneutics, and exegesis of Scripture. The *International Standard Bible Encyclopedia* captures the significance of studying and correctly interpreting Scripture: "The moment the Bible student has in his own mind what was in the mind of the author or authors of the Bib. books when these were written, he has interpreted the thought of the Scriptures."[7] This is what every student of the Scripture should strive to do.

BELIEF CAN PRODUCE AMAZING RESULTS

Your view of the end times will necessarily affect how you plan for the future. If you believe the world as you know it is crumbling and will fall apart soon, you will be short-sighted in your thinking. However, if you see hope for a better future, if you believe you can (with the help of God) change the world for the better, you will act accordingly.

Belief can produce amazing results. Belief is the idea, the persuasion, the conviction, faith, trust, and confidence in yourself, your ideas, or in God. Belief is a six-letter word causing people to excel and do the impossible. Belief in an idea drove the pilgrims and pioneers to cross oceans, plains, and mountains, to battle countless foes, to build, to plant, to love the unlovable. Belief has built hospitals, orphanages, schools, and colleges. However, throughout history, misguided belief has also caused mass destruction and the deaths of millions and millions of people. Belief can lead you to succeed or fail, give you drive, or leave you apathetic.

There is always a link between belief and action. This is true in the sports world, the business world, and the realm of the Church. Belief in your goal is the primary ingredient that will allow you to attain it. Every athlete who has ever won a gold medal believed he could win or had someone who believed in him, and that belief eventually found its way through the mind and heart to the body. Everyone who has ever accomplished anything in this world believed they could succeed. The person who sets their mind on a goal will either achieve it or die trying.

Shawn Johnson was a 20-year-old Olympic star who took home gold and silver medals in the 2008 Beijing Games. In a brief article about her life, the author states:

> U.S. gymnast Shawn Johnson is once again going for gold. And just like her previous attempts to achieve success in her sport, she knows that win or lose, there is one person who will always be cheering her on: her mom.

In the Yahoo! original video series, "Raising an Olympian," Johnson talks about how her mom, Teri, provided her with constant motivation in her pursuit of a gold medal. "My mom taught me from when I was little that you have to have a balance in life. If there's something that you're dedicated to, that you have to enjoy it …"[8]

Her secret to success is this simple: no motivation, no belief = no gold medal.

The immutable belief in Darwinian evolution by anthropologists and others in the scientific community put Ota Benga in a monkey cage with an orangutan at the Bronx Zoo. Ota was a pygmy from the Belgian Congo. He was born in 1883 in central Africa. He had been married twice. His first wife and two children were murdered in a campaign of terror by the Belgian government against the "evolutionarily inferior natives." His second spouse died from a poisonous snakebite. Ota was later captured and sold into slavery.

Noted African explorer Samuel Verner was in Africa looking for several pygmies to display at the Louisiana Purchase Exposition when he spotted Ota at a village slave market. Verner purchased Ota, and eventually, Ota was presented by Verner to the Bronx Zoo director, William Hornaday. Shortly afterward, Ota ended up in the cage with an orangutan named Dohong. This grotesque display of the "missing link" was so successful that 40,000 visitors swarmed the New York Zoological Park on September 16, 1906, to see "Ota Benga the Pygmy." Because the crowds were so enormous, they assigned a police officer to guard Ota full time. Although many black ministers protested, the atrocity went on.

"The spectacle of a black man in a cage gave a *Times* reporter the springboard for a story that worked up a storm of protest among Negro ministers in the city. They made their indignation known to Mayor George B. McClellan, but he refused to take action."[9]

Why should Mayor McClellan have acted any differently, when he, along with many in the scientific community, believed people evolved from apes? The belief in evolution was growing, and many newspaper stories were being written with titles like *"Pygmies of the Congo"*:

The earliest type of humanity which entered the Dark Continent, and these too, urged on by the pressure of superior tribes, were gradually forced into the great forests. The human type, in all probability, first emerged from the ape in south-eastern Asia, possibly in India. The higher types forced the Negro from the continent in an eastward direction, across the intervening islands, as far as Australia, and westward into Africa. Even today, ape-like Negroes are found in the gloomy forests, who are doubtless direct descendants of these early types of man, who probably closely resembled their simian ancestors ...

They are often dirty-yellowish brown in color and covered with a fine down. Their faces are fairly hairy, with great prognathism, and retreating chins, while in general they are unintelligent and timid, having little tribal cohesion and usually living upon the fringes of higher tribes, among the latter, individual types of the lower order crop out now and then, indicating that the two were, to certain extent merged in past ages.[10]

Mayor McClellan et al. simply acted on their belief that Ota was a "missing link," and not really human. There is much more to this story. For a more complete history see the book *One Blood,* written by Ken Ham. But just imagine how this poison added fuel to the fire for those racists who read and believed what was written.

The belief in evolution also provided a rationale for the wholesale slaughter of thousands of Australia's Aboriginal people. Countless graves were plundered so the bones of these victims could be sent to museums. Some were even killed, skinned, and stuffed prior to exhibition. Pickled Aboriginal brains were in great demand. Mounted police in New South Wales murdered dozens of Aboriginal men, women, and children. They boiled down forty-five heads, saving the ten best skulls for overseas museums. Many children were taken from the "racially inferior Aborigines" and given to missions to lead a better life than was thought possible with their families. This separation policy continued until the 1960s. These systematic atrocities are well documented (again, read *One Blood*). Why did this happen? The reasons are found in just one word: *belief.*

Where was the Church when all this happened? Where was the Church in Germany when the blatantly evolutionary fascist doctrine formed the script to rid the world of the "unfit"? First went the genetically "inferior," the mentally and physically disabled, then the gypsies, Jews, Christians, and others. So where was the Church? It was rendered inert, as it still is today, by the false belief of evolution. Some Christians in Germany, like Dietrich Bonhoeffer, spoke out against Hitler and what was going on. However, to a large extent, the Church acquiesced to this deadly teaching.

In sharp contrast, because of his belief in God and love for the Lord, William Carey sailed to India as a missionary in 1793. He encountered so much hardship it is amazing he didn't abandon his mission and go home. But his belief and faith were strong, so he did not abandon his calling.

Carey was tormented by one horrific practice of the Indians known as "sati"—whereby widows were expected to burn themselves alive after their husbands died. If they refused to submit to this grotesque custom, they were forced to do so. Ten thousand women a year died this way. This sadistic ritual was practiced for many generations and was prevalent among Hindu communities and within aristocratic Sikh families. Sati is mentioned and defended in the Rig Veda 10.18.7 and Atharva Veda, two sacred texts in the Hindu tradition.

Carey would not rest until this practice was stopped. Largely because of his passionate belief, sati is a thing of the past. (See Appendix D for Dr. Peter Hammond's historical account of the life of William Carey.)

Viktor E. Frankl's book *Man's Search for Meaning*[11] is based on the years of unspeakable horror he endured in Nazi death camps. Frankl explains why belief and a reason for living are so important. He wrote as his premise, "The prisoner who had lost faith in the future—his future—was doomed."[12] He also shared deep insights into the human character rendered so vulnerable in the context of these brutal, primitive, and horrible death camps. As Frankl related, even in those hellish places some prisoners were able to develop a deep spiritual life. "They were able to retreat from their terrible surroundings to a life of inner riches and spiritual freedom. Only in this way can one explain the apparent paradox that some prisoners of a less hardy make-up often seemed to survive camp life better than did those of a robust nature."[13] Viktor Frankl witnessed how belief could make the difference between life and death.

Kenneth Gentry, in his book *He Shall Have Dominion*, quotes R. J.

Rushdoony on what effect a positive eschatology can have on Christian endeavor and life. "A study of hospital patients in relationship to their life expectancy reportedly concluded that there was a strong correlation between life expectancy and future-oriented thinking. A man whose mind looked ahead to activities a year hence was more likely to live than one whose thinking was only in terms of the daily hospital routine. Those without a future in mind had no future, as a rule."[14]

Through their awful trials, all these people learned the same lesson: having a positive outlook and believing there is a future here on earth, promotes a more productive and meaningful life.

Concerning the interpretation of Biblical prophecy, Iain Murray wrote: "The fact is that what we believe or do not believe upon this subject will have continual influence upon the way in which we live. The greatest spiritual endeavors and achievements in the past have been those energized by faith and hope."[15]

I could go on with examples of what belief did in Soviet Russia, about the communists' repression of the Russian people—arguably the greatest horror story in human history. Those who are interested in the brutality of the Soviet regime can read Aleksandr I. Solzhenitsyn's book *The Gulag Archipelago 1918–1956*.[16]

WHAT THE DISPENSATIONAL BELIEF HAS WROUGHT

Has *belief* in the pessimistic Dispensational view of the future made Christians ineffective in our culture? I believe it has. Dispensational teaching leads to the belief we do not have time to change the world. The Dispensational notion of an imminent departure holds that all we can do with the time left is to pull a few souls out of the fire before Jesus pulls His Church out of this world.

Tim LaHaye stated it well when he wrote:

Most knowledgeable Christians are looking for the Second Coming of Christ and the tribulation period that He predicted would come before the end of the age. Because present world conditions are so similar to those the Bible prophesies for the last days ... they conclude that a takeover of our culture by the forces of evil is inevitable; so they do nothing to resist it.

One Dispensationalist told me after reading Tim LaHaye's words, "This is where they are wrong. We are called to be faithful servants working until He comes, regardless of world conditions." I agreed wholeheartedly. However, when you teach a fatalistic future, you get people who believe and behave as Tim LaHaye stated. If you preach and teach faith, you will get people who have faith. If you preach and teach love, you will get people who have love. If you preach and teach Dispensationalism, you will get pessimistic and fatalistic people. And if you teach victory and hope for all Christians, victory and hope would prevail.

Gary North also writes about Dispensational belief and the paralyzing effect of the anticipated rapture that has permeated most fundamentalist Churches:

> For over 160 years, pastors and authors have been telling Bible-believing Christians that Jesus is coming soon to "rapture" His Church to heaven.
>
> This means that nothing a person can do to build a legacy on earth will survive the 3.5–year Great Tribulation period that will begin 3.5 years after the "secret" Rapture. This means that an investment in graduate school or any other long-term capital project is a very high-risk investment.
>
> Here is a major reason why modern fundamentalism has not built universities, medical schools, law schools, and all the other institutions that produce wealth and leadership in the modern world. This is why fundamentalist Christians have been sitting in the back of humanism's bus for over a hundred years. They believe that the Church's time on earth has just about run out. They are willing to make sacrifices only for projects that will pay off in the short term. They have been paralyzed by Rapture Fever.[18]

Many understand the Dispensational mindset very well. On the Quora forum, a question-and-answer site found on the internet (8/2019), was this question; Do you fear the events the Bible says will occur? Peter Wheeler answered this way:

> Not really. What I do fear, however, are the Evangelicals who are so convinced that we're nearing the "End Times" that they don't give a damn about protecting the planet, our environment, and resources for the future, since they don't see the need. Or, that they're so eager for the coming "End Times" that they seek to hasten the fulfillment of the "prophecies" in the hopes that they'll bring about the Second Coming, thus escalating conflicts and wars in the Middle East.
>
> I'd much prefer a world run by non-believers, since they're the ones eager to protect the planet for future generations.

SALVATION BELIEF

There are very few beliefs our salvation hinges upon. The thief on the cross alongside Jesus probably knew nothing about God creating the world in six literal days. He probably knew nothing about Jewish history or about the virgin birth of Jesus. What was important in his final moments was his repentance and confession of faith in Jesus as his Lord and Savior. This he learned right there at the cross, beholding the Lord suffer and die.

There are many doctrines that are fundamental to Christianity we must, however, learn as we grow in Christ. There are things we must do to complement our faith, "[A]*dd to your faith virtue; and to virtue knowledge ... temperance ... patience ... godliness ... brotherly kindness ... charity*" (II Peter 1:5–7).

It is important we not "major on minors" when dealing with the faith, but balance our teaching concerning the various doctrines that define our walk with the Lord. The belief in seven literal days of creation is vital. But let us suppose you believed the "days" in the first few chapters of the Book of Genesis are long periods of time and not literal days. What if you believed that, but also believed in the Lord Jesus as your Savior and were born again. Would you be damned? No, of course not! It is the same concerning the Dispensational (future) view versus the preterist (historical) view of the Scriptures. You are neither saved nor lost because you cleave to one particular eschatological stance versus another.

My thesis attempts to establish the notion of salvation, recognizing that the world with its billions of souls is at stake. Millions more innocent people may be lost to communists, evolutionists, and Islamists because of the defeatist, pessimistic, escapist belief of the Dispensationalists who lack a future vision of victory.

Let us compare the Dispensationalists' faith to the faith of a communist. The communists have a victorious faith that cannot be swayed; this is the reason for much of the success they have had in the last one hundred years. The communists believe, "They are the wave of the future. Their victory is as certain as the rising of the sun because the same material law that causes the sun to rise in the morning has ordained that they shall conquer and rule the world. Of this they have no vestige of doubt."[19]

Dispensationalists, however, are not for victory but escape. They want to escape this world and its evils with as many souls as possible. They know they cannot win, for the Antichrist is coming and he will put an end to all their plans. The Dispensationalist believes the rise and rule of the Antichrist is the wave of the future. His rule is as certain as the rising of the sun. On this topic, Dispensationalists are immovable.

The communists believe "... their convictions are undisturbed by any evidence to the contrary that may appear day by day ... The idea that their faith can be shattered by anything they see at present is naive to the point of imbalance."[19]

In contrast, the Dispensationalist looks at the world and its present condition and thinks the end is near. My former pastor "knows," along with most Dispensationalists, that the end is near because of "the present state of affairs"—whatever that means. By merely looking at the world, they have concluded we are running out of time. They are relying on sight, not faith. Even after a hundred years of failed predictions, forecasts, and prophecies, their faith remains the end is near. Communists do not look at world conditions. They rely on faith, not sight.

The Book of James says, "*A double minded man is unstable in all his ways*" (James 1:8). This applies to the Dispensationalist view of eschatology. They are double-minded, basing their belief we are living in the Last Days by what they see in the world around us. Meanwhile, the Bible proclaims victory (Dan. 2:44), despite whatever questionable evidence people choose to see.

The communist paradigm invariably looks to the future. "It is this future in which he is interested and in which he firmly believes. In the last analysis, he believes in the inevitable triumph of Communism not because of the evidence, but because of his faith in the dialectic. As a true believer, he has lived and labored during forty years of sacrifice, danger, and brutality."[19] The Dispensationalist does not believe in a future beyond the next ten or twenty years. He dares not, if he is consistent with his belief that we are running out of time. The Rapture could be less than ten or over twenty years away. This depends on who is telling the tale, but it is always "soon," "very soon," "very near," "could be any time"—imminent.

BELIEF EQUALS ACTIONS

The link between *belief* and action was vividly demonstrated on September 11, 2001, when hijacked jetliners plunged into the World Trade Center. Carl Wieland wrote an editorial for *Creation* magazine concerning this horrific event. It was entitled *THE POWER OF IDEAS—What you believe does matter.* He described the enormous force of the planes that plunged into and sliced through the concrete and steel of the towers in milliseconds. "Yet driving this atrocity was something far more potent— the ideas and beliefs of those who perpetrated it."[20] He also addressed the outcome of the evolution-fueled ideologies [beliefs] of Hitler and Marx— the murder of 100 million people. Remember: belief equals action. If there really are millions of Christians in this country, as polls indicate, why are thousands of babies being aborted each day? Why the rise and acceptance of homosexuality? Why all the senseless brutality and crime? Why does racism still abound? And why is the filth on TV still being shown and tolerated?

Author and researcher Dave MacPherson also writes concerning the correlation between belief and action:

> The pre-Trib Rapture view has caused the deaths of thousands
> of persons. Veteran missionary H. A. Baker shares his experiences
> of thirty-four years on the mission field in China in several of his

books, including *Through Tribulation, Tribulation to Glory, Visions Beyond the Veil, and God in Ka Do Land*. He graphically points out the link between beliefs and actions.

Baker and other post-trib missionaries warned many Chinese Christians that Antichrist would come before Christ returns. Many heeded the warning and, before the Communist takeover, fled to the mountains where they have been able to continue witnessing for many years.

On the other hand, many pre-trib missionaries assured believers they would be raptured away *before* any time of persecution and history tells us tens of thousands of Chinese Christians have been murdered since 1949! ... tens of thousands of Christians are now languishing in prisons in China and Russia and other Communist countries ...

Corrie ten Boom has also spoken of the Chinese Christians and their suffering: "The Christians were told that they didn't have to go through tribulation and we all know how it is in China." She added ... that those teaching "there will be no tribulation" and "the Christians will be able to escape all this" are really "the false teachers Jesus was warning us to expect in the latter day."[21]

For every action, there is a cause and effect. Although the belief in and teaching of Dispensations have not caused all the aforementioned horrors, I am fairly certain they have contributed to the world's thorniest problems. It seems the Christians living in the USA have settled out of the culture and sunk to the "bottom of the barrel." We Christians have ceased, to a large extent, to be what Christ said we should be: "the salt and light of this world." Instead of changing the world, we have allowed the world to change the Church. When the view of the future is wholly pessimistic, what kind of actions would one expect from such a narrow-minded belief?

As you read through this book, you will not find a discussion of every view, just two: the most important, dominant, and significant views of the last days and end times. One view of the future is pessimistic, which can only generate a feeling of despair. This is the Dispensational view. The only hope it provides is escape (the Rapture) from the world and its (seemingly) ever-growing troubles. The other, a view of the past, provides hope for the future. This is the traditional preterist view of eschatology, held by Christians for millennia.

The preterist believes the Olivet prophecy has been fulfilled. That the *parousia* (presence, arrival) Jesus talked about was intended as a spiritual coming to judge the Jews that rejected Him. This happened in AD 70 when the temple and city of Jerusalem were destroyed. The first Church believed Jesus would come to judge Israel in their generation. That is the reason the Christians fled Jerusalem before it was destroyed, and not one perished.

The preterist believes we can build a legacy and leave a godly inheritance for our children that will not be swallowed up by an Antichrist during the prescribed tribulation. The preterist believes we can do more in this generation than just snatch a few souls out of the fire before the supposed return of Jesus.

The kingdom of God was established when Christ rose from the dead, and Christ is now reigning and will continue to reign "*till he hath put all enemies under his feet*" (I Cor. 15:24–25; see also Eph. 1:20–23). Christ's kingdom will continue to grow and break in pieces all the kingdoms of this world until it fills the whole earth (Dan. 2:35, 44). Because the kingdom of God is a present reality, Christians can change the world's cultures and make all nations the disciples of the Lord (Matt. 28:19). Governments and every other entity that exalts itself against the knowledge of Christ can, and one day will be obedient to the Lord.

Much of the Church's teaching today about the soon-to-come "end" sounds like the nightly news—all gloom and doom. There is already enough despair of the future without the Church echoing the sentiments and fears of the rest of humanity. Christians down through the ages have faced lions, persecutions, torture, and death. Nevertheless, they persevered, won the victory, and changed the world.

If you believe what I have written here—what many before me have believed—your worldview will change and you will have new hope for the future. This book will show that Dispensational teaching is devoid of hope, and the Scripture is infused with the promise of a better world. What Viktor E. Frankl said bears repeating: "... it is hoped that an 'optimism' for our future may flow from the lesson learned from our 'tragic past."[22]

Today, it seems for many, the only hope for the future is for Jesus to rapture them out of this world of pain and misery. Many Christians are counting on it. Escape from never-ending problems would make anyone happy. That is probably the reason some people do drugs, to escape from life's downturns. However, did Jesus ever speak about an escape from all problems and trials? On the contrary, He prayed, *"I do not pray that You should take them out of the world, but that You should keep them from evil"* (John 17:15). If you are a Christian and you die, all your difficulties will be over, as you will be with the Lord. But what about your friends and family? Life will still go on for them. Meanwhile, for 150 years, hope for an "airlift" (the Rapture) out of this world has been in vain. Is that not defined as a dashed hope? Indeed, Scripture says, *"Hope deferred maketh the heart sick"* (Prov. 13:12).

This book will help you unravel some confusing teaching about the end times and the copious predictions (prophecies) offered by Dispensationalists that were never fulfilled (see Dwight Wilson's book *Armageddon Now!*).[23]

The following chapters will help you understand why every date set, and every future date that might be set for the "soon" coming of the Lord, will fail; and why everyone who teaches and believes "this is" or "we are" the generation that will be raptured out of the world *will be wrong* and *can never be right.* It will also help you understand the many Bible verses that seem to teach a soon return of Jesus. In addition, again, we will spend some time analyzing the detrimental beliefs of the Dispensational doctrine and the paralyzing effect it has had on the Christian Church.

If I would have read this book twenty years ago, I would have disagreed with most, if not all, of what I present here. If you have been taught the standard Dispensational line as I was, and embraced the writings of Hal Lindsey, Tim LaHaye, and Dave Hunt, this book will have you shaking your head and muttering under your breath, "How could they have been so wrong"! Hopefully, you will have enough curiosity and courage to finish reading this book and take the time to consider its message.

FOOTNOTES

1. International Preterist Association, *What Is the Preterist View?* (Bradford PA 16701–1515: 122 Seaward Avenue) Web Site: http://www.preterist.org.

2. Fred J. Foster, *Think It Not Strange, A History of the Oneness Movement* (St. Louis, MO: Pentecostal Publishing House, 1965) p. 13.

3. Dr. Kenneth L. Gentry, Jr., *He Shall Have Dominion* (Institute for Christian Economics, Tyler, Texas, 1992) p. 59.

4. John F. MacArthur, *The Second Coming* (Crossway Books, A Division of Good News Publishers, 1300 Crescent Street, Wheaton, Illinois 60187, 1999) p. 137.

5. W. Herschel Ford, *Decision Magazine*, January 2001, p. 27.

6. John L. Bray, *Matthew 24 Fulfilled* (John L. Bray Ministry, Inc., P.O. Box 90129, Lakeland, Florida 33804, 2000) p. 209.

7. *The International Standard Bible Encyclopedia* (Massachusetts: Wm. B. Eerdmans 1956) vol. III, p. 1489.

8. Shine website from Yahoo! *Raising an Olympian: Shawn Johnson* by Charlene Prince Birkeland, Team Mom.

9. Ken Ham, Carl Wieland, Don Batten, *One Blood. The Biblical Answer to Racism* (Green Forest, AR: Master Books, 1999) p. 145.

10. Ham, Wieland, Batten, *One Blood*, p. 131.

11. Viktor E. Frankl, *Man's Search for Meaning* (New York, NY: Washington Square Press Pocket Books, 1985).

12. Frankl, *Man's Search for Meaning*, p. 95.

13. Frankl, *Man's Search for Meaning*, p. 56.

14. Gentry, *He Shall Have Dominion*, p. 48.

15. Gentry, *He Shall Have Dominion*, p. 48.

16. Aleksandr I. Solzhenitsyn, *The Gulag Archipelago 1918-1956* (New York, NY: Harper & Row, 1985).

17. Tim LaHaye, *The Battle for the Mind*, quoted in, *He Shall Have Dominion*, Kenneth L. Gentry, p. 24.

18. Gary North, *Rapture Fever/Why Dispensationalism is Paralyzed* (Institute for Christian Economics, P. O. Box 8000, Tyler, Texas 75711, 1993) Back cover.

19. The Schwarz Report, *The Dialectic Faith* (Manitou Springs CO: 80829. PO Box 129, Website, www.schwarzreport.org, October 2001) p. 3, 4.

20. *Creation magazine* (Florence, Kentucky: Answers in Genesis, December 2001-February 2002) p. 6.

21. Dave MacPherson, *The Incredible Cover-Up* (Medford, Oregon: Omega Publications, 1980) p. 103.

22. Frankl, *Man's Search for Meaning,* p. 17.

23. Dwight Wilson, *Armageddon Now!* (Institute for Christian Economics, P. O. Box 8000, Tyler, Texas 75711, 1991).

CHAPTER TWO

DISPENSATIONALISTS DISTORT BIBLICAL WORDS

———⊶⊷———

RULES OF INTERPRETATION

The Dispensational doctrine distorts words and terms the Bible uses and replaces them with non-Biblical meanings and explanations. They build their dogma on false or altered contexts that are detached from all the Bible teaches. This chapter will show how Dispensationalism persists in misconstruing and modifying the Scripture.

Before we endeavor to expound or interpret Scripture, it is necessary to understand a few things about the principles of interpretation. Rules and laws are of paramount importance. Whether you are playing football, arguing in a court of law, or studying the Bible, without rules and laws, chaos will result. When we interpret Scripture we are not talking about a game, but something of ultimate importance: God's words of life.

Guy Duty, in his book *If Ye Continue*, had this to say about the rules of interpretation: "Exact rules are needed for an exact result. You cannot get a sure meaning with an uncertain rule. The Bible student must not only study the Scriptures, he must decide *how* he will interpret them. Two persons can read the same texts and get different ideas from them because they put different meanings upon the words."[1]

Duty's book laid out eight rules of interpretation.[2] The rules that follow are adapted from his book and come from the foremost interpretive authorities, both in law and theology. They can apply to a court of law or the Word of God. These rules will be important as you continue to read the rest of this book.

1. *Rule of Definition*

Any study of Scripture must begin with a study of words. Define your terms and keep to the terms defined.

2. *Rule of Usage*

The whole Bible may be regarded as written "for the Jew first," and its words and idioms ought to be rendered according to Hebrew usage. Christ accepted this usage and did not seek to alter it.

3. *Rule of Context*

Many passages of Scripture will not be understood at all without the help afforded by the context. Many a sentence derives its point and force from the sentences surrounding it. Every word you read must be understood in light of the words that come before and after it. The words of Scripture, when used out of context, can prove almost anything. Some interpreters twist them from a natural to a non-natural sense.

4. *Rule of Historical Background*

Even the general reader must be aware that some knowledge of Jewish life and society at the time of writing is necessary for understanding Gospel history. Theological interpretation and historical investigation can never be separated from each other. The strictest historical scrutiny is an indispensable discipline to all Biblical theology.

5. *Rule of Logic*

Interpretation involves logical reasoning. The use of reason in interpreting of Scripture is everywhere to be assumed: *"Come now, and let us reason together, saith the Lord"* (Isa. 1:18). The Bible comes to us in the form of human language and appeals to our reason. It invites investigation, and it is to be interpreted, as we interpret any other volume, by a rigid application of the same laws of language and grammatical analysis.

6. *Rule of Precedent*

We must not violate the known usage of a word and invent another usage for which there is no precedent.

7. *Rule of Unity*

It is fundamental to an accurate interpretation of the Scripture that each part of a document, law, or instrument is to be construed with reference to the significance of the whole.

8. *Rule of Inference*

In adjudicating evidence, an inference is a fact that can be reasonably implied from another fact. It is a logical consequence. It is a process of reasoning. It derives a conclusion from a given fact or premise. It is the deduction of one proposition from another proposition. It is a conclusion drawn from the evidence. An inferential fact or proposition, although not expressly stated, is sufficient to bind. This principle of interpretation is upheld by courts of law. Jesus even proved the resurrection of the dead, to the unbelieving Sadducees, by this very rule (Matt. 22:31–32).

DISPENSATION: THE BIBLICAL MEANING

Since Dispensational teaching is such an important part of end-time eschatology, we need to look at how the Bible uses and defines the word *dispensation*—and how Dispensationalists have consistently misused this word, the very word, and description of what they consider themselves. We will also examine other keywords and phrases.

First, let us see how Dispensationalists use the word *dispensation*. Accelerated Christian Education, Inc. employs the PACE system (Presenting Accelerated Christian Education) as its mode of instruction. This method has been used by many denominations and Church schools. At one church I attended, I took a class in the Old Testament using the PACE curriculum. It defined a dispensation as "A period of time during which God deals in a particular way with man in respect to sin and man's responsibility."[3]

Another publishing house, Search for Truth Publications, Inc., via their home Bible study manual, *Search for Truth* (used by the United Pentecostal Church), defined dispensation as, "a period of time in which God deals with man in a particular way. It is a probationary period of time that has always ended in judgment because of the sins of man."[4]

Now let us look at an example of how the Bible uses the word "dispensation." The Greek word for dispensation is *oikonomia*. It is used seven times in the New Testament and translated as "dispensation" four times (I Cor. 9:17; Eph. 1:10, 3:2; and Col. 1:25); and three times as "stewardship" in Luke 16:2–4. Clearly, dispensation is a Biblical word. Paul says in Ephesians 1:10 *"That in the dispensation of the fulness of times he might gather together in one all things in Christ, both which are in heaven, and which are on earth, even in him."* In this verse, *dispensation* means a process of dealing or transacting, an administrative system. It carries the same meaning in the other verses stated above. The definitions that follow will verify this meaning.

Now let us see how some Greek lexicons define the word "dispensation." In *Strong's Concordance*, dispensation is defined as: "administration (of a household or estate); spec. a (religious) 'economy':- dispensation, stewardship." # 3622.[5]

Thayer's Greek-English Lexicon of the New Testament defines "dispensation" as "the management of a household or of household affairs; specifically, the management, oversight, administration, of others' property; the office of manager or overseer, stewardship."[6]

In *Vine's Expository Dictionary of New Testament Words*, we read "A dispensation is not a period or epoch (a common, but erroneous, use of the word), but a mode of dealing, an arrangement or administration of affairs. Cp. *oikonomos*, a steward, and *oikonomeo*, to be a steward."[7]

As demonstrated by the Bible and the definitions cited, we see that dispensation never means a period of time. It would seem Dispensationalists have changed the meaning of dispensation, assigning it a non-Biblical interpretation. And they use it in a way other than Scripture sets forth.

Thus, the question remains and continues to mushroom: how many rules have the Dispensationalists broken in just this one instance?

RIGHTLY DIVIDING THE WORD OF GOD

II Timothy 2:15 says, *"Study to shew thyself approved unto God, a workman that needeth not to be ashamed, rightly dividing the word of truth."* The word *dividing* in this passage means "to expound, to teach the truth correctly." Dr. Jack Van Impe's interpretation of "rightly dividing," offered in his book *Everything you always wanted to know about PROPHECY,* states "This dividing has to do with dispensations and enables one to arrive at accurate conclusions."[8] As Dr. Van Impe never arrived at an accurate definition of the word "dividing," how can he arrive at an accurate conclusion?

Again, we will see that Dispensationalists, like Van Impe, are guilty of "wrenching" the Scripture (breaking rules of interpretation) and giving non-Biblical meanings to Bible words, whenever it suits their purpose. The following definitions will verify how thoroughly he erred in his use of "dividing."

Thayer's Greek English Lexicon defines the word "dividing" as "to teach the truth correctly and directly."

Vine's Expository Dictionary explains the word "dividing," as "handling aright (the word of truth); the meaning passed from the idea of cutting or dividing, to the more general sense of rightly dealing with a thing. What is intended here is not dividing the Scripture from Scripture, but teaching Scripture accurately."

"And a certain Jew named Apollos, born at Alexandria, an eloquent man, and mighty in the scriptures, came to "Ephesus ... And he began to speak boldly in the synagogue: whom when Aquila and Priscilla had heard, they took him unto them, and expounded unto him the way of God more perfectly" (Acts 18:24–26). Being "mighty in the Scriptures" does not necessarily mean being accurate in the Scriptures.

DO THE WORDS "SOON," "QUICKLY," AND "SHORTLY" IMPLY A DELAY?

Anyone attending a church adhering to Dispensational doctrine will, before long, overhear the words; *"the coming of the Lord is soon," "very soon,"* or *"near."* For example, one Sunday morning Church service I attended on December 3, 2000, the visiting evangelist said, "We have less than 25 years until the second coming of the Lord." Then we heard about all the signs of His coming and prophecies that are being fulfilled. Of course, that prediction is not heard in every sermon or on every Sunday, but it is a major subject in many evangelical churches.

So, what do the words *soon*, *quickly*, and *shortly* mean? Does the Bible use those words differently from the way we do? Remember Rule Number One: define your terms and keep to the terms defined. So, let us look at the dictionary and Bible lexicons to see what these words truly mean and how they should be used.

Noah Webster's 1828 *American Dictionary of the English Language* defines the word "soon" as "In a short time; shortly after any time specified or supposed; as soon after sunrise; soon after dinner; I shall soon return; we shall soon have clear weather; or early; without the usual delay; before any time supposed. How is it that ye have come so soon to-day? Exodus ii. 9"[9]

The following verses were chosen at random. Moreover, I could have picked any Scripture with the word "soon" and it would have conveyed the same meaning:

> *And when he saw a fig tree in the way, he came to it, and found nothing thereon, but leaves only, and said unto it, Let no fruit grow on*

thee henceforward for ever. And presently the fig tree withered away. And when the disciples saw it, they marvelled, saying, How soon is the fig tree withered away (Matt. 21:19–20).

Now as soon as it was day, there was no small stir among the soldiers, what was become of Peter (Acts 12:18).

And Moses said unto him, As soon as I am gone out of the city (Ex. 9:29).

Then Martha, as soon as she heard that Jesus was coming, went and met him (John 11:20).

As we can see, Webster's Dictionary and the Bible use the word "soon" the same way everyone does today.

The word "shortly" is used in the Book of Revelation in verses 1:1 and 22:6. *Thayer's Greek-English Lexicon* defines the word "shortly" as "quickness, speed, speedily, soon." *Strong's* defines the word "shortly" as "a brief space (of time), in haste, quickly, speedily."

The words "quickly" and "shortly" are also used in describing something the first Christians believed was imminent. It is important to understand how the Bible uses these words; then we will see to what degree the Dispensationalists have misused them.

The word "quickly" is translated from four different Greek words. It is translated as "quickly" seventeen times in the New Testament. Here are the other Greek words for "quickly," their meanings, and the numbers from *Strong's*:

> #5035 tachu – without delay, soon, or (by surprise) suddenly, or (by impl.) of ease. It is also translated as lightly and quickly.
>
> #5030 tacheos – briefly, (in time) speedily, or (in manner) rapidly. It is also translated as hastily, quickly, shortly, soon, and suddenly.
>
> #5032 tachion – more swiftly, (in manner) more rapidly, or (in time) more speedily out [run]. It is also translated as quickly, shortly, and sooner.
>
> #5034 tachos – a brief space (of time) in haste. It is also translated as quickly, shortly, and speedily.

The word "quickly" is used seven times in the Book of Revelation, in verses 2:5, 2:16; 3:11; 11:14; 22:7,12 and 22:20. *Thayer's Greek-English Lexicon* defines the word "quickly" as, "quickly, speedily, (without delay)." That is the actual and only meaning in every verse in the Book of Revelation.

HAS CHRIST'S COMING BEEN DELAYED?

The Scripture is clear. The word "soon," as used in the Scripture, means soon—no delay or long period of time was ever meant or implied. The word "quickly" means quickly, without delay, speedily. There is also no hint or suggestion of a delay or lapse of time implied in the word "quickly" or the word "soon" in ANY context in Scripture.

The word "delay," as defined by *Webster's*, means, "to put off; postpone or to make late; detain; to stop for a while."[10] MacArthur, in his book *The Second Coming*, uses the word "delay" six times on pages 57 and 58 to explain why the Lord purportedly has not yet returned: "I suppose it is also possible that Christ could **delay** His coming another 2,000 years or longer ... He still could **delay** His coming ... or **delays** longer than we think possible ... In other words, the real reason for the Lord's **delay** ... He is longsuffering and kind, **delaying** Christ's coming ... the long **delay** before Christ's appearing."[11] (emphasis added)

Dave Hunt takes up the same lament as MacArthur. For he also wonders: "Why has it taken so long for our Lord to return? Could it be another 2000 years, or even more, before His promise is fulfilled?"[12] Hunt also states: "As the months after His ascension stretched into years, however, and the years into decades, the early Christians must have pondered with increasing wonder the meaning of *a little while*—a phrase which seems all the more incomprehensible to us nearly 2000 years later."[13] (emphasis his)

Contrary to Hunt's contention, the early Christians never pondered the meaning of "*a little while*," which is so confusing, mystifying, and bewildering to Hunt and all other Dispensationalists. The early Christians simply believed what Jesus said, and when those signs came to pass, they knew what to do. Thus, not one Christian perished when the temple in Jerusalem was destroyed!

So where does the Scripture even hint or imply Christ's coming might be delayed? Nowhere, not one verse! If there was going to be a delay the words "tarry," "linger," or "postpone," could and would have been used. "In fact, notice the very words of Jesus and what He had to say concerning Him not tarrying but that He would come before their generation had passed away. *"This generation shall not pass away, till all be fulfilled"* Luke 21:32; see also Matthew 24:34; Mark 13:30).

In the Book of Hebrews, the author tells his readers of an imminent occurrence, the soon coming of the Lord. That day they could readily discern—as they see Him coming on the horizon. *"Not forsaking the assembling of ourselves together as the manner of some is; but exhorting one another: and so much the more, as ye see the day approaching"* (Heb. 10:25). They were to get ready because they would bear witness, and still be alive, when that day came! There is no hint or talk of a delay in any of these verses.

Later on, the timing becomes more definitive: *"For yet a little while, and he that shall come will come, and will not tarry"* (Heb. 10:37). The word "tarry" is the same word translated "delayeth" (#5549 *Strong's*), which means "to take time, linger." The Lord was not planning to delay or linger. It was aptly foretold He *"will come and will not tarry."* Who would possibly believe, in the absence of any evidence to the contrary, that that day of the Lord has not come? Would not an interval of 2,000 years constitute something of a delay? If someone called you and said they will be there shortly, would you expect them shortly; or one-hundred or a thousand years from now?

We can see how the Bible and *Webster* use the words "soon," "shortly," and "quickly." The Scripture also uses these synonymous terms: *"for the time is at hand"* (Rev. 1:3; 22:10), *"the time is fulfilled"* (Mark 1:15), *"must shortly come to pass"* (Rev. 1:1), *"Surely I come quickly"* (Rev. 22:20), *"Behold I come quickly"* (Rev. 22:12), *"is nigh at hand"* (Luke 21:31), *"the day is at hand"* (Rom. 13:12), *"the time is short"* (I Cor. 7:29), and *"the end of all things is at hand"* (I Peter 4:7). These phrases all indicate something amazing was about to take place in the faithful's lifetime who either heard them, or read them in Epistles.

We know how the dictionary defines "soon" and how that pivotal word is used in Scripture. So, when Dispensationalists say, "Jesus is coming soon," what, precisely, does that mean to them? It is obvious they do not apply the words "soon," "quickly," and "shortly" in the same way as

Scripture and the English language. Dispensationalists have given these words new, non-Biblical meanings that have confused many people. The first Christians certainly believed Jesus's coming would be soon, but to us 2,000 years later, "soon" is a very different matter.

The word "soon" lost its intended meaning around the turn of the twentieth century; when the Dispensationalists preached the soon coming of the Lord in a radically different way. They began to use "soon" to mean "delay," "tarry," or "postponement"—thereby distorting the word's original meaning. Dispensationalists can say, "Jesus is coming soon" all they want, but Christ's coming can only be perceived as a past historical event for it to have been *soon* to those First Century Christians.

You may disagree with that last statement, that Jesus's coming was a past historical event. If so, you are in good company, for many people would disagree on this point. However, please do not stop reading until you have read the rest of this book and examined the Scriptural evidence. The key to understanding the "coming" of Jesus is what *He* meant, not what some people *think* He meant—two thousand years later. We will deal more with that salient point in the chapters that follow. And you will be surprised at what you will discover.

For now, consider this question: Was the early Church deceived when they thought Jesus's coming would be (soon) in their lifetime? The first Christians knew something monumental would happen in their lifetime. The disciples believed Jesus would come in their lifetime because He told them He would: *"Ye shall not have gone over the cities of Israel, till the Son of man be come"* (Matt. 10:23). *"Verily I say unto you, There be some standing here, which shall not taste of death,* [who must be getting very old by now!] *till they see the Son of man coming in his kingdom"* (Matt. 16:28). *"Jesus saith unto him, Thou hast said: nevertheless I say unto you, Hereafter shall ye see the Son of man sitting on the right hand of power, and coming in the clouds of heaven"* (Matt. 26:64; Mark 14:62). *"[A]nd they shall see the Son of man coming in the clouds of heaven with power and great glory ... this generation shall not pass, till all these things be fulfilled"* (Matt. 24:30–34). We know the early Christians believed this event would be soon, as clearly stated throughout the New Testament. What then should we conclude? Categorically, Christ's coming was believed imminent by the early Church in the First Century; and that event happened a long time ago.

In Matthew 24:34, Jesus said, "*this generation shall not pass, till all these things be fulfilled.*" Some believe this verse only references the destruction of the temple, not the Lord's coming. But one cannot just chop up Matthew 24 like a salad by saying verse 34 refers solely to the temple, while other verses refer to a "second coming." In Matthew 24, Mark 13, and Luke 21, all the words Jesus said up to "*this generation shall not pass, till all these things be fulfilled,*" are a complete unit. There is no break in His discourse. He did not say, "now I am teaching about the temple," and "now I am talking about a different subject, a second coming." We will have more to say about the second coming in Chapter 8.

Jesus perpetrated a lie if he had any foreknowledge His coming would not be soon, as He plainly said it would be. And His followers would have been deceived if He did not correct their misunderstanding of what He meant by His coming. The real problem is most people misunderstand what He meant. Jesus did come soon—in the lifetime of the First Century Church—as He said He would. What if I write a letter to you and say, "I want to come as quickly as possible, so shortly I will pack up my things and soon be on my way"? What if I did not show up for a year, five years, fifty years, or 1,950 years—assuming you lived that long (maybe you got hold of some good nutritional advice from a late-night infomercial!). If that was me waiting, I would wonder what had happened and why you did not come *soon*—as you said you would?

GOD'S TIME OR MAN'S TIME

If Jesus has not come back for 1,950 years, which of the following five reasons would explain why He didn't return, as the First Century Christians believed? Did He forget? Did He lie? Did Jesus have a problem and could not make it on time, and then forget to tell us? Is He dead? Or did the authors of Scripture misunderstand and preach a lie, saying he was coming soon when, after 1,950 years and counting, he has yet to return?

MacArthur, in his book *The Second Coming*, tries to explain the Lord's apparent delay this way: "The amount of earthly time that passes is of no consequence. It is certainly irrelevant from God's timeless point of view. A moment is like many aeons in His mind, and aeons pass like moments. He is not bound by time as we are, and no amount of time can ever nullify His faithfulness ... the fact that 2,000 years have elapsed is utterly irrelevant to the doctrine of Christ's imminent return."[14]

What MacArthur says about God's eternal nature is certainly true; God is timeless. However, if language is to convey God's thoughts and will, then the length of time that has elapsed is of serious consequence and relevance. God created time, and time is the way the eternal Supreme Being deals with mortal, transient, sinful humans. The whole Bible is full of examples of God using time as we know it.

In the Old Testament, there are many prophecies, and events linked to specific amounts of time. The Israelites were to wander in the wilderness for 40 years (Num. 14:34). God gave Joseph the ability to interpret dreams (Gen. 40:8; 41:16). Using his God-given gift, Joseph interpreted for Pharaoh's butler and baker each of their dreams and stipulated a specific number of days until they would be fulfilled (Gen. 40:8–19). Joseph also interpreted Pharaoh's dreams and gave a specific number of years before events would unfold (Gen. 41:15–32). God told Abraham of a specific amount of time (400 years) his seed (Israel) would be in Egypt (Gen. 15:13, 14).

Jeremiah the prophet foretold of a period of time (70 years, no more, no less) Israel would be in captivity in the city of Babylon, reiterating, "*This captivity is long*" (Jer. 29:28). Then, after 70 years had elapsed, they would be allowed to return to their land. "*For thus saith the LORD, That after seventy years be accomplished at Babylon I will visit you, and perform my good word toward you, in causing you to return to this place*" (Jer. 29:10, 25:11–13; II Chron. 36:21; Ezra 1:1). Daniel read this prophecy when he was a captive in Babylon and knew all Israel's (Dan. 9:11) captivity would shortly end. If time is irrelevant to God, how would Daniel have known such a finite fact?

To continue, in the Book of Daniel, Daniel knew Israel's seventy years of captivity was just about finished. How? "*I, Daniel, understood by books the number of years, whereof the word of the LORD came to Jeremiah the prophet, that he would accomplish seventy years in the desolations of Jerusalem*" (Jer. 25:12, 29:10; Dan. 9:2).

When King Hezekiah was dying, the prophet Isaiah came to see him with a message from the LORD. "*Thus saith the LORD, Set thine house in order: for thou shalt die, and not live*" (Isa. 38:1). However, Hezekiah did not die, for he prayed earnestly for his life, and God heard and answered his prayer. God told the King He would add fifteen years to his life and gave Hezekiah a sign this would happen. The sun returned ten degrees on the sundial. God, in communicating His message to Hezekiah, used a precise, absolute, and determinate amount of time.

In these examples, there are no delays or gaps in the time that is specified. When God sets a date and gives time limits, most assuredly, the event will happen within the time frame God has set. These dates and time limits are to let people know God alone can accurately foretell the future.

So, is it true we must look at the word "soon" from God's perspective? Does not the Bible say, *"that one day is with the Lord as a thousand years, and a thousand years, as one day"* (II Peter 3:8)? Peter, in this verse, was quoting from Psalm 90:4 where it also says a thousand years is *"as a watch in the night."* Yes, it is true with God all time is as nothing, because in His presence, all is eternity. In addition, compared to eternity, when the longest ages have passed, it is but a moment.

However, Peter is not applying some obtuse mathematical formula where a thousand years equals one day, and one day equals a thousand years. The Book of Genesis (7:17) says, *"And the flood was forty days* (in "God's time," the flood lasted forty, 24-hour days) *upon the earth"*. Using the logic of one day equals a thousand years, we would still be inundated as the flood would have lasted forty thousand years. Moreover, what did it mean when Jesus said, *"after three days I will rise again"*? If one day "is as a thousand years," then we still have a thousand years to go before Jesus is resurrected.

Though patently absurd, this line of reasoning corresponds perfectly with MacArthur's interpretation of the word "soon." It lacks logic and violates many rules of interpretation. You cannot just take one word or verse of Scripture and drop it in the middle of a different portion and have it retain the same meaning. Again, every verse has to be taken in context. Peter, in this portion of Scripture, is talking about unbelievers who mock God by denying judgment will ever come. Remember, God deals with people in time: hours, days, and years.

The point is, if the Bible meant to say the "Rapture" was a long time into the future, it would have used similar language (e.g., "the latter days," or "years"). God can clearly show when an event is close at hand or when it is far into the future. God is able, and at times does specify the dates and times of tasks He wants to accomplish. He sets these dates so when they come to pass, people will know He is God.

We have seen from Scripture how the Bible uses the word "soon." It means within a short time, with no delay implied. We have seen from Scripture God uses time, days, and years in precisely the same way as we use them. So, when MacArthur applies the argument that "The amount of earthly time that passes is of no consequence ..." and says that it is "... irrelevant from God's timeless point of view,"[15] he violates the rule of definition, the rule of usage, the rule of context, the rule of logic, and the rule of unity—each so essential to Biblical interpretation.

COVENANTAL APPROACH TO THE BIBLE

Is there a way to study Scripture that retains its meaning, rather than distorting it based on human reasoning? Yes. It is found in one word: Covenant. Covenants are the way God has always dealt with His people from the very beginning of time (Gen. 6:18, 9:9–17, 15:18, 17:2, 21:27; Ex. 2:24, 6:4, 19:5, 24:7). The Hebrew word *berith* is used 291 times in the Old Testament. It is translated as "covenant" 273 times and 18 times as "confederacy" or "league." The Greek word for covenant is *diatheke*, which is translated 20 times as "covenant" and 14 times as "testament" in the New Testament. In both the Old and New Testaments, where the word "covenant" is used, it usually refers to God's dealing with man through various transactions.

Properly speaking, a covenant is a compact between man and man or between tribes or nations, where each party binds itself to fulfill certain conditions advantageous or beneficial to each party. However, because man is incapable of being an independent covenanting party with God, the agreement is not strictly mutual; it is a promise from God to arrange His providences for the welfare of those who render obedience or service to Him.

The Biblical way to teach God's mode of administering His affairs with mankind is the Covenantal approach, not the Dispensational method. Each covenant builds upon and overlaps the others. God did not chop history into compact units of time. He deals with us in time as we know it.

There is unity and flow to history. Thus, if you want to study and teach the Scripture, why not use the Bible? What the Dispensationalists do, is detach the Bible from its covenantal framework in favor of an artificial scheme. When they do, the Bible can be made to teach anything. Correct Scriptural interpretation rests on an understanding of the covenants between God and His people.

SUMMARY

When studying Dispensational teaching, one thing becomes immediately clear: their canon is consistent, but consistently wrong. They start with an error at the very foundation of their doctrine. Since the foundation is faulty, everything that is built upon it will come crashing down—eventually.

So far, we have seen Dispensationalists have changed the meaning of key Biblical words: "dispensation," "soon," "shortly," and "dividing." To understand the Bible correctly, we must use Scripture to interpret Scripture and use Biblical words the way the authors of Scripture used them.

Those who do not are guilty of "wresting" (perverting) the Scriptures. To distort Scripture is a very serious matter. As we continue to study this subject, we will see these deliberate alterations have caused much harm to the Church and its overall mission to uplift our cities, states, nation, and world.

FOOTNOTES

1. Guy Duty, *If Ye Continue* (Minneapolis, Minnesota 55438: Bethany Fellowship, Inc., 1966) p. 180.
2. Duty, *If Ye Continue,* p. 182.
3. Accelerated Christian Education, Inc. Written and Edited by Earl B. Wise, #109 Old Testament Survey, 1978, p. 1.
4. Teachers' Manual, *Search for Truth* (Search for Truth Publications, 10929 Almeda-Genoa Rd., Houston, Texas, 77034, 1965) p. 75.
5. *Strong's Exhaustive Concordance of the Bible* (Nashville, New York: Abingdon Press, 1974).
6. Joseph H. Thayer, *Thayer's Greek-English Lexicon of the New Testament* (Grand Rapids, Michigan: Baker Book House, 1979).
7. *W.E. Vine, An Expository Dictionary of New Testament Words* (Fleming H. Revell Company, Old Tappan, New Jersey, 1966).
8. Jack Van Impe, *Everything you always wanted to know about PROPHECY* (Jack Van Impe Ministries, Box J, Royal Oak, Michigan, 1980) p. 31.
9. Noah Webster, *1828 American Dictionary of the English Language* (San Francisco, California: Foundation for American Christian Education, 1980).
10. *Webster's New World Dictionary,* Compact Desk Edition, 1963.
11. John F. MacArthur, *The Second Coming* (Crossway Books, A Division of Good News Publishers, 1300 Crescent Street, Wheaton, Illinois 60187, 1999) p. 57, 58.
12. Dave Hunt, *Whatever Happened to Heaven* (The Berean Call PO Box 7019, Bend, OR 97708, 2011) p. 259.
13. Hunt, *Whatever Happened to Heaven,* p. 43.
14. MacArthur, *The Second Coming,* p. 58.
15. MacArthur, *The Second Coming,* p. 58.

CHAPTER THREE

DISPENSATIONALISM: A NEW VIEW THAT SEES THE FUTURE PESSIMISTICALLY

ORIGIN OF DISPENSATIONALISM

What shocked me when I studied the origins of the Dispensational doctrine was its recent vintage. I always thought Dispensational teaching with its pre-trib (tribulation) Rapture was the eternal truth of the Scriptures. Nevertheless, all Christians need to examine how this theological belief came into existence. This book looks at Dispensational teaching in light of the Scriptures. However, a good source for an in-depth study of the Dispensational thesis can be found in Dave MacPherson's books *The Incredible Cover-Up* and *The Great Rapture Hoax*.[1]

The Dispensational view being taught today (by Hal Lindsey, Dr. Jack Van Impe, Tim LaHaye, Dave Hunt, and others of their ilk) has only been around for 150 years, but it became popular only within the last 100 years or so. LeRoy Edwin Froom, in his four-volume set of books, *The Prophetic Faith of Our Fathers*, writes:

> It was not until the first decade of the twentieth century that Dispensationalism, with its rapture theory, and the separation of the seventieth week from the previous sixty-nine weeks of years of Daniel 9, became general in the then newly forming Fundamentalist wing of Protestantism. This was largely brought about by the acceptance of Dr. C. I. Scofield's bold and revolutionary thesis,

and the aggressive support given this postulate by the Moody Bible Institute of Chicago.[2]

Author and evangelist Ralph Woodrow writes that during the Reformation, many, if not all, of the reformers (men like John Foxe, John Wycliffe, John Huss, Martin Luther, Huldrych Zwingli, William Tydale, John Wesley, Roger Williams, Cotton Mather, Jonathan Edwards) preached and taught:

> … that the prophecies concerning the man of sin or Antichrist have found their fulfillment in the Papacy—the succession of popes that rose to power in Rome following the fall of the Roman Empire.[3]

This teaching is also referenced in the Epistle Dedicatory of the King James Version of the Bible:

> … that the zeal of your Majesty toward the house of God doth not slack or go backward, but is more and more kindled, manifesting itself abroad in the farthest parts of Christendom, by writing in defence of the Truth, (*which hath given such a blow unto that man of sin, as will not be healed*). (emphasis added)

The reformers hammered away at the Roman Catholic Church, which they believed was "the man of sin" (or "Antichrist") mentioned in Scripture. To parry the reformers' preaching, which was having a devastating effect on the Papacy, a counter interpretation of the Antichrist was needed. This was supplied by a commentary written by the Jesuit priest Francisco Ribera.

Here's Froom again regarding the origin of the rapture theory, vis-à-vis Ribera:

> Thus in Ribera's commentary was laid the foundation for that great structure of Futurism, built upon and enlarged by those who followed, until it became the common Catholic position. And then, wonder of wonders, in the nineteenth century this Jesuit scheme of interpretation came to be adopted by a growing number

of Protestants, until today Futurism, amplified and adorned with the rapture theory, has become the generally accepted belief of the Fundamentalist wing of popular Protestantism.[4]

What is amazing to me, most Protestant churches reject many of the traditions of the Roman Catholic faith, yet they accept without question the teaching of a Catholic Jesuit priest, Francisco Ribera. Froom, continuing his research, quotes Joseph Tanner, a Protestant writer, dealing with a future antichrist:

> On the other hand the Jesuit Ribera tried to set aside the application of these prophecies to the Papal Power by bringing out the Futurist system, which asserts that these prophecies refer properly not to the career of the Papacy, but to that of some future supernatural individual, who is yet to appear, and to continue in power for three and a half years. Thus, as Alford says, the Jesuit Ribera (circa 1580) may be regarded as the Founder of the Futurist system in modern times.[5]

David K. Bernard, in a paper on Dispensationalism, states:

> Dispensationalism as a distinct theological system began with John Nelson Darby (1800–82), chief organizer and leader of the Plymouth Brethren. Early teachers who popularized it in America were C. I. Scofield, editor of the Scofield Reference Bible, and L. S. Chafer, founder of Dallas Theological Seminary ... For the most part, the emerging fundamentalists of the early 1900s embrace dispensationalism, and the two systems became almost synonymous. Today many evangelicals, spiritual heirs of the early fundamentalists, have modified or abandoned the system.[6]

Pastor and author Wayne E. Rohde questions the acceptance of the Dispensational doctrine:

> How will you respond if you learn you are embracing a teaching that was not believed by any of the early Church or Church Fathers including Origen, Eusebius, Athanasius or Augustine?

What if your present belief was rebuffed by Puritans including Thomas Goodwin, John Owen, and John Cotton and all the great ministers of the Reformation, including John Wycliffe, John Knox, John Calvin, John and Charles Wesley, Jonathan Edwards, George Whitfield, Charles Spurgeon and many others? Further, what if the teaching you believe to be true was not endorsed by a single Protestant before the 1830s? Would you ignore these serious concerns, or would you at least want to be like a Berean and *"search the scriptures daily to find out whether these things were so?"*[7]

The Dispensational teaching of what is commonly called the "Rapture" was not an integral doctrine of the early Church. Even as the faithful were looking for Jesus's coming, they were not envisioning an airlift from earth to heaven prior to a tribulation.

Bullinger defines the word "coming" as, "the being present, to be present, presence, arrival, a coming which includes the idea of a permanent dwelling from that coming onwards."[8] *Strong's Concordance* defines coming as "advent (often, return; spec. of Christ to punish Jerusalem, or finally the wicked)."[9]

In the Mount Olivet Discourse, the disciples did not ask Jesus about His "Second Coming" (we will discuss this further in Chapter 8). The Bible never uses that terminology! What they wanted to know was when the temple was going to be destroyed; and what sign of His presence should they look for?

The word "rapture" is not even in the Bible. In addition, if Dave MacPherson is right, rapture originated from a source that was anything but Biblical. In his tract *The Rapture Hoax,* MacPherson states:

> **Even the language of Prior Rapturism came from the OCCULT!** During the Middle Ages mystics at times were mysteriously lifted up bodily before witnesses. They would sometimes float for hours above the floor or ground. Whenever this occurred, the levitation was called (gulp) a **"rapture!"**[10] (emphasis his)

Evangelist John L. Bray spent many years studying eschatology. As he asserted, "I find no reference anywhere in any document, by any author, or anybody in this whole world who ever preached on the pre-tribulation rapture before 1788. That date stands. If anybody can find it, I would like to know."[11]

Bray had at one time offered to pay $500 to anyone who could find an earlier date than 1812 of anyone who first taught the pre-tribulation rapture, which has always been a key part of the Dispensational credo. Bray was looking for a text "which taught that the second coming of Christ will be divided into two stages (Rapture and Revelation) and separated by a period of time, such as 45 days, three and one-half years, or seven years."[12] Finally, in 1995, someone found a book that espoused this notion. Evangelist Bray then sent the man a check for $500, and subsequently published a book called *Morgan Edwards and the Pre-Tribulation Rapture Teaching (1788)*.

The recent origin of this Catholic Jesuit construct should be enough to make the Dispensational teaching suspect. If this thesis was indeed God's truth, we would probably find it in writings that are much older. Trying to make a case for or against a certain doctrine from a position of silence is a dubious exercise. Therefore, I intend to do as the Scripture says, "*[Y]e should earnestly contend for the faith which was once delivered unto the saints*" (Jude 3). In achieving that ideal, this book will clearly demonstrate the Dispensational teaching is not found anywhere in the Scriptures.

DEFEAT OF THE CHURCH / WHAT KIND OF HOPE IS THAT?

In 1973, prophecy, end times events, and the second coming of Jesus from a Dispensational view were the topics that led me to become a born-again Christian. My curiosity concerning end times moved me to go to my friend's church to hear a preacher sermonize on the subject. It was there, at that church, I received a conviction of sin and repentance.

I was excited to know, in a short time, the Lord would come back and rapture me—along with the rest of His Church—out of this world. But Jesus entreated just the opposite: "*I pray not that thou shouldest take them out of the world, but that thou shouldest keep them from the evil*" (John 17:15). That would be great: no more bills, no more problems, no more work. As

I recall, I don't know if I was more excited to see Jesus or to know all my troubles would soon be over.

I was overjoyed the Rapture would be soon (at the time of this writing, I have been waiting for over forty-eight years). The world was getting worse and worse (or so I thought). In 1948 Israel had again become a nation, and all the signs the Bible prophesied had seemingly come true. To me, this was as clear an indication as possible that *"this generation shall not pass till all these things be fulfilled."*

A Biblical generation is considered to be about 40 years, so the Lord's return had to be soon. I also believed the Antichrist was alive and just waiting to make himself known. Dr. Jack Van Impe certainly believed the Antichrist was alive. In his book *Everything you always wanted to know about Prophecy*, he answered the question: "Do you think the Antichrist is alive at this moment?" Van Impe unreservedly declared, "Yes."[13] Hal Lindsey wrote in his book *The Late Great Planet Earth* that he believed the Antichrist "is alive today—alive and waiting to come forth."[14] Since both books were written over four decades ago, the Antichrist had better make his move soon or he will die of old age!

Accepting these teachings as fact, there was not much we could do to change the world because the time window was so short. The defeat of the Church was already prophesied, so we could not change that. Moreover, even if we did change or improve things, all was still going to be destroyed (or at least misused) by the devil and the Antichrist after the Rapture. So why plan or build for the future? The world was a sinking ship, and you do not waste time polishing brass when the ship is going down, or paint your back porch when your house is on fire. Of course, I witnessed for the Lord, brought people to church, and taught Bible studies. However, I never really thought the Church could win or change the world, for as one pastor I knew told me, "The Church is the *spiritual bus stop* to which we bring people to wait for Jesus to come back."

I was not alone in my beliefs. I had heard many express similar thoughts. A friend of mine recently wrote to admonish me concerning my belief in a victorious eschatology:

> You are wrong. There is nothing that you can or will ever
> be able to do to change my mind on this subject ... You will

NOT persuade me to change my mind ... I can see the road to Revelation forming up in front of us (I do not know how many years it will take to come to fruition before evil's conquering of the world, followed by Christ's triumphant return, or even if I will live to see it) and way too many people I care about or who I know have the power to influence things who are in denial of the truth about the rise of evil....

The reason millions and I believed in the Dispensational doctrine was it was widely taught by most Evangelical, Apostolic, Pentecostal, and Baptist churches. The *Scofield Reference Bible*, which many still use, has long been one of the major exponents of Dispensationalism. And most, if not all, major Christian television and radio stations incline toward Dispensationalism and will not air any teaching contradicting this theology.

What kind of hope for the future does such a teaching offer? The Church will not be going out of the world in victory if it is destined to fail! Will not the preaching of the Gospel through the power of the Spirit be powerful enough to convert the world to the kingdom of God? God's Church would be defeated and need to be rescued via the Rapture by Jesus, like a dog with its tail between its legs!

Is this the faith that carried Christians singing triumphantly as they faced certain death in the Roman coliseum? Is this *"the faith which was once delivered unto the saints"* (Jude 3)? Is this the faith we are to *"contend for"*? Is this the faith that once *"turned the world upside down"* (Acts 17:6)? Will God's Word fail with our hopes voided? Does this dark view correctly define Scripture and glorify God? Heavens no! Thus, let us call this teaching what it really is: *pessimistic, escapist, defeatist,* and *unscriptural*!

POWER AND VICTORY FOR THE CHURCH

Some might ask, "What will constitute defeat of the church"? Is it not victory if we are going to be with Jesus? Victory? What will we have victory over? Just our problems and trials? No, we will be gone before Jesus can teach us to overcome our struggles. Did the world ever become the kingdom of God? No, the majority still need to repent and believe in Jesus.

Did the Church gain victory over the devil? No, for he will rule through the Antichrist as soon as the Church is gone. Dispensationalists teach the Church will be spirited away so the devil can play.

Jesus said, *"Lo, I am with you alway, even unto the end of the world"* (Matt. 28:20). He said He would be with us through our problems, not airlift us out of our troubles. If Jesus has to transport us because the Antichrist and devil rule the world for a span of time, would that not constitute a defeat? At the very least, it would be a retreat.

Nowhere does the Bible teach defeat or retreat of the Church. Should the Church ever depart (be raptured), it would mean the devil was ruling this world, and God's Spirit would be gone. For seven years of the tribulation, Christ would not be ruling on earth. However, the Bible says He shall reign and His kingdom shall have no end (Luke 1:32–33). *"Of the increase of his government and peace there shall be no end"* (Isa. 9:7; Dan. 7:14). The Scriptures do not teach a gap of time in the kingdom of Jesus. There will never be a time the Church will be absent from the earth. The Church was established on Christ (The Rock) and will continue here on the earth to the end of time (whenever that end may be).

One kind of victory the Bible talks about is the triumph of one who beats back all challenges: *"Him that overcometh will I make a pillar in the temple of my God"* (Rev. 3:12). *"And they overcame him by the blood of the Lamb, and by the word of their testimony; and they loved not their lives unto the death"* (Rev. 12: 11). *"These things I have spoken unto you, that in me ye might have peace. In the world ye shall have tribulation: but I have overcome the world"* (John 16:33). *"For whatsoever is born of God overcometh the world: and this is the victory that overcometh the world, even our faith. Who is he that overcometh the world, but he that believeth that Jesus is the Son of God"* (I John 5:4–5).

The Book of Hebrews (Chapter 11) tells us that victory is *"by faith."* In the Book of Revelation (12:11), we learn how victory was achieved: *"And they overcame him by the blood of the Lamb, and by the word of their testimony; and they loved not their lives unto the death."* And let us not forget that *"greater is he that is in you, than he that is in the world"* (I John 4:4).

The Holy Spirit was given to the Church on the day of Pentecost. He was given to every believer as empowerment to overcome the world, the flesh, and the devil. Paul says, *"Let this mind be in you, which was also in Christ Jesus"* (Phil. 2:5). We need the "supply of the Spirit of Jesus Christ."

The Holy Spirit has endowed each believer with the power to overcome the kingdom of Satan and every idol we may still have in our lives. Anything that takes the place of or is put above God is an idol or false god. Paul explained idolatry to the Church at Corinth (I Cor. 8:5–6), teaching them there were many called gods, and many called lords, but they were all false. To the Christian, there is only one true God, the Lord Jesus Christ. Accordingly, it is the true God, Jesus, who reigns supreme over this planet. Not the false god, the devil.

THE DEVIL'S KINGDOM

Many assume (as I always did) when Paul wrote of the *"god of this world"* in II Corinthians 4:4 he was writing about Satan. *"In whom the god of this world hath blinded the minds of them which believe not, lest the light of the glorious gospel of Christ, who is the image of God, should shine unto them."* But is the devil really the one Paul was referencing? Is Satan the only being (with God's permission) that can blind the mind or harden the heart? Who alone has the power to give people over to a reprobate mind? (see Rom. 1:18–32) I now concur with what Adam Clarke wrote about this verse: "I feel considerable reluctance to assign the epithet "THE *God*" to Satan."[15]

Let us not forget, as we sometimes do, that God is a God of justice and judgment and, because of the perverseness of man's heart, can give individuals over to a reprobate mind. Cannot God do with us anything He wishes?: *"O house of Israel, cannot I do with you as this potter? Saith the LORD. Behold, as the clay is in the potter's hand, so are ye in mine hand, O house of Israel"* (Jer.18:6). Since God is sovereign, He may take His mercies away from those who abuse them. You will find throughout Scripture it was God who blinded the eyes and hardened the hearts of those who were already corrupt:

> *And Moses and Aaron did all these wonders before Pharaoh: <u>and the LORD hardened Pharaoh's heart</u>, so that he would not let the children of Israel go out of his land* (Ex. 11:10).

Go, and tell this people, Hear ye indeed, but understand not; and see ye indeed, but perceive not. Make the heart of this people fat, and make their ears heavy, and shut their eyes; lest they see with eyes, and hear with their ears, and understand with their heart, and convert, and be healed (Isa. 6: 9–10; see also Matt. 13:14–15; Mark 4:12; John 12:40; Rom. 11:8–10).

Because they did not receive the love of the truth, that they might be saved. And for this reason <u>God will send them strong delusion, that they should believe a lie</u>, that they all may be condemned who did not believe the truth but had pleasure in unrighteousness (II Thess. 2:10–12).

Adam Clarke, commenting on these verses, writes:

Now all this is spoken of the same people, in the same circumstances of willful rebellion and obstinate unbelief; and the great God of heaven and earth is he who judicially blinds their eyes; makes their hearts fat, i.e., stupid; gives them the spirit of slumber; and bows down their back, &c. On these very grounds it is exceedingly likely that the apostle means the true God by the words "the god of this world."[16]

Clarke continues: "Some, and particularly the ancient fathers ... have read the verse (II Cor. 4:4) ... But God hath blinded the minds of the unbelievers of this world ... Irenaeus, Tertullian, Chrysostom, Theodoret, Photius, Theophylact, and Augustine, all plead for the above meaning; and St. Augustine says that it was the opinion of almost all the ancients."[17]

You may not agree with Clarke's view that the god of this world is the one true God, but he certainly shows we should not automatically assume our interpretation of Scripture is correct without a lot of prayer *and* study behind that assumption.

The devil has a kingdom (Luke 11:18) from which he rules the thoughts and deeds of evil men and demons. He is the ruler of the world of darkness, the world of sin, the world of wicked thoughts, the world of lies, and of everything that exalts itself against the authority of the Lord Jesus. The devil's "world" is amoral and ethereal. But it also has physical properties

(Rom. 12:2); its cares (Matt 13:22); its sons (Luke 16:8, 20:34); its rulers (I Cor. 2:6, 8); its wisdom (I Cor. 1:20, 2:6, 3:18); and its fashion (Gal. 1:4).

Satan is called the "power of darkness" (Luke 22:53) and the "prince of the power of the air." *"And you hath he quickened, who were dead in trespasses and sins; Wherein in time past ye walked according to the course of this world, according to the prince of the power of the air, the spirit that now worketh in the children of disobedience"* (Eph. 2:1–2).

Satan is not called the King of the earth or King of the planet for a very good reason: He is not either one! Adam Clarke, commenting on Eph. 2:2, writes, "Satan is termed prince of the power of the air, because the air is supposed to be a region in which malicious spirits dwell, all of whom are under the direction and influence of Satan, their chief."[18] Matthew Henry concurs with Adam Clarke on Ephesians 2:2 when he writes:

> Those who walk in trespasses and sins, according to the course of this world, walk according to the prince of the power of the air. Satan, or the prince of devils, is thus described.

In opposing the devil, Jesus said, *"I will build my church: and the gates of hell shall not prevail against it"* (Matt. 16:18). Joseph H. Thayer's remarks on the word "prevail" in Matthew 16:18 are very enlightening: "... to be strong to another's detriment; to prevail against; to be superior in strength; to overpower: (meaning, 'not even the gates of Hades—than which nothing was supposed to be stronger—shall surpass the church in strength.')"[19]

All Christians need to do what Paul and John taught:

> *Casting down imaginations* (reasonings) *and every high thing that exalteth itself against the knowledge of God, and bringing into captivity every thought to the obedience of Christ* (II Cor. 10:5). *Love not the world, neither the things that are in the world. If any man love the world, the love of the Father is not in him. For all that is in the world, the lust of the flesh, and the lust of the eyes, and the pride of life, is not of the Father, but is of the world. And the world passeth away, and the lust thereof: but he that doeth the will of God abideth for ever* (I John 2:15–17).

Each Christian also needs to remember Christ triumphed over the devil and his works: "*And having spoiled principalities and powers, he made a shew of them openly, triumphing over them*" (Col. 2:15).

GOD IS KING AND LORD OF THIS PLANET

The devil does not own this planet; he is not the prince of this world; he is a defeated foe. Jesus vanquished the devil on the cross. I sometimes wonder if Dispensationalists have ever read the Book of Psalms. This book leaves no doubt about who reigns as King. Over and over, it tells us:

> *Who is this King of glory? The LORD strong and mighty, the LORD mighty in battle* (Psalm 24:8). *The heavens are thine, the earth also is thine: as for the world and the fulness thereof, thou hast founded them* (Psalm 89:11). *For the LORD is a great God, and a great King above all gods* (Psalm 95:3). *For the LORD most high ... he is a great King over all the earth. The earth is the LORD'S and the fulness thereof; the world, and they that dwell therein* (Psalm 24:1).

Many verses tell us God is the King and judge of the earth. These include Ex. 9:29, 19:5; I Chron. 16:8–36; Psalms 24:1, 47:2, 7, 83:18, 97:5; Isa. 37:16, 54:5.

In the New Testament, Jesus celebrates the Lord of this world: "*I thank thee, O Father, Lord of heaven and earth*" (Matt. 11:25). In Matthew 28:18 Jesus says, "*All power is given unto me in heaven and in earth.*" The one who is all-powerful (I will give you a hint, it isn't the devil) is the one in charge—the true and eternal ruler. In Colossians, Paul tells us everything is God's:

> *For by him were all things created, that are in heaven, and that are in earth, visible and invisible, whether they be thrones, or dominions, or principalities, or powers: all things were created by him, and for him: And he is before all things, and by him all things consist. And he is the head of the body, the church: who is the beginning, the firstborn from the dead; that in all things he might have the preeminence ... And, having made peace through the blood*

of his cross, by him to reconcile all things unto himself; by him, I say, whether they be things in earth, or things in heaven (Col. 1:16–20).

Jesus is King of Kings and Lord of Lords. I Timothy 6:15–16 says Jesus *is* King of Kings, not will be. In the Book of Revelation, chapter 17, verse 14, we read of the ten Kings and the beast making war with the Lamb, and the Lamb shall overcome them. This war was considered a future event when John wrote the Book of Revelation (about AD 68). Moreover, as John was writing Revelation, it was known and accepted that Jesus was already Lord of Lords and King of Kings; not that Jesus would become King sometime in the future. Paul and Silas were not falsely accused of *"saying that there is another King, one Jesus"* (Acts 17:7).

The Jews rejected their King: *"Pilate saith unto them, Shall I crucify your King? The chief priests answered, We have no King but Caesar"* (John 19:15). *"Pilate ... washed his hands before the multitude, saying, I am innocent of the blood of this just person: see ye to it. Then answered all the people, and said, His blood be on us, and on our children"* (Matt. 27:24–25).

Nathanael recognized who Jesus was: *"[T]thou art the Son of God; thou art the King of Israel"* (John 1:49). On Christ's ride into Jerusalem, the people recognized who Jesus was, *"and cried Hosanna: Blessed is the King of Israel"* (John 12:13). Zechariah prophesied that the King, Jesus, would ride upon a colt (Zech. 9:9). And the wise men asked, *"Where is he that is born King of the Jews"* (Matt. 2:2)?

Since Christ is King, He also has a kingdom and subjects. When one becomes a Christian he enters into the kingdom of Christ. *"Who hath delivered us from the power of darkness, and hath translated us into the kingdom of his dear Son"* (Col. 1:13). Please note, the Scripture says "hath," which is past tense; the Christians of the city of Colosse were already in the kingdom of Christ. When the Apostle John was exiled on the isle of Patmos, he wrote he was then in the kingdom of Jesus (Rev. 1:9). This teaching does not deny any future glories of God's kingdom.

The word shall means something will happen in the future; it does not refer to present reality. In Isaiah 7:14 we read, *"a virgin shall conceive, and bear a son, and shall call his name Immanuel."* Does that verse mean we are still to look for a future fulfillment because the word shall is in it? No, of course not! So why, when people read in Luke 1:32–33 that Jesus *"shall* reign over the house of Jacob for ever, and of kingdom his there shall be no end," do they still think His supremacy is a future event? We need to realize Jesus has already been crowned King of Kings and Lord of Lords—as He is reigning even now!

CHRIST REIGNS AS LORD AND KING NOW

Jesus reigns now? Some may consider this a little confusing, for Christ said to Pilate: *"My kingdom is not of this world: if my kingdom were of this world, then would my servants fight, that I should not be delivered to the Jews: but now is my kingdom not from hence"* (John 18:36). Christ's kingdom is not secular in nature. His chosen ones do not do battle with tanks, guns, or an air force. *"For though we walk in the flesh, we do not war after the flesh: For the weapons of our warfare are not carnal, but mighty through God to the pulling down of strong holds. Casting down* <u>imaginations</u> (Greek: reasonings), *and every thing that exalteth itself against the knowledge of God, and bringing into captivity every thought to the obedience of Christ"* (II Cor.10:3–5).

Peter preached on the day of Pentecost that Christ, after the resurrection, had taken his seat on the throne of his father, David. Peter said, *"God … would raise up Christ to sit on his throne; He seeing this before spake of the resurrection of Christ"* (Acts 2:30–31, 5:31). Paul says we are now in the kingdom of Christ (Col. 1:13). In his epistle to the Church at Ephesus, Paul tells us when Jesus was raised from the dead, He was set at the right hand of God *"Far above all principality, and power, and might, and dominion, and every name that is named … and hath put all things under his feet"* (Eph. 1:20–22).

The first Christian martyr, Stephen, delivered a message about Jesus to the council of Jewish leaders. It filled their hearts with such hatred and rage they stoned him. Just before the stones began to fly, Stephen *"looked up steadfastly into heaven, and saw the glory of God, and Jesus standing on the right hand of God"* (Acts 7:55).

What did Stephen see? No less than "The *Shekinah*, the splendor or manifestation of the Divine Majesty."[20] The phrase, "right hand" metaphorically means power or authority. Stephen saw just one person, Jesus, with the glory of God shining out from Him. This meant Jesus reigned as King as a present reality, not that His reign as King would begin sometime in the future.

Jesus now sits at the right hand of God. *"But this man, after he had offered one sacrifice for sins forever, sat down on the right hand of God"* (Heb. 10:12). Jesus will also reign until *"his enemies be made his footstool"* (Heb. 10:13).

Psalm 2:8–9 is a prophecy about the resurrected Jesus ruling all the kingdoms of the world: *"Ask of me, and I shall give thee the heathen for thine inheritance, and the uttermost parts of the earth for thy possession. Thou shalt break them with a rod of iron; thou shalt dash them in pieces like a potter's vessel."*

There are many verses of Scripture that teach Jesus is King now, He is reigning now, and His kingdom is a present reality. If Jesus had not been crowned King, He would not be reigning. Consider the following:

> *"[W]e have a great high priest, that is passed into the heavens, Jesus the Son of God, let us hold fast our profession. For we have not an high priest which cannot be touched with the feeling of our infirmities ... Let us therefore come boldly unto the throne of grace, that we may obtain mercy, and find grace to help in time of need"* (Heb. 4:14–16).
>
> *"For through him we both have access by one Spirit unto the Father"* (Eph. 2:18).
>
> *"Having therefore, brethren, boldness to enter into the holiest by the blood of Jesus, By a new and living way, which he hath consecrated for us, through the veil, that is to say, his flesh; and having an high priest over the house of God; Let us draw near with a true heart in full assurance of faith"* (Heb. 10:19–22).
>
> *"All power is given unto me in heaven and in earth ... lo, I am with you always, even unto the end of the world"* (Matt. 28:18–20).
>
> *"For where two or three are gathered together in my name, there am I in the midst of them"* (Matt. 18:20).
>
> *"Then cometh the end, when he shall have delivered up the kingdom to God, even the Father; when he shall have put down all rule and all authority and power. For he must reign, till he hath put all enemies under his feet"* (I Cor. 15:24–25).

"The eyes of your understanding being enlightened; that ye many know ... the exceeding greatness of his power to usward who believe ... Which he wrought in Christ, when he raised him from the dead, and set him at his own right hand in the heavenly places, Far above all principality, and power, and might, and dominion, and every name that is named, not only in this world, but in that which is to come: And hath put all things under his feet, and gave him to be the head over all things to the church, Which is his body, the fulness of him that filleth all in all" (Eph. 1:18–23; see also; Matt. 28:18–20; Eph. 2:18)

These verses clearly delineate the fact, the setting up of Christ's kingdom is a past historical event, for He is now seated upon His Throne. He holds all power and has dominion over every earthly king and kingdom.

After Christ's resurrection, Cleopas and a companion were traveling to the village of Emmaus. As they journeyed, they spoke about the recent events concerning Jesus of Nazareth. He was the one they had trusted to redeem Israel, but was condemned to death by the chief priests and was crucified. As they communed and reasoned together, Jesus himself drew near and joined them. He then initiated a series of probing questions about their conversation.

Choosing not to reveal His identity, Cleopas and his friend remained unaware the Lord was among them. Jesus's companions ended their recount of the last three days by stating certain women had been at the sepulcher earlier that morning, and they had reported the tomb was empty, and they had seen a vision of angels. Jesus then offered these words: *"O fools, and slow of heart to believe all that the prophets have spoken: Ought not Christ to have suffered these things, and to enter into his glory"* (Luke 24:25–26)?

Then, beginning with Moses, Jesus expounded every Scripture that pertained to the Christ. Later that same day, He appeared to His gathered disciples and told them, *"These are the words which I spake unto you, while I was yet with you, that all things must be fulfilled, which were written in the law of Moses, and in the prophets, and in the psalms, concerning me"* (Luke 24:44). Would not the fulfilling of "all things" also include Jesus sitting on His throne and reigning over His kingdom?

Dispensationalists Dave Hunt and (popular radio Bible teacher) J.

Vernon McGee would disagree, arguing that, at present, Christ is a king without subjects or a kingdom to rule, i.e., "There can be no kingdom without the king being personally present."[21] They believe Christ's kingdom will not be established until the supposed Millennium, for Christ needs to be physically present to rule:

> All Christians admit this to be the case when it comes to the spiritual kingdom in their hearts. Christ must reign there. And the same is equally true of the outward manifestation of His kingdom upon earth during the millennium. He must personally reign there as well.[22]

Hunt quotes Micah 5:2, to wit: "Jesus Christ did not fulfill that Scripture when He was here the first time. To do so He must come again personally to this earth … Then and not until then shall His earthly kingdom be established."[23]

The very idea that Christ cannot reign unless He is physically present is farcical, perhaps ridiculous, in view of the Scriptures referenced. Let us consider the practicality, no matter the physical location of His throne. Does He have any less authority here on earth if His throne is in Heaven? Would His power be further enhanced if He sat on a throne in Jerusalem?

There are about 7.7 billion people (as of August 2019) residing on this earth. Even if Jesus was physically ruling from Jerusalem, very few could actually see Him. Each day, throngs of unimaginable size would be cueing up to meet Him. Crowd control would be impossible, and chaos would reign supreme!

Dispensationalists are akin to the apostles before the Holy Spirit changed them; and similar to the many Jewish leaders who did not understand the nature of the kingdom of God. The Jews expected a kingdom of political power, of ceremony and pomp, just as Dispensationalists expect during the Millennium. Just after Jesus had passed through Jericho and before His triumphal entry into Jerusalem, many thought the kingdom of God would immediately appear (Luke 19:11). The Pharisees thought the kingdom would reflect all the glory and glamor of great military power. They demanded to know of Jesus *"when the kingdom of God should come"* (Luke 17:20). Jesus replied to them, *"The kingdom of God cometh not with observation* [with outward show; margin]: *Neither shall they say, Lo here! or, lo there! for behold, the kingdom of God is within you."* Or as the margin says, *"among you."* Just before Jesus ascended into heaven the apostles asked Him, *"Lord, wilt thou at this time restore again the kingdom to Israel?"* (Acts 1:6). The Pharisees did not yet perceive, *"the kingdom of God is not meat and drink; but righteousness, and peace, and joy in the Holy Ghost"* (Rom. 14:17).

Christ's reign will not start in the Millennium, as some mistakenly think. For Christ is King now. He is on the throne now, and He reigns now! His kingdom is a present reality. *"Who hath delivered us from the power of darkness, and hath translated us into the kingdom of his dear Son"* (Col. 1:13). *"Therefore being a prophet, and knowing that God had sworn with an oath to him, that of the fruit of his loins, according to the flesh, he would raise up Christ to sit on his throne; He seeing this before spake of the resurrection of Christ"* (Acts 2:31–32). *"[W]ho is the blessed and only Potentate, the King of Kings, and Lord of lords"* (I Tim. 6:15). Many have read those verses without understanding what they proclaim.

Jesus as King does not have to be physically present to reign. If it were a requirement for Jesus to be seen, we would be relying on sight, not faith. As Jesus stated, *"blessed are they that have not seen, and yet have believed"* (John 20:29). He reigns now, in His ordained place at the right hand of His father.

I have met none of our presidents face to face. I have seen them on TV and heard them on the radio, but never in person. I do not have to "see" the president to know he exists. The Bible says Satan has a kingdom and rules his demons and imps. However, I have never seen his throne room or even a photograph. Nor has anyone else. Yet most people believe Satan has a domain or kingdom over which he rules, although they have never seen it.

Christ's kingdom is here now, and at any time we are welcome before the throne of the King: *"Let us therefore come boldly unto the throne of grace, that we may obtain mercy, and find grace to help in time of need"* (Heb. 4:16). We can while on earth join with Christ in his celestial realm: *"And hath raised us up together, and made us sit together in heavenly places in Christ Jesus"* (Eph. 2:6).

DISPENSATIONALISTS SEE THE NEAR
FUTURE PESSIMISTICALLY

Because Dispensational authors believe the devil will rule the world for a short period of time, they write books with a decidedly pessimistic outlook. Dr. Jack Van Impe, Tim LaHaye, John F. Walvoord, Hal Lindsey, and others teach the world is getting worse as the devil grows stronger. Television specials like *Israel, America's Key to Survival* (the early 1980s) promote the Dispensational view.

Lindsey's books *The Late Great Planet Earth* and *Satan Is Alive and Well on Planet Earth* are eulogies to Dispensationalism. The *Left Behind* series of novels by LaHaye and Jerry Jenkins, which have given rise to several dreadful movies, illustrates the pretribulation rapture view. The sixteen books comprising the series have sold more than 65 million copies. Volume 7, *The Indwelling: The Beast Takes Possession*, set a record when eager readers snapped up 1.9 million books in just two weeks.

What do Dispensationalists really believe about the present? Do they think Christ's Church will prevail and change the world? The following quotes represent the belief system of most Dispensational teachers:

Christians have no immediate solution to the problems of our day.[24]

To attempt to establish a long-term change of institutions before Christ returns will only result in the leaven of humanism permeating orthodox Christianity.[25]

I suppose it is also possible that Christ could delay His coming another 2,000 years or longer. Given the rapid decline of society I do not see how that is possible.[26]

The pre-trib rapture view puts forward that the world will grow worse and worse. The Church will be removed from earth, then God's judgment will begin to fall on rebellious earth-dwellers.[27]

The late Harold Lindsell, who was editor-in-chief of *Christianity Today*, may not have been a Dispensationalist but he still echoed the same sentiments when he pointed out "This present world is doomed. The scent of death is upon it. It is committing suicide and nothing can save it ... until the coming of Jesus Christ."[28]

A song that fits right in with Dispensational teaching is *Hold the Fort*. I can hear their minions singing it now:

> See the mighty host advancing, Satan leading on;
> Mighty ones around us falling, courage almost gone!
> "Hold the fort, for I am coming," Jesus signals still;
> Wave the answer back to Heaven, "By Thy grace we will."

Some Dispensational leaders write as though all hope and courage are gone. They see themselves as a little band of desperate survivors just hoping Jesus will return to save them before it is too late.

Here are a few more uplifting Dispensational nuggets:

> I do not believe in inevitable progress toward a much better world in this dispensation, and God's church has no right to take an optimistic, triumphalistic attitude.[29]

> Apostasy grows worse and worse as time goes on. We live in the last days and we know that our Lord prophesied that in our days there would be few in the world that believe.[30]

Tim LaHaye seems to sum up the feelings of many in the Christian community when he writes:

> Most knowledgeable Christians are looking for the Second Coming of Christ and the tribulation period that He predicted would come before the end of the age. Because present world conditions are so similar to those the Bible prophesies for the last days ... they conclude that a takeover of our culture by the forces of evil is inevitable; so they do nothing to resist it.[31]

I realize a few of the authors I have quoted may not like being lumped in with the likes of Hal Lindsey and Dr. Jack Van Impe. They would probably deny they are Dispensational in their beliefs. That may be true. The point is, whatever doctrinal camp they are in, they have a pessimistic view of the future. Therefore, what I have done in this book is to combine every fatalist and pessimist into the Dispensational mix—as they are all in the same defeatist camp. They are free to sort out their doctrinal beliefs however they want; but I will not sort out those differences here.

After reading through such dire sentiments, how could anyone conclude Dispensationalists portray a positive viewpoint or a victorious theme? What verse or book in the New Testament displays such a pessimistic, hopeless outlook as the one Dispensationalists have? That wholly negative attitude is nowhere to be found in Scripture. The Dispensational doctrine that spawned it needs to be abandoned as it is not of God. It is a sin to be so defeatist and joyless.

The Apostle Paul was a man who knew adversity. He wrote to the Church at Corinth about his ministry, saying:

> *I am more; in labours more abundant, in stripes above measure, in prisons more frequent, in deaths oft. Of the Jews five times received I forty stripes save one. Thrice was I beaten with rods, once was I stoned, thrice I suffered shipwreck, a night and a day I have been in the deep; In journeyings often, in perils of waters, in perils of robbers, in perils by mine own countrymen, in perils by the heathen, in perils in the city, in perils in the wilderness, in perils in the sea, in perils among false brethren; In weariness and painfulness, in watchings often, in hunger and thirst, in fastings often, in cold and nakedness. Beside those things that are without, that which cometh upon me daily, the care of all the churches* (II Cor. 11:23–28).

After all Paul suffered, he could still say,

> *We are troubled on every side, yet not distressed; we are perplexed, but not in despair; persecuted, but not forsaken; cast down, but not destroyed; always bearing about in the body the dying of the Lord Jesus, that the life also of Jesus might be made manifest in our body* (II Cor. 4:8–9).

The Dispensationalist viewpoint cannot even approximate the message of hope Paul delivers. Paul did not discourage the Church—which seems to be the province of the Dispensationalists.

HAS THE WORLD GROWN WORSE
AND WORSE FOR CHRISTIANS?

When Dispensationalists say things such as, "Christ could delay His coming another 2,000 years or longer. Given the rapid decline of society, I do not see how that is possible,"[32] I wonder where their faith is? I also wonder what they mean when they write, "[O]ur Lord is warning that before He returns, the world will become more and more hostile to the people of God ... The world's hostility to Christ will not diminish but will increase dramatically ..."[33]

The Scriptures do not teach an ever-increasing hostility to the Church. There has often been—at certain times and specific places—great resistance to the Church's agenda. The Jews and Romans beset and plagued the early Church. Down through the ages, the Roman Catholic Church beleaguered the followers of Christ. After the rise of Islam in the 7th century to this very day, Muslims have been fierce adversaries of the Church. I ask you, is the world more hostile to Christianity now, or was it more hostile in the beginning?

If we could go back in time, what was the world like on the day of Pentecost? Before that day there was no Christian Church. That day, when Peter preached, there were no teachers, pastors, missionaries, or ministers of the Gospel. There were no evangelists or even a New Testament to read. The churches, to whom many of the epistles addressed, had not yet come into existence. The Apostle Paul, who at first persecuted the Christian Church, did not even know what a Christian was. The field was white unto harvest, but had no laborers to bring it in, and no barns to store such bounty.

What lay before those in one accord, when they were all filled with the Holy Spirit? What did the 3,000 who were added to the Church on Pentecost see in their future? As *"they continued stedfastly in the apostles' doctrine and fellowship ... And the Lord added to the Church daily such as should be saved"* (Acts 2:42, 47), what did tomorrow hold for them?

For the early Church, the entire world lay barren. It was like a desert—windswept, hot, and dry. No oasis awaited the weary traveler to cool his perspiring brow. The Gospel, however, would make this parched land come alive, as the Church labored with joy and hope.

Author and theologian Dr. Elton Trueblood, when asked the question, "Sighting the final third of the Twentieth Century, what do you think it offers the church?" replied, "By the year 2000, Christians will be a conscious minority surrounded by an arrogant militant paganism."[34] Based on their beliefs, MacArthur and most Dispensationalists would concur with that statement.

Dispensationalists look at the world—with its wars, crimes, famines, and earthquakes—and conclude the end must be near. They see the moral climate and think the Church no longer holds sway over anyone. The wicked appear to be in control of most governments and many of the world's institutions.

But is it really worse today than it was for the early Church?[35] Today there are millions and millions of believers worldwide. Christians are no longer being thrown to the lions, burned at the stake, or pulled apart on the rack. There are no Jewish mobs stoning Christians or putting them in jail. There are TV ministries and Christian radio programs. You can travel from coast to coast in the USA and hear Christian programming all the way. Churches exist by the thousands around the globe. There are outreach programs, campaigns, and rallies all over the world. The Church is expanding in many countries. It is growing behind the former Iron Curtain in Europe and behind the Bamboo Curtain in China.

While the previous paragraph is certainly true, it can also be rightly argued that more Christians are being persecuted and martyred for their faith today than in the early days of the Church. A bit of historical evaluation is needed. According to the most recent United Nations estimates elaborated by Worldometers, as of December 2017 the current world population is close to 7.6 billion. At the time of the birth of Jesus, the earth's entire population was just 300 million (smaller than the current number of inhabitants of the U.S.A.), and of that number, about 45 million lived within the Roman Empire.

Let us return to the Church on the day of Pentecost. Everything— and I mean everything—was standing in the way of the Church. The establishment in Rome was hostile right from the beginning. The world was seemingly being ruled by the devil. Even "God's people," the Jews, targeted every Christian and, allied with the power of Rome, stopped at nothing (including murder and deceit) to terminate the small band of believers.

The early Christians were indeed "a conscious minority surrounded by an arrogant militant paganism."

With many Christians still besieged today, what an opportunity we have for growth! The whole world lay before the early believers, and they saw this as a great opportunity. So should we. The fields are white unto harvest. Do we share Paul's philosophy or the pessimistic and hopeless Dispensational outlook of men like Cornelius Vanderwaal, who said, "God's church has no right to take an optimistic triumphalistic attitude."³⁶ But I will say, in lockstep with the early Church, we have every right to a triumphant attitude, for all power is given unto us through Christ (Matt. 28:18). *"And greater is he that is in you, than he that is in the world"* (I John 4:4).

Have we forgotten what was given to the early Church? Power! *"But ye shall receive power, after the Holy Ghost is come upon you"* (Acts 1:18). *"For the kingdom of God is not in word, but in power"* (I Cor. 4:19). *"And what is the exceeding greatness of his power to usward who believe, according to the working of his mighty power, which he wrought in Christ"* (Eph. 1:19–20). *"For our gospel came not unto you in word only, but also in power"* (I Thess.1:5). *"For God hath not given us the spirit of fear, but of power, and of love, and of a sound mind"* (II Tim. 1:7). The early Church also recognized God was with them. *"If God be for us, who can be against us?"* (Rom. 8:31).

The early Church knew the Spirit gives life, and along with that life came the power: the power to live for the Lord and the power to change the world. The entire world? Yes, because when an individual changes, that changes the whole family; when the family changes, that changes the community; when the community changes, that changes the city; when the city changes, that changes the state; and on and on until the whole world becomes the kingdom of God.

This nation may have seemed to turn its back on God, but *"If my people, which are called by my name, shall humble themselves, and pray, and seek my face, and turn from their wicked ways; then will I hear from heaven, and will forgive their sin, and will heal their land"* (II Chron. 7:14). In addition, as author Ayn Rand has said, "There are no 'waves of the future'... and any trend can be stopped." And "Any step can be retraced if men understand where they're going."³⁷ Any portion of life the devil has taken can be retaken. To the Dispensationalist I would offer another thought from Ayn Rand: "It is not as late as you think."[37] The world is not coming to an end. So wake up and get to work assembling the kingdom!

I asked one minister of a church I attended why he thought we had only a few years left. He said, "Because of what we see around us." Well, what do we see around us? Corruption, wickedness in high places, evil men and women, much as we have seen in the past.

As we survey the history of the Christian Church, we find that persecution then peace, then more persecution followed by peace has been the lot of the Church down through the ages. In the United States, it has long appeared morals are going down the drain, but there really is not a lot of persecution of Christians. Some were jailed by the powers that be on false or unfair charges. Pro-life people are consistently abused and villainized in the press. Sometimes, Christian gun owners have been unduly hounded. Occasionally, Christians have had their doors broken down by the police for no apparent reason, or been arrested on trumped-up charges. However, I do not know of anyone who has been murdered by our government just for being a Christian. Thankfully, America's Christians still have a lot of freedom and can fight the system and the government in the courts. And sometimes we win.

Of course, it is not only Christians to whom these things happen. The unjust also suffer abuses. Therefore, we really cannot say persecution is getting worse and worse, at least in the USA. While persecution is a daily reality in many countries across the earth, it is not a sign of anything prophetic, an indicator of decline, or the so-called last days or time of the end. So why the growth of Dispensationalism in the United States?

For the first 30 years of the Church, it was the Jews (with help from the power of Rome) who hounded and persecuted the Church. God then destroyed those unbelieving sons of Abraham and scattered them to the four corners of the earth, with no promise of ever restoring the nation of Israel again (Deut. 4:23, 26–27). Then, after the great tribulation and destruction of Jerusalem in AD 70, it was the Roman Empire that persecuted the Church for many years.

Ultimately, it was the Church that conquered the Roman Empire from the inside out. Emperor Constantine converted to the faith in AD 310, and peace reigned for a long while. [In retrospect, the supposed conversion of Constantine to the faith, might have been one of the worst things for the Church, with his mixture of pagan and the sacred and the subsequent watering down of the faith.] Then the papacy arose, and for hundreds of years cruel and heartless popes tried to crush the life out of the Church. When the Reformation was born during the dark days of the Inquisition, the Church revived and went forth to proclaim the Gospel. For much of the last century, communism has held numerous nations under its evil grip, and the teaching of evolution continues to poison impressionable minds. From Christianity's beginning, the kingdom of the Lord has waxed and waned in all places on this globe. Based on what history has shown us, should we not anticipate another triumph and renewed flowering of the Church?

We can compare the growth of the Church to the way a carpenter hammers a nail into a joist. The carpenter holds the hammer above the nail. He then swings the hammer through the air as it descends toward the nail. It hits the head of the nail, and the nail is forced violently into the wood. The carpenter then reverses the course of the hammer to its starting point high above the nail and begins the process again, until the nail's head is flush with the wood.

The Gospel's spread and the growth of the Church are like a nail slowly driven into the world, penetrating our thoughts and consciousness. Now that the Church has been wedged into our domain, it is impossible to remove. Every institution and art form in our land and across the globe has been influenced by Christianity.

The process of hammering a nail, unless understood in terms of its effect, will seem to make no sense. We can understand as the hammer strikes the nail and drives it into the wood, but then the hammer is moved away from the nail and goes in the opposite direction.

At times, the progress of Christianity has slowed to the point of inertia. Many of the faithful were martyred, and the Church was seemingly reduced in number. But because of these martyrs the Church grew, prospered, and has continued as an immense engine of unstoppable change.

The history of the Church shows us all is not lost; there remains tremendous hope. Societies can be rebuilt, and people can and will be born again. And when someone is changed on the inside, everything around that individual is renewed as well.

D. James Kennedy and Jerry Newcombe in their 1994 book *What if*

Jesus Had Never Been Born?, spell out in great detail the amazing changes, the innumerable positive contributions Christianity has made in this world through the centuries. This is a book everyone should read, for it truly shows true Christianity will triumph and Christ's Church will continue to grow no matter what is transpiring.

THE DISPENSATIONAL HOPE
FOR THE FUTURE

Quotes from Vanderwaal and the other Dispensational believers leave one with a cold and hopeless feeling for the future. Of course, Dispensationalists still cling to their overriding expectation—the Church being zapped out of the world. But if you take away this idea of their magic carpet ride to heaven (which the Bible does not teach and, if you think about it, is remarkably selfish), Dispensationalists would be singing the blues in unison with everyone else with nowhere to turn.

Just look at the hope Dispensationalists give to the ones who stay behind should they miss the great airlift. For, after the Rapture, all hell will be loosed upon the earth. What a wonderful prospect to think about!

Rather than me laying out this dismal future, I'll let Dr. Jack Van Impe, from his book *Everything You always wanted to know about PROPHECY,*[38] relate what those left behind can anticipate:

- The world's greatest dictator
- The world's greatest war
- The world's greatest famine
- The world's greatest persecution
- The world's greatest ecological disaster
- The world's greatest hour of fear
- The world's greatest fire
- The world's greatest oceanic disturbance
- The world's greatest storm
- The world's greatest plague

Added to this list of horrors are the world's greatest pollution of water, perpetual darkness, a pestilential invasion, invading armies, an epidemic, a ferocious scorching, and the greatest earthquake this planet has ever known. I sure hope these hapless remainders all have homeowner's insurance!

This darkest possible view of the future is immeasurably disheartening. Think about the millions, maybe billions, who would be left behind to die in awful ways. All your work for the Lord would be destroyed. Everything you built would be taken and used by the devil and the Antichrist.

Moreover, all the Church has accomplished over the last two millennia would come to nothing. Yes, millions of souls will have been saved, but the world will be given to the devil. And what about all the destruction that will be caused by bowling ball-sized hail (even a hard hat would be of little value); the rivers and lakes turning to blood, and most sea life dying from the polluted water. If you are at all concerned about other people and about this planet (and God is concerned about this planet—He even knows "when a sparrow falls"), this scenario does not seem very victorious to me.

Of course, all these disasters happen to the ones left behind because they rejected Christ. And God's Church will be in heaven enjoying the Marriage Supper of the Lamb (reward for failure?). But why are we the only ones who will benefit from this coming of the Lord? What have we done that is so special Jesus will remove us from our problems, including the curse of death? Why are we more deserving than all the other believers throughout the ages?

Why weren't the Christians who were thrown to the lions in the Roman colosseum raptured? Why weren't the Christians who suffered through the terrors of the Inquisition raptured? Why haven't the Christians who, even today, suffer in communist prisons, been raptured out of their pain and misery? Many Christians in this country exhibit what I term "American arrogance." They think God would never allow such persecution to happen here.

Renowned evangelist Leonard Ravenhill writes, "God did not have any such rapture for the Chinese Christians in 1940, nor for His dear children in Hungary, nor for His blood-washed who were again blood-washed in the uprisings in Russia. But we darlings—fat, faint, and flourishing— think to get to heaven without a scar or even a scratch, if you please."[39]

Foxe's Book of Martyrs is a history of those Christians who sacrificed all from the time of Stephen (Acts 7:59) through the 17th century. *By Their*

Blood by James C. Hefley and Marti Hefley details the history of many Christians who were martyred in the 20th century. If any group deserved a rapture out of this world, it was the countless millions of Christian men, women, and children who yielded up their lives for their faith in Jesus.

In exploring the past, it may seem that evil will surely triumph as we move into the future. However, Christianity shall grow, for the blood of the martyrs is the seed of the Church. Ravenhill had this to say about Christ's power to overcome:

> The Lord Christ not only delegated His grace to His disciples; He also bequeathed them His Power! "I give unto you power ... over all the power of the enemy!" To this we have another great promise: "Resist the devil, and he will flee from you." Here we have a clear revelation of the Christian having the whip hand over the devil. The believer is to be the head in this battle and not the tail.[40]

Without question, Dispensationalists must recognize Christians are to have dominion over all the earth. Jesus said, *"Go and make disciples or Christians of all nations"* (Greek rendering Matt. 28:19). Moreover, Jesus is the one who has *"all power in heaven and in earth"* (Matt. 28:18). Does it seem at all rational Christ would let His Church be defeated? Of course, Dispensationalists readily believe the Church will be defeated simply because they are pessimists. I cannot help but wonder where this belief comes from. Perhaps Dispensationalism comes from our old adversary, the devil, for—to reiterate—the Bible certainly does not uphold this doctrine.

FOOTNOTES

1. Dave MacPherson, *The Incredible Cover-Up. The Great Rapture Hoax* (Medford, Oregon: Omega Publications, 1980).

2. LeRoy Edwin Froom, *The Prophetic Faith of Our Fathers: The Historical Development of Prophetic Interpretation, 4 vols.* (Washington, DC: Review and Herald, 1978) vol. IV, p. 1203.

3. Ralph Edward Woodrow, *Great Prophecies of the Bible* (Riverside, CA: Ralph Woodrow Evangelistic Association, 1971) p. 128.

4. Froom, *The Prophetic Faith of Our Fathers,* vol. II, p. 493.

5. Froom, *The Prophetic Faith of Our Fathers,* vol. II, p. 487.

6. David K. Bernard, *Dispensationalism and Oneness Pentecostal Theology* 1987 p. 1.

7. Wayne E. Rohde, *A Future, A Hope, An Expected End* (Xulon Press, 11350 Random Hill Center, Suite 800, Fairfax, VA 22030, 2001) p. 3.

8. Ethelbert W. Bullinger, *A Critical Lexicon and Concordance to the English and Greek New Testament* (Grand Rapids, Michigan: Zondervan Publishing House, 1980).

9. *Strong's Concordance,* # 3952.

10. Tract, *The Rapture Hoax.* (Chatsworth, California: Christian Tract Service, P.O. Box 5082 91313).

11. John L. Bray, *A Southern Baptist's Prophetic Pilgrimage* (John L. Bray Ministry, Inc., P.O. Box 90129, Lakeland, Florida 33804, 2000) p. 19.

12. Bray, *A Southern Baptist's Prophetic Pilgrimage,* p. 19.

13. Dr. Jack Van Impe, *Everything you always wanted to know about PROPHECY* (Jack Van Impe Ministries, Box J, Royal Oak, Michigan, 1980) p. 38.

14. Gary DeMar, *Last Days Madness* (Brentwood, Tennessee: Wolgemuth & Hyatt, 1991) p. 72.

15. Adam Clarke, *Clarke's Commentary, combined edition* (Nashville: Abingdon) Matthew—Revelation vol. III, p. 328.

16. Clarke, *Clarke's Commentary,* p. 329.

17. Clarke, *Clarke's Commentary,* p. 329.

18. Clarke, *Clarke's Commentary,* p. 437.

19. Joseph H. Thayer, *Thayer's Greek-English Lexicon of the New Testament.*

20. Clarke, *Clarke's Commentary,* Matthew—Revelation p. 735.

21. Dave Hunt, *Whatever Happened to Heaven* (The Berean Call PO Box 7019, Bend, OR 97708, 2011) p. 259.

22. Hunt, *Whatever Happened to Heaven,* p. 259.

23. Hunt, *Whatever Happened to Heaven,* p. 266.

24. John F. Walvoord, *Why Are the Nations in Turmoil?* Quoted in, *He Shall Have Dominion,* Dr. Kenneth L. Gentry, Jr. p. 18.

25. *House and Ice, Dominion Theology* quoted in, *He Shall Have Dominion,* Kenneth L. Gentry, Jr. p. 19.

26. John F. MacArthur, *The Second Coming* (Crossway Books, A Division of Good News Publishers, 1300 Crescent Street, Wheaton, Illinois 60187, 1999) p. 57.

27. Rapture Ready – website. The Rapture-*Answering the Critics* by Terry James.

28. John Wesley White, *Re-entry,* (Minneapolis, Minnesota: World Wide Publications, 1971) p. 59.

29. Cornelius Vanderwaal, *Hal Lindsey and Biblical Prophecy,* quoted in *He Shall Have Dominion,* Kenneth L. Gentry Jr. p. 21.

30. Arie den Hartog, *Hope and the Protestant Reformed Churches' Mission Calling,* quoted in *He Shall Have Dominion,* Kenneth L. Gentry Jr. p. 24.

31. Tim LaHaye, *The Battle for the Mind,* quoted in, *He Shall Have Dominion,* Kenneth L. Gentry Jr. p. 24.

32. MacArthur, *The Second Coming,* p. 57.

33. MacArthur, *The Second Coming,* p. 83.

34. Leonard Ravenhill, *Sodom had no Bible* (Zachary, La.: Ravenhill Books 1971) p. 13.

35. Some would answer that question in the affirmative. And depending upon your perspective they could be correct. There are many ministries like Richard Rumbrand's "Voice of the Martyrs", Brother Andrews' "Open Doors", and Wally Magdangal's "Christians in Crisis", that record the persecutions of our brothers and sisters across the world. It is recorded that persecution for a believer in about 53 countries happens to the tune of one every

three minutes or 300 per day. You can see some of the statistics here: http://christiansincrisis.net/. and here:http://www.newsweek.com/christian-persecution-genocide-worse-ever 770462

36. Cornelius Vanderwaal, *Hal Lindsey and Biblical Prophecy*, quoted in *He Shall Have Dominion*, Kenneth L. Gentry Jr. p. 21.

37. "*Letters of Ayn Rand*." p. 225 [1945].

38. Van Impe, *Everything you always wanted to know about PROPHECY*, p. 25–26.

39. Ravenhill, *Sodom had no Bible*, p. 103.

40. Ravenhill, *Sodom had no Bible*, p. 118.

CHAPTER FOUR

WHOOPS! WRONG AGAIN!

A MYRIAD OF DATE-SETTERS

I realize many of the people who have set dates for Christ's return were not Dispensationalists, seeing the Dispensational teaching has only been around since 1830. Dispensational believers have, however, built their doctrine on the errors of the past.

The Dispensational view has always produced a bumper crop of people who casually foretell end time events (and dates) for the coming of the Lord. And when these events fail to occur (as is always the case), these individuals become what everyone who has ever set a date for the coming of the Lord has become: false prophets and teachers. The year 1988 was no exception.

That was the year Edgar C. Whisenant's two-part book, *88 Reasons Why the Rapture Will Be In 1988–On Borrowed Time,* caused quite a stir in the fundamentalist world, and in the church I attended. Many of the Christians I knew felt a newfound zeal for the Lord, and many more people started to attend church. The end was at hand. I even heard a sermon titled "Cramming for the Finals," shortly before September, when the Rapture was supposed to take place.

Whisenant's book was everywhere—in my church bookstore and every other Christian bookstore I checked. Even my pastor proclaimed, "Can anyone guarantee that Jesus will not come back on the date Whisenant has set?" If I knew then what I know now, I would have stood up at once.

(Well, I really do not know if I would have had the courage to stand up and speak the truth in front of that large congregation.) But now, I would certainly say, "Yes, I can guarantee it!"

As it turned out, all of Whisenant's 88 Reasons proved false. Consequently, he became yet another false prophet. (Interestingly, I never heard one word condemning the doctrine of Dispensationalism, which Whisenant used as the foundation for his date-setting). Not having learned his lesson, he then wrote *The Final Shout: Rapture 1989*, in which he admitted, predictably, to an arithmetic mistake that made him wrong by a year. This publication was subsequently re-titled *The Final Shout—Rapture Report 1990* and was issued yearly as *The Final Shout—Rapture Report 1991, 1992, 1993*, and *1994*. At present no Whisenant website exists, for he passed away in 2001. Whisenant and his 88 Reasons are now considered part of the lore of false prophecies of the 20th century.

Many other soothsayers have tried their hand at setting dates: Tichonius (an early Christian writer), AD 381; Hippolytus and Lactantius, AD 500; Isaac Newton, 1715; William Whiston, 1734; William Miller (Adventist), October 22, 1844; Charles Taze Russell (Jehovah's Witness), 1914; William Branham, 1977; Bill Maupin, June 1981; Mikkel Dahl, April 4-5, 1982; S. G. Norris, (Apostolic Bible College), 1986; Cha Dang-Ho, October 28, 1992; Harold Camping, on or between September 15 and 27, 1994, then May 21, 2011;[1] Chen Heng-Ming, 10 a.m. on March 31, 1998; and Marvin Byers, 2000; plus a host of others.

Over the years, many people have set dates for the second coming of the Lord. Some date-setters have produced a large following; others, few, if any. Some are well known (Billy Graham);[2,3] others obscure. However, all the soothsayers have one thing in common: They have ALL been wrong! (Or, rather, they have all been proven "false prophets.") *"But the prophet, which shall presume to speak a word in my name, which I have not commanded him to speak, or that shall speak in the name of other gods, even that prophet shall die ... When a prophet speaketh in the name of the LORD, if the thing follow not, nor come to pass, that is the thing which the LORD hath not spoken"* (Deut. 18:20–21). **I predict—No, I mean I guarantee—that every date that anyone has or ever will set for the second coming and end time events will fail!**

There is a major problem when intelligent, well-meaning, and knowledgeable men and women continue to set dates for these monumental Biblical events. Scholars, too, have not been immune to the false doctrine of date-setting. Dwight Wilson, in his book *Armageddon Now!*, surveys the history of ill-fated forecasts and prophecies from 1917 to 1977. He shows none of the identifications of the Beast, Antichrist, 666, or numerous other "literal fulfillments" of Biblical prophecy have come to pass. Francis X. Gumerlock, the author of *the Day and the Hour*, chronicles the perennial fascination many Christians have had with predicting the end of the world. He shows there were very few years when "end time events" or "signs of the end" were not predicted. It should be obvious by now that every date-setter and every end time teacher since AD 70 has misunderstood Jesus's own words concerning His coming and the end of the age. Clearly, this stubborn ilk never will, nor ever can be, right!

After King David had committed his great sin of adultery with Bathsheba, and murdered her husband to cover it up, the Lord waited for him to repent. When he didn't, God sent Nathan the prophet with a story about an unabashed sinner. The story so moved David he gave sentence upon the man in the tale. Nathan then said, "*Thou art the man.*" This convinced David of his sin, and he repented. But Nathan pronounced God's judgment on David and his kingdom. Part of his punishment was the death of his son "*because by this deed thou hast given great occasion to the enemies of the LORD to blaspheme*" (II Sam. 12:14). In each instance, does not the onerous presence of false prophets empower the enemies of the Lord?

WHAT SIGNS?

According to Dispensational doctrine, the first Church believed Christ could come at any hour. For example, MacArthur writes, "A solid conviction that Christ could return at any time permeates the whole New Testament."[4] Dave Hunt further states, "… the early church, in obedience to His clear commands, was waiting and watching for Him to come at any moment."[5] Arthur W. Pink says, "... the Scripture presents the Second Coming of Christ as something that may happen at any hour ..."[6] These statements notwithstanding, the early Christian Church **never** believed in the "imminent return of Christ" that is taught so prevalently today.

They knew certain events (prophecies) had to be fulfilled first. In Matthew 24:5–6, our Lord says, *"For many shall come in my name, saying, I am Christ; and shall deceive many. And ye shall hear of wars and rumours of wars; see that ye be not troubled: for all these things must come to pass, but the end is not yet."* These upheavals were not assumed to presage the coming of the Lord. Jesus then talks of pestilences, earthquakes, persecutions, many false prophets, iniquity abounding, the gospel of the kingdom preached in all the world for a witness, and then the end would come. The end of what? The end of the world? No! He was talking about the "end of the age." Jesus could not come back before these prophecies were fulfilled. We will address these points more fully in Chapter 8, when we critique and examine Matthew 24.

Considering these momentous events, MacArthur writes:

> First, all the general "signs of the times" given in the New Testament have been fulfilled and are being fulfilled before our eyes. They are, in fact, characteristics of the entire church age. Apostasy and unbelief, self-love and sin, wars, rumors of wars, and natural disasters have been common throughout the church age.[7]

A "general sign"? A general sign of what? A sign has to indicate something, or it is not a sign. If the leaves on the trees in my backyard never fell off, staying green all year round, like an evergreen tree, what would that be a sign of? Maybe mutant trees? However, when they start to change color, it is a sign autumn is near, and that winter will be arriving shortly thereafter.

MacArthur says apostasy is a sign, a sign of ... more apostasy? He also says that sin and wars and unbelief "are characteristics of the entire church age." However, when did such events not occur during any age after Adam and Eve's original sin? Knowing this, how can the aforesaid "general signs" signal anything of note? Indeed, MacArthur states all this upheaval would occur after the Rapture: "There are indeed many signs that must precede His final coming with the saints in glory. But the aspect of Christ's return we look for today is the Rapture—His coming for the saints ... there are no signs whatsoever that will precede the Rapture."[8]

Where are these signs MacArthur references? Either there are signs or there are not signs; you cannot have it both ways. What does MacArthur mean when he says, "all the general signs of the times given in the New Testament have been fulfilled and are being fulfilled before our eyes"?[9] LaHaye and Jenkins, in their book *Are We Living in the End Times?*, claim that "Many ancient prophecies are unfolding before our eyes ... but they could not be fulfilled until Israel was back in her land, as she is today."[10]

If the statements by MacArthur and LaHaye are taken at face value, then the Rapture has never been imminent at any point over the last 1,950 years. For if these requisite signs (prophecies) needed to be fulfilled, and are still being fulfilled, the Rapture could not have happened before they were completed. In sum, if prophecy is only being realized now, how could the Rapture happen before the prophecy is entirely fulfilled? Thusly, if all these prescribed events had to be fulfilled first, then the Rapture could not have been imminent at any time prior.

So, if the early Church believed the Rapture (parousia) was imminent (and they did!), even though it was still at least 1,950 years away, it would seem they were wrong—at the very least, misled. In addition, if more prophecy must be fulfilled before the parousia, then the great airlift is not imminent today—or any day. Furthermore, since the Rapture will not be imminent until the entire prophecy comes to pass, that would mean Jesus was wrong as well! What confused teaching this is!

DISPENSATIONALISTS TEACH THE THIRD COMING IS THE SECOND COMING OF JESUS

Some errors on the teaching of Christ's second coming are common to all Dispensationalists, while some are distinct to MacArthur and other would-be "prophets." The following discussion deals with the general Dispensational teaching on the second coming of Christ.

MacArthur says, "Scripture suggests that the Second Coming occurs in two stages–first the rapture, when He comes for the saints and they are caught up to meet Him in the air (I Thess. 4:14–17) and second, His return to earth, when He comes with His saints (Jude 14) to execute judgment against His enemies."[11]

Christian theologian Charles C. Ryrie says of the second coming, "At the close of this age, Premillennialists believe that Christ will return for His Church, meeting her in the air (this is not the Second Coming of Christ), which event, called the rapture or translation, will usher in a seven-year period of tribulation on the earth. After this the Lord will return to the earth (this is the Second Coming of Christ)."[12]

Dispensationalists say when Christ returns for His Church—in what they call "the Rapture"—that is not the second coming. They believe when Jesus comes for a third (and final) time with His Church, this is the second coming. However, when Jesus comes back with His Church after the Rapture, it would have to be His *third* coming because it takes place seven years after His second coming.

Nowhere does Scripture speak of two "second comings"; thus, the Dispensational thesis disregards the Bible. In fact, to be extremely candid, the Bible never speaks of a "second coming" of Christ—period. The very closest it comes is in Hebrews 9:26, 28. He came the first time to die on the Cross for our sins, to save us (we are told, *"at the end of the ages"*—1,985 years ago). Then, the second time, we are told, He comes to deliver that salvation, personally—to make that salvation retroactive and activated in you when you receive Him, by believing in Him, for you to actually experience it. *"Once at the end of the ages, He has appeared* (Greek: phaneroó: to make clear or known) *to put away sin by the sacrifice of Himself ... Christ was offered once to bear the sins of many. To those who eagerly wait for Him He will appear* (Greek: horaó: be experienced, be discerned, be perceived) *a second time, apart from sin, for salvation."*

Dispensationalists say, as does Scripture, no man or angel knows the day or the hour of the coming of Jesus. But every Christian and angel would know *"the times and the seasons which the Father hath put in his own power"* (Acts 1:7), as well as the day and the hour of his final coming. How? According to most Dispensationalists, the tribulation is seven years long. Therefore, all the Christians (and angels) would have to do is count the days from the time the Christians were raptured and, when seven years had passed, the Lord would return in what they call the second coming.

Dispensationalists believe the second and final coming of Jesus is the great hope of the Christian. Jesus said, *"Watch therefore: for ye know not what hour your Lord doth come"* (Matt. 24:42). But, if the Rapture is not the second and final coming, what sense would it make to "watch" for Jesus? What would be the point? We would not have to wait because the

Church would already have been with the Lord for seven years, and would be coming back with Him at His second coming (i.e., His third coming). Is this not clear? As mud! And you thought a life insurance policy was confusing!

Here is how Dispensationalists layout the various "comings" of the Lord:

> 1st. His birth in Bethlehem. His baptism by John the Baptist in the Jordan River and His triumphal entry into Jerusalem were not comings because He had already come (or arrived) at His birth.
>
> 2nd. His next coming or return is from heaven, which is called the Rapture, when Jesus comes for His Church.
>
> 3rd. His third coming or return is also from heaven, but with His saints seven years after the first return, which was the Rapture event.

Any way you slice it, Dispensationalists teach a second and then a third coming of Jesus. This position sounds so bizarre, it is a wonder anyone would teach it, let alone believe it. This is not what I would ever impart, nor what the Bible says. Nevertheless, this is the hodgepodge Dispensationalists look to instill out of the teachings of the Lord.

DISPENSATIONALISM—A FAILED INTERPRETIVE MODEL

Harold Camping would not quit, even after successive failed predictions starting in September 1994 and continuing to May 21, 2011. He followed up with the audacious statement that the actual apocalypse was set to occur on October 21, 2011. Of course, the cataclysmic event never occurred. Camping had probably heard the old adage "Never give up." However, he really should have given heed to "Do not beat a dead horse." I really pray his fellow false prophets would stop this date-setting nonsense.

Shortly before his death on December 15, 2013, he admitted in a private interview he no longer believed anybody could know the time of the Rapture or the end of the world. That was in blatant contrast to his former staunch position on the Rapture subject.

It is not only important to show where Harold Camping and others (such as William Miller and Edgar C. Whisenant) were wrong in their predictions. It is also crucial to understand they were using an interpretive model that leads otherwise intelligent people to make false predictions repeatedly.

The history of Dispensationalism/premillennialism is littered with hopelessly inaccurate prophecies, erroneous speculations, and a growing list of fundamental errors. As to this panoply of failed predictions, Dwight Wilson wisely states in *Armageddon Now!*:

> The current crisis was always identified as a sign of the end, whether it was the Russo-Japanese War, the First World War, the Second World War, the Palestine War, the Suez Crisis, the June War, or the Yom Kippur War. The revival of the Roman Empire has been identified variously as Mussolini's empire, the League of Nations, the United Nations, the European Defense Community, the Common Market, and NATO. Speculation on the Antichrist has included Napoleon, Mussolini, Hitler, and Henry Kissinger ... The "kings of the east" have been variously the Turks, the lost tribes of Israel, Japan, India, and China ... The restoration of the latter rain has been pinpointed to have begun in 1897, 1917, and 1948. The end of the "times of the Gentiles" has been placed in 1895, 1917, 1948, and 1967...[13]

Irvin Baxter,[14] Tim LaHaye, and John MacArthur, along with many other Dispensationalists, have not set a specific date for the Rapture or second coming of Jesus. In fact, many Dispensationalists denounced Harold Camping for his false prophecy. Camping's fallacious predictions drew the ire of many within the Dispensational community, as well it should. However, because all Dispensationalists use the same interpretative grid and the same basic reasoning, they have, in essence, set a firm date and time for the final coming of the Lord: before our generation passes away. Thus, in reality, they are just as culpable as Harold Camping, for in just a few years their erroneous speculations will have failed to come to pass. In addition, as these events fail to happen—akin to their predecessors—they will be deemed guilty of bearing false witness to Jesus's final return.

Every Dispensational commentator, preacher, and pastor who denounced Harold Camping's failed predictions of Judgment Day have all missed the boat. They all still believe we are living in the end times or last days. They teach the coming of the Lord is soon, just around the corner, and within our generation. They decry Camping's setting of a specific date; however, they are just as guilty, and maybe more so, of bearing false witness by misinterpreting, ignoring, and/or taking out of context the passages of Scripture that deal with eschatology.

Irvin Baxter had this advert on his "Endtime Ministries" website as recently as June 2011:

> APOCALYPSE–Beware of False Prophets! Do you want to understand the timeline of *ENDTIME EVENTS just ahead*? (emphasis added)

Anyone who called the toll-free number could get seven hours of DVDs, a 113-page manual, and an interactive prophecy timeline—all for just $125! But I guarantee that everyone who obtained this material and studied it diligently was still just as confused, just as ignorant, and just as wrong about end time events as they were before they received these prophetic insights. Why? Because it will be confirmed (when the days of this supposed last generation run out), that Baxter is part of the ever-growing list of failed prophets who thought they were living in the last days and had it all figured out, but were sadly mistaken. Baxter already is—what all end times preachers are destined to become—false witnesses of events that will never occur. [15]

What makes these end times preachers so sinister is most are blind to their error and unable to see the fact that, sooner or later, they all become false prophets—which God so profoundly *hates*!

There is no way to get around the fact that if you teach and preach Jesus is coming soon to spirit us off this earth—for it is we who are pegged the "terminal generation"—you are in the same camp as Harold Camping, for you have the same mindset and are using the same interpretative grid to predict the end date arriving within our generation.

The teaching we are living in the last days and we are the generation that Jesus will spirit off this planet has been the mainstay of most evangelical churches for the last 50 years. As president of American Vision, Gary DeMar states:

> Entire ministries, seminaries, churches, and publishing companies are built on it. Of course, we don't find today's popular prophecy teachers arguing for a particular day or hour, but we do find them assuring us that we are the terminal generation and Jesus is returning "soon."[16]

ALL FROM THE SAME TREE

Today's prophecy teachers, be they Harold Camping, Irvin Baxter, John MacArthur, or a host of others take their doctrine of the end times from the same Dispensational tree.

Every tree, even within the same species, is slightly different from another. Each fruit of an orange tree differs slightly from all the other fruit on that given tree. Each orange is unique. Some will be larger, some smaller, some sweeter, and some a different color or shape. Each branch on the tree will be slightly different from all the other branches. Though the fruits, leaves, and branches may vary a bit, one from another, they still all belong to the same tree. If the tree is a good tree, it will bear good fruit. If it is a diseased tree, it will bear rotten fruit.

End times teaching, be it Harold Camping's distinct brand of date-setting, or the generational date-setting of Irvin Baxter, Tim LaHaye, and John MacArthur, has all been plucked from the same diseased tree.

The Dispensational tree features three different "fruits" on the rapture branch: pre-trib, mid-trib, and post-trib. There are also different lengths of time on the tribulation branch: 3.5 years, 7 years, 14 years, and 21 years. So too, different shapes and colors of fruit appear on the date-setting branch: day-specific and generational date-setting. However, whether a branch produces a Camping fruit, a Baxter fruit, or a LaHaye fruit, each fruit, the leaves, and the branches all belong to the same toxic tree.

The Dispensational tree is diseased because it has always produced rotten fruit: people who are pessimistic, escapist, defeatist, and retreatist. Sooner or later, all those who teach a "soon coming" bring forth a harvest of false witness, which gives great occasion to the enemies of the Lord to blaspheme.

Decade after decade, Dispensational teachers have shouted, *"He Is Coming Soon!"* They never retract their words but continue their argument until death claims them. Others, such as the specific date-setters (like Camping and Whisenant), retract their predictions the day after they fail to happen. These "prophets" then abashedly claim they made a mistake in their calculations, their timing was off, or they find some other excuse to explain why the Lord did not come or why the judgment of God did not fall. However, the date-setters continue to labor on and on bearing successive fresh crops of false witness.

TWO BRANDS OF DISPENSATIONAL ERROR

1. Specific date-setting

All modern specific date/end time prophecy teachers, such as Camping, Smith, Whisenant, and others are, in reality, engaging in speculative activities … not unlike tea leaf and tarot card readers and other occultists who claim they can tell the future. Instead of using the usual tools of the trade (tea leaves, tarot cards, crystal balls, bat wings, dice), these last days speculators employ more biblically sounding hocus-pocus. They "look into" current events to determine the future and "discern the times." They tell us they are privy to special knowledge and anointed information which they alone can use to divine and unlock the Scriptures dealing with end time and last days events. While it is true some are sincere in their endeavors to expound the Word of Life to those who are thirsting, others are just plain charlatans, hustlers, and deceivers—hawking their latest prophetic DVDs and books. However, whether or not they are true believers, they are still serving up a toxic brew of error that harms the Church of God.

2. Generational date-setting

The other brand of Dispensational error known as generational date-setting—which Irvin Baxter, Tim LaHaye, John Hagee, Dr. Jack Van Impe, and many others dogmatically assert—is a much more insidious venom. These modern-day prognosticators turn a blind eye to the multitudinous hordes of those who have gone before. They speculate not where "no man has gone before," but where myriads have already trod and been found wanting. Their concocted plots of end time scenarios and events—such as cataclysmic war between China and the USA—continue to produce fearful, pessimistic, escapist, and defeatist Christians. Tim LaHaye confirms as much when he writes:

> Most knowledgeable Christians are looking for the Second Coming of Christ and the tribulation period that He predicted would come before the end of the age. Because present world conditions are so similar to those the Bible prophesies for the last days ... they conclude that a takeover of our culture by the forces of evil is inevitable; so they do nothing to resist it.[17]

However, whether a teacher is a charlatan or sincere expounder of the Scripture, whenever he sets a specific date for the Rapture or uses a generational date method, the message is inherently worthless. Therefore, they are, to that extent, false witnesses! Their erroneous speculations are more than deceitful for those who swallow their poisonous fruit; the effects can be jeopardizing.

For instance, some of those who partook of Harold Camping's toxin quit their jobs, gave away many of their possessions, and spent their entire life-savings promoting his folly.[18] Others who follow the generational date-setters become, as stated earlier, fearful, pessimistic, and defeatist. Instead of rendering useful service for the Lord, they withdraw from the very institutions founded by their illustrious Christian forefathers: institutions such as Harvard, Princeton, Yale, and Oxford, which once trained men and women in the ways of God.

Many of those who study history see the putrid results the teaching of Dispensationalism has produced. They lament the vision of victory the recent crop of preachers has failed to deliver to their flocks. They long for the days of old, when our nation was young, when the teaching and preaching was a diet of Biblical principles, a comprehensive worldview, and the main course of dominion and victory.

The Dispensational doctrine of defeat cannot sustain the governmental system and moral foundation painstakingly built by our wise forefathers.

Pastor Roger Anghis, in his article "Defining America's Exceptionalism," cogently states:

> The pastors of America were more important than any one group of people from the establishing of the Colonies to the developing of our governmental system, education system and defining the moral foundation that all of it was grounded upon and defending it with their very lives. Oh, to have that kind of pastor today throughout America![19]

Organizations like the YMCA and YWCA[20] were places of refuge and Christian service until Christians abandoned them to the forces of secular humanism (i.e., with its potential for evil). Why did this happen? I suspect it is due to the burgeoning influence of the pessimistic doctrine of Dispensationalism, which teaches this world will grow worse and worse, and there is nothing we can do to change it. Unfortunately, those deceived by this malignant error will continue to partake of the end time fraud until they are open to reassessing their beliefs.

ROOT CAUSE OF ERROR FOR ALL DATE-SETTING

Throughout history, there have always been those who have set dates for the second coming and other end time events. Long before the Johnny-come-lately doctrine of Dispensationalism (around 1830), hundreds, probably thousands, tried their hand at predicting the "end of the world." Unfortunately, it has been a perennial fascination within Christianity. Francis X. Gumerlock catalogs many of the prognosticators in his detailed book *the Day and the Hour.*

Why is it that every prediction of end time events has failed and *always will* fail? The reason is simple. Modern prophecy experts and end time diviners are still predicting events that have already happened—but which they mistakenly think are still in the future. In II Peter 3:3, Peter aptly called unbelievers "*scoffers.*" Moreover, would not those who *intentionally* deny, misread, twist, disregard, and refuse to believe the numerous, clear *time statements* found in Scripture, also be correctly called scoffers?

The Mount Olivet Discourse and the Book of Daniel's Prophecy of Seventy Weeks were future events when originally written. But they were duly fulfilled and are now history. The Book of Revelation has, likewise, been fulfilled and is now history. As Gary DeMar points out in the foreword to *the Day and the Hour*:

> The biblical writers are straightforward in their claim that certain prophetic events were to happen "soon" for those who first read the prophecies. The eschatological events were near for them. No other interpretation is possible if the words are taken in their "plain, primary, ordinary, usual, or normal" sense; that is, if they are interpreted literally.
>
> If the biblical authors had wanted to be tentative, vague, or ambiguous in the way they described the timing of future events, they would have equivocated by using words expressing probability... .[21]

For Dispensational Christians to keep making the same errors over and over has to be a form of insanity. And if they are not insane, these "prophets" are very slow learners. The reality is that all those who predict (wrongly, 100% of the time) the second coming still use the same failed methods and interpretations, while determinedly expecting different results!

THE LAST DAYS HAVE A BEGINNING AND END

Let us delve a little deeper into the teachings of Van Impe, LaHaye, Hagee, and their ilk by examining their take on the last days and their penchant for setting dates for the coming of the Lord, just as Harold Camping did.

Applying global statistics, the average lifespan is about 72 years. During each lifetime, there is a beginning, middle, and an end. These individuals' last days are not their teenage years or when they are 40 or 50 (and probably going through some kind of a "midlife crisis"). Nor are their last days what some call the "golden years." Their last days, the end of days for them, are the last few months or days of life spent here on this earth.

The Greek phrase *in the last days,* as found in many passages such as II Timothy 3:1 refers to the prophesied "End of Days," sometimes called *acharit ha-yamin* in Hebrew. Similarly, as in a person's lifetime, this Biblical phrase implies both a starting point and an ending point in time. It does not mean an indefinite period, with no beginning or end. It does not mean "enduring" or "to continue on and on with no end in sight." When the last day of the *last days* has finished the apocalypse would be over, and the next age would start.

WHEN WAS THE ALARM CLOCK SET?

Those who teach Jesus is *coming soon*—that we are living in the *last days* and we are the *terminal generation*—are just as deceived as Harold Camping, for they also have set a future date for the coming of the Lord. When you set a timer or an alarm clock, it will continue to wind down until it gets to the precise time which you have set. When the alarm goes off the time is up. To those who teach these are the last days, when did their timer start? When was the alarm clock set? When did the countdown begin?

Most modern-day soothsayers use the founding of the nation of Israel in May 1948 for their point in time when the alarm clock was set. In the *Search for Truth* teachers' manual used by the United Pentecostal Church, you will read, "The return of the Jews to the land of Palestine is another of the most recent signs which have been fulfilled."[22]

Evangelist Donald Perkins states on his website:

One of the greatest signs of our day occurred on May 14, 1948, when the nation of Israel was reestablished after nearly 2,000 years of desolation. The Word of God prophesies the future for this nation in the latter days. Israel's birth in 1948 was by divine appointment.[23]

Some use Israel's Six-Day War (June 5–June 10, 1967) as the pretext for setting the alarm clock for the end times and the last days generation. In writing about this event, Dwight Wilson states:

> The initial response of the premillenarians has solidified into an enduring disposition in favor of the war and Israel. A 1973 article in "Christian Life" claimed that the war was a fulfillment of Psalm 83:1-8 and that the territories conquered (Jerusalem, the West Bank, the Gaza Strip, and the old city of Samaria) had been predicted by Obadiah 17–20. Isaiah 19:1–17 was interpreted as a prophecy of Egypt's economic plight as a result of the war.[15] S. Maxwell Coder in an article entitled "Jerusalem: Key to the Future" emphasized the war's significance: "Gentile times were fulfilled when Gentiles ceased to control Jerusalem in 1967." The world, he said, was now in a period of transition which would bring the time of the Gentiles to its ultimate end.[24]

Just to make this clear, Israel becoming a nation again is just one of the "signs" Dispensationalists use to pinpoint the start of the last day's generation. However, the regathering of the Jews to Palestine and the rebirth of the nation of Israel has always played a key part in end time and last days scenarios. As these prognosticators believe and teach, the generation that sees these signs—the regathering of the Jews back to Israel and Israel's rebirth—is the last (terminal) generation that will see the coming of the Lord.

HOW LONG IS A BIBLICAL GENERATION?

As I was searching for the answer to this question, I determined most end time scholars and theologians consider a generation as lasting for 40 years. According to Dr. Jack Van Impe, "... a generation is anywhere from 35 to 40 years."[25] So, using the 1948 date as our starting point and adding 40 years, we arrive at 1988 as the year by which the last generation should have ended. This date has long passed, Christ did not come, and we are still here (as some may have noticed). If we use 1967 as our starting point and add a Biblical generation of 40 years, we end up in the year 2007, which is also in the past. Clearly, the timing of these so-called scholars and theologians is more than a bit fishy.

However, instead of pondering why the last day's generation has run out of time with so little notice and arguing about the length of a generation, we will extend our discourse. Let us give these prophets enough rope to hang themselves, using any practical means to try to make their scheme possible. To do so, we will use what I call "rubber band theology" to stretch out the prophetic timeline for as long as we need it to be.

Instead of using the Biblical generation of 40 years [or Psalms 90:10 lifespan of seventy to eighty years], we will cite the longest-lived person in modern history to establish the length of a generation. According to Wikipedia, the person with the longest confirmed lifespan was Jeanne Calment of France (1875–1997), Having lived to the astonishing age of 122 years and 164 days, we will use 122 years as the length of time of our last days generation. Now, on to the next question.

STARTING POINT FOR THE
LAST GENERATION

When did this present last day's generation begin? As noted before, some authors believe 1948 is the correct starting point, while others hold to 1967. Some even use the November 2, 1917, Balfour Declaration (a statement of British support for the establishment in Palestine of a national home for the Jewish people) as the correct point in time. According to pastor and premillennialist Dwight Wilson:

> The Balfour Declaration was viewed by the Premillennialists as the beginning of the restoration of Israel to Palestine, the opening scene of the end-time saga which would culminate in the early reign of Christ for the millennium. This unveiling of the divine drama was enthusiastically applauded by the Premillennialists.[26]

Rather than quibble, let us just use 1967 (Israel's consolidation of Jerusalem in the Six-Day War) as the starting point of the terminal or last day's generation.

We have now arrived at 122 years as the longest possible length of a generation. We have also determined 1967 is the latest possible starting time of the last day's generation. Using these benchmarks, what is the final feasible moment for our terminal generation to end? When does the alarm clock that was wound up in 1967 finally wind down?

To give the soothsayers the full benefit of the doubt, we have stretched the last possible date in time to its breaking point. Adding 122 years to the start of the terminal generation (1967) brings us to 2089. This is the date ALL Dispensationalists have, by default or by implication, set as the absolute last possible year Jesus could come back. Remember, they teach the Lord must come back before the last days generation passes away. (Actually, their final date would have to be at least seven years before 2089, for Dispensationalists believe Jesus will come invisibly for His Church seven years before His second coming.)

Whether or not you accept my timing of the last generation, there is no getting around the fact John Hagee and his fellow prognosticators continue to teach the generation that saw Israel become a nation is the terminal generation, and this generation's time will predictably run out—whether they know it or not. I have given them oodles of time with my scenario, probably much more than they themselves allow. Whatever number Dispensational prophets want to arbitrarily pick out of thin air for the length of a generation; and whichever preset date they prefer for the fulfillment of the birth of modern Israel—1917, 1948, 1967, or some other—the fact remains the last day's generation they envision must end very soon, for their game is almost over!

It is unconscionable and blatant hypocrisy for Dispensationalists to condemn Camping for setting a specific future date, and then with the same breath turn around and set yet another future date (2089, the last possible year) for the end of a generation. The Bible plainly condemns such behavior: "*Thou therefore which teachest another, teachest thou not thyself? Thou that preachest a man should not steal, dost thou steal? Thou that sayest a man should not commit adultery, dost thou commit adultery*" (Rom. 2:21–23)? And to all Dispensationalists, I offer, "Thou therefore which sayest, thou shalt not set a date, dost thou set a date?" Unfortunately, the answer to that question is a resounding *yes*!

THE CREDIBILITY OF JESUS

There are many reasons the doctrine concerning the last days, end times, and the second coming is so important. The number one reason is the credibility, reliability, and truthfulness of Jesus's words are at stake.

In Chapter 2 we saw how Scripture and the dictionary used and defined the word "soon." With this knowledge, we now know, when Jesus talked about His pending coming, soon can never have meant 1,950 years in the future!

I have heard that Jesus is coming *soon* for over forty-eight years. Now my grandchildren are hearing it. So many years have passed that the word "soon" is no longer relevant to anyone's messianic expectation.

Skeptics, such as Muslims, Jews, and atheists, have not overlooked this point. Atheist Bertrand Russell, in his essay *Why I Am Not a Christian*, rejects the inspiration of the New Testament:

> I am concerned with Christ as He appears in the Gospels ... there one does find some things that do not seem to be very wise ... For one thing, He certainly thought that His second coming would occur in clouds of glory before the death of all the people who were living at the time. There are a great many texts that prove that ... He believed that His coming would happen during the lifetime of many then living. That was the belief of his earlier followers, and it was the basis of a good deal of his moral teaching.[27]

Russell would have had a legitimate dispute if Christ did not come before the death of all the people who were living at the time.

There is another important reason the word "soon" must be interpreted as Jesus intended. When Christians continually set dates and make predictions that do not come to pass (is that not what false prophets do?), they give the world a justification to mock and ridicule Jesus and His Church.

Why didn't the church I attended denounce Edgar C. Whisenant as a false prophet? In addition, why do not Christian churches, TV, or radio stations publicly identify Whisenant and his fellow oracles as false prophets? Even Peter was called to account for an error in judgment he made (Gal. 2:11).

The reason most churches did not and cannot is that they cleave to the same erroneous doctrinal foundations (Dispensationalism) as Whisenant. The only difference is Whisenant crossed the line by setting a specific date—which Christian churches (even those with Dispensational inclinations) generally do not do. However, to say continually the end is near (inevitably followed by "Whoops! I guess we were wrong again") and still teach that "the stage is being set" is not the God-given mission of the Church—and certainly not what the early Church taught. All the early Christians had to do was wait for Jesus' own words to be fulfilled and hurriedly leave the doomed city of Jerusalem before it was destroyed.

Every date-setter and end time preacher has something in common: they have been wrong 100% of the time and will always be wrong. With the dawn of the 21st century, every end-time event that was supposed to have happened has failed. "Rapture fever" (as Gary North calls it) has died down, but many are still afflicted. There will be further outbreaks, as the *Left Behind* movie and book series attest. In addition, if any new prophetic events take place in the Middle East, such as a war involving Israel, or a particularly large earthquake, many false prophets will rush to get more books into print to fan the flames of Rapture fever once more. The desire for fame, so rampant among these deceivers, is a terrible thing.

Dispensational eschatology is, at bottom, a teaching framework distilled from myriad reports of current calamities, famines, earthquakes, wars, and ever-present violence (while turning a blind eye to any good events). The concept then twists and distorts Christ's clear Scriptural teachings presented in His Olivet Discourse. Misapplying our Lord's clear, time-sensitive statements is nothing short of reprehensible. Misapplying Jesus' warnings (which clearly reflect historically documented events of 1,900 years ago), and arguing those warnings point to events still in our future, is theological hogwash.

FOOTNOTES

1. Only months before the year 2011 started, Harold Camping published on his website, *WeCanKnow.com*, that the rapture would take place on May 21, 2011. His site stated:

   "This website serves as an introduction and portal to four faithful ministries which are teaching that WE CAN KNOW from the Bible alone that the date of the rapture of believers will take place on May 21, 2011 and that God will destroy this world on October 21, 2011. Please take your time and browse through the teachings of Harold Camping, President of Family Radio. Visit EBible Fellowship, Bible Ministries International, and The-Latter-Rain to read and listen to many faithful teachers give scriptural insight on the doctrines that God is teaching His people. Learn about the Biblical Timeline of History, the correct method of Bible interpretation, the End of the Church Age and God's command to believers that they must depart out of the churches. Study the proofs that God has so graciously given in His Word showing us that these dates are 100% accurate and beyond dispute...."

   Some dismissed Camping as a "prophecy" crank with limited audience reach. But he was the president of the California-based Family Radio, a worldwide conglomerate of dozens of radio stations broadcasting a conservative and somewhat idiosyncratic Christian message. The network's website homepage in early 2011 included a banner that read "Judgment Day: May 11, 2011."

2. Gary DeMar, *Last Days Madness* (Brentwood, Tennessee: Wolgemuth & Hyatt, 1991) p. 9.

3. In John Noë's 1999 book, *Beyond the End Times*, published by Preterist Resources, he says on page 22, "In 1950, *U.S. News & World Report* magazine commented on Dr. Graham's "youthful exuberance" at a rally in Los Angeles and quoted him as saying, 'Two years and it's all going to be over.' Since then, Graham has become more cautious regarding apocalyptic timetables."

4. John F. MacArthur, *The Second Coming* (Crossway Books, A Division of Good News Publishers, 1300 Crescent Street, Wheaton, Illinois 60187, 1999) p. 52.

5. Dave Hunt, *Whatever Happened to Heaven*, (The Berean Call PO Box 7019, Bend, OR 97708, 2011) p. 39.

6. MacArthur, *The Second Coming*, p. 197.

7. MacArthur, *The Second Coming*, p. 54.

8. MacArthur, *The Second Coming*, p. 137.

9. MacArthur, *The Second Coming*, p. 54.

10. Tim LaHaye, Jerry B. Jenkins, *Are We Living in the End Times?* (Tyndale House Publishers, Inc., Wheaton, Illinois) p. 47.

11. MacArthur, *The Second Coming*, p. 87.

12. Dr. Kenneth L. Gentry, Jr., *He Shall Have Dominion* (Institute for Christian Economics, P. O. Box 8000, Tyler, Texas 75711, 1992) p. 59.

13. Dwight Wilson, *Armageddon Now!* (Institute for Christian Economics, P. O. Box 8000, Tyler, Texas 75711, 1991) p. 216.

14. Irvin Baxter, pastor and televangelist of Endtime Ministries died on Tuesday, November 3, 2020, of complications from Covid-19. He was 75. His ministry's purpose is to prove that we are now at the end of the era of human government and very near the beginning of the prophesied Kingdom of God. It's a purpose he never lived to see, nor will any such ministry.

15. Irvin Baxter published the following prediction. *The Coming War with China*, a full-page advertisement in the May 22, 2000 edition of *USA Today*. "The Bible prophesies a war for the near future in which two billion people will die." How near? "The next few months."

16. Gary DeMar, May 24, 2011, American Vision website article. *Before Harold Camping, there Were Hal Lindsey and Chuck Smith*.

17. Tim LaHaye, *The Battle for the Mind*, quoted in *HE SHALL HAVE DOMINION A Postmillennial Eschatology*, Kenneth L. Gentry Jr. (Institute for Christian Economics, P. O. Box 8000, Tyler, Texas 75711, 1991) p. 24.

18. There were many stories on the Internet dealing with this: "New York Man Spends Life Savings Ahead of May 21 Doomsday," New York Post, May 21, 2011; "Apocalypse almost: World waits for Rapture," AFP/File, May 21, 2011.

19. Pastor Roger Anghis, NewsWithViews.com, October 30, 2011 article "Defining America's Exceptionalism" Part 24.

20. The first YMCA was concerned with Bible study, although the organization has generally moved on to a more holistic approach to youth work. Around six years after its birth, an international YMCA conference in Paris decided that the objective of the organization should become "Christian discipleship developed through a program of religious, educational, social and physical activities." More recent objectives as found on the YMCA UK website include no reference to discipleship. From Wikipedia, the free encyclopedia.

21. Francis X. Gumerlock, *The Day and the Hour* (American Vision P.O. Box 220 Powder Springs, Georgia 30127, 2000) p. xxiv.

22. Teachers' Manual, *Search for Truth* (Search for Truth Publications, 10929 Almeda-Genoa Rd., Houston, Texas, 77034, 1965) p. 109.

23. Evangelist Donald Perkins, website, *According To Prophecy Ministries, The Signs of the Times; How Close are We?*.

24. Wilson, Armageddon *Now!*, p. 192.

25. Dr. Jack Van Impe, *Everything you always wanted to know about PROPHECY* (Jack Van Impe Ministries, Box J, Royal Oak, Michigan, 1980) p. 40.

26. Wilson, *Armageddon Now!*, p. 15.

27. John Noë, *The Only Solution to the Liberal/Skeptic Attack on the Bible* (Fishers IN: Prophecy Reformation Institute, 2000). p. 1.

CHAPTER FIVE

THE HISTORIC CHURCH BELIEVED IN VICTORY

—∞∞∞—

VICTORY: THE HISTORIC VIEW OF THE CHURCH

Down through the ages, the Church knew she would be victorious in changing the world with the help of the Holy Spirit. Believers knew there would be trouble, persecution, and death for many of them; but they also knew they would overcome in the end! Not just victory in eternity (Psalms 78:69, 93:1, 96:10, 104:5, 119:90; Eccl. 1:4; Eph. 3:21) but **victory on earth**, taking the Gospel worldwide to fashion the kingdom of our Lord.

Origen (AD 185–254) was a notable church father of considerable influence who believed Christianity would gain dominion over all:

[I]t is evident that even the barbarians, when they yield obedience to the word of God, will become most obedient to the law, and most humane; and every form of worship will be destroyed except the religion of Christ, which will alone prevail. And indeed it will one day triumph, as its principles take possession of the minds of men more and more every day.[1]

John Calvin (1509–1564), although a devout amillennialist, was clearly optimistic about the success of the Gospel:

Our doctrine must tower unvanquished above all the glory and above all the might of the world, for it is not of us, but of the living God and his Christ whom the Father has appointed King to 'rule from sea to sea, and from the rivers even to the ends of the earth ...' And he is so to rule as to smite the whole earth with its iron and brazen strength, with its gold and silver brilliance, shattering it with the rod of his mouth as an earthen vessel, just as the prophets have prophesied concerning the magnificence of his reign.[2]

Attorney and law professor John Eidsmoe, in his book, *Christianity and the Constitution*, says "Postmillennialism was the predominant eschatology of the 1600s, 1700s, and early 1800s."[3] According to Eidsmoe, postmillennial eschatology "... assumed an upward direction of history–God was using believers to prepare the world for the return of Christ."[4] This was the eschatology adopted by most Puritans.

Well-known intellectual Puritan divine, the Reverend Jonathan Edwards, described his thoughts on New England's postmillennialism role in his sermon *The Latter-Day Glory Is Probably to Begin in America*. In that sermon he believed the New World, particularly North America (as opposed to the Old Worlds of Europe and Asia) would be the place of honor to host the second coming:

He noted that the "sun of righteousness" had been traveling from east to west, and therefore when the time comes of the church's deliverance from her enemies, so often typified by the Assyrians, the light will rise in the west, till it shines through the world like the sun in its meridian brightness.

... And if we may suppose that this glorious work of God shall begin in any part of America, I think, if we consider the circumstances of the settlement of New England, it must needs appear the most likely, of all American colonies, to be the place whence this work shall principally take its rise... .[5]

Protestant theologian Philip Schaff completed his eight-volume set, *History of the Christian Church,* sometime before 1893—just as the pessimistic tentacles of Dispensationalism started to strangle the expected burgeoning of the kingdom of Christ here on earth. Schaff wrote with the belief prevalent in his day that Christ's kingdom would continue to grow and change the world:

> It is a continuous commentary on the Lord's twin parables of the mustard-seed and of the leaven. It shows at once how Christianity spreads over the world, and how it penetrates, transforms, and sanctifies the individual and all the departments and institutions of social life ... From Jesus Christ, since his manifestation in the flesh, an unbroken stream of divine light and life has been and is still flowing, and will continue to flow, in ever-growing volume, through the waste of our fallen race; and all that is truly great and good and holy in the annals of church history is due, ultimately, to the impulse of his spirit.[6]

In *He Shall Have Dominion*, ordained minister and reformed theologian Kenneth L. Gentry Jr. lists many noteworthy adherents to the postmillennial view of the Scriptures, from the early church fathers up to the present.[7] I don't necessarily reside in the postmillennial camp, but I certainly share their view that He shall reign from sea to shining sea and "far as the curse is found."

This victorious theme is also apparent in many of the hymns written in the past. "Joy to the World" celebrates victory and dominion of Christ's kingdom here on earth. This hymn, written by Isaac Watts, comes from a paraphrase of Psalm 98, verses 4 through 9. It was published in *Psalms of David Imitated in the Language of the New Testament* in 1719.

The melody by Lowell Mason was taken from different sections of *Handel's Messiah*. Mason's uplifting music was published for the first time in 1836. Isaac Watts had a brilliant mind, having authored several books on philosophy and religion. He had a burning desire to elevate the singing in English congregations and make the Scriptures relevant to lay people. He saw hymns as the perfect way to do this.

Below are verses three and four of "Joy to the World." Notice the last part of the third verse, "Far as the curse is found." Watts believed, along with most of the Church, that everything on earth—people, nations, plants, animals—would one day be under God's control and would fully submit to Him:

> No more let sins and sorrows grow,
> Nor thorns infest the ground;
> He comes to make His blessings flow
> Far as the curse is found,
> Far as the curse is found,
> Far as, far as, the curse is found.
>
> He rules the world with truth and grace,
> And makes the nations prove
> The glories of his righteousness,
> And wonders of His love,
> And wonders of His love,
> And wonders, wonders of His love.

Isaac Watts published over 600 hymns, including "O God, Our Help in Ages Past," "When I Survey the Wondrous Cross," "Marching to Zion," "Am I a Soldier of the Cross?," "At the Cross," and "Jesus Shall Reign," which are still popular today. His hymn "Jesus Shall Reign" also shows victory and dominion. The first verse reads:

> Jesus shall reign where'er the sun
> Does his successive journeys run,
> His kingdom stretch from shore to shore
> Till moons shall wax and wane no more.

One reason for the happy, glorious, and triumphal theme of these hymns from the past is the writers knew and used the Scriptures. The Scriptures are the only way to see what the Church should be and what attitude the Church should have. These hymn writers were just echoing what the Scriptures plainly taught: Victory! Of the Church! On earth!

"Onward Christian Soldiers" is another song of victory and dominion. Christ's Church will conquer until all is placed at His feet! In this hymn, Satan and his kingdom are defeated and forced to flee! Christ and His soldiers press on to victory until all is the Lord's. However, incredible as it seems, Dispensationalists have it completely backward. They have the Church and Christ's kingdom fleeing, rather than securing victory.

Onward Christian soldiers, marching as to war,
With the cross of Jesus going on before!
Christ the royal Master, leads against the foe;
Forward into battle, see his banner go!

At the sign of triumph Satan's host doth flee;
On, then, Christian soldiers, on to victory!
Hell's foundation's quiver, at the shout of praise;
Brothers, lift your voices, loud your anthems raise!

Like a mighty army moves the church of God;
Brothers, we are treading where the saints have trod;
We are not divided; all one body we,
One in hope and doctrine, one in charity.

Crowns and thrones may perish,
Kingdoms rise and wane,
But the church of Jesus constant will remain.
Gates of hell can never against that church prevail;
We have Christ's own promise,
And that cannot fail.

Onward, then, ye people, join our happy throng,
Blend With ours your voices in the triumph song;
Glory, laud, And honor, unto Christ the King,
This thro' countless ages men and angels sing.

Chorus:

Onward, Christian soldiers, Marching as to war,
With the cross of Jesus Going on before!

The 1849 hymn "Faith of Our Fathers" also shows holy zeal and a robust belief the Church will win the world for Christ:

> Faith of our fathers, we will strive
> To win all nations unto thee;
> And through the truth that comes from God,
> Mankind shall then indeed be free.
> Faith of our fathers! Holy faith!
> We will be true to thee till death!

Yes, the hymn says, "we will strive," where striving does not necessarily guarantee an inevitable outcome. Nevertheless, Christians of ages past believed they would be victorious here on earth, not just in eternity.

THEME OF VICTORY IS ALL THROUGH THE BIBLE

The theme of victory is found throughout the Old Testament (Gen. 1:28; Isa. 9:6, 11:4; Dan. 2:44), especially in the Book of Psalms (Psalms 2:8–9, 9:17, 22:27–31, 37:9,11, 47:2–4, 66:3–4, 67:1–7, 72:8,17, 86:9, 89:27–29, 36, 102:15, 110:1). It is also found in the New Testament. In I Cor. 15:24–25, we read: *"Then cometh the end, when he shall have delivered up the kingdom to God, even the Father; when he shall have put down all rule and all authority and power. For he must reign, till he hath put all enemies under his feet."*

Some may say that verses in the Psalms do not apply to us today. After all, that is the Old Testament, when the Law of Moses was still enforce, and now that Christ has come, we are under grace. However, many erroneously believe the four gospels, starting with Matthew chapter one, initiates the chronicle of the New Testament. Although each of the gospels is considered New Testament, the majority of each gospel is under the jurisdiction of Old Testament law. Thus, the New Testament does not commence until Christ's resurrection. *"And for this cause he is the mediator of the new testament, that by means of death, for the redemption of the transgressions that were under the first testament, they which are called might receive the promise of eternal inheritance. For where a testament is, there must also of necessity be the death of the testator. For a testament is of force after men are dead; otherwise it is of no strength at all while the testator liveth"* (Heb.

9:15–17). So, most who may have considered the Old Testament as not applicable to modern times must now re-evaluate that belief.

However, if the Old Testament is not applicable to modern times, why did God put it in His Bible for all posterity? The New Testament is full of quotes, allusions, and examples from the Old Testament. The eight authors of the twenty-seven New Testament books correctly interpreted the Old Testament as teaching victory for the Church.

The Apostle Paul certainly believed in such a victory. In I Corinthians 15:24–25, Paul quotes from Daniel 7:14 and Psalm 110:1, with each verse referring to Jesus. This fact is validated by my King James Bible, which states, "A star immediately following a verse in the Old Testament indicates that in the concurrent opinion of many scholars and theologians, the verse embodies a prophetic reference to Christ."

In Chapter 2 in the Book of Daniel, King Nebuchadnezzar had a dream only Daniel could interpret. Nebuchadnezzar had envisioned a large image with a head of gold, breast and arms of silver, thighs of brass, and legs of iron, with feet part iron and part clay. Then a stone smote the image at its feet and broke it in pieces, and the stone that smote the image became a great mountain and filled the whole earth.

Daniel told the king each of the image's materials represented a different kingdom, with Babylon being the head of gold. History shows us there were three other "World kingdoms" after the kingdom of Babylon: the Persian Empire, the Greek Empire (under Alexander the Great), and the Roman Empire.

One of the objections Dispensationalists and others have to the preterist view is its assertion that this whole world will inevitably be transformed into a heavenly realm—Christ's protectorate, domain, and territory—where most people willingly submit. The Scripture, as correctly interpreted by the preterists, says the kingdom (the stone, God's kingdom) will indeed fill the earth, but this kingdom was established long ago at Christ's resurrection (Dan. 2:35, 43, 44; Acts 2:30–31).

The kingdom of the stone had to be set up *"in the days of these Kings"* (Dan. 2:44), meaning the Kings of the fourth monarchy, the Roman Empire. God's kingdom grew from the small stone and *"became a great mountain, and filled the whole earth."* And this kingdom *"shall break in pieces and consume all these kingdoms and it shall stand forever"* (Dan. 2:35,

44). This is God's kingdom. At the resurrection of Christ, the stone began to break in pieces in fulfillment of Daniel's prophecy *"according to the working of his mighty power, which he wrought in Christ, when he raised him from the dead, and set him at his own right hand in the heavenly places, far above all principality, and power, and might, and dominion, and every name that is named, not only in this world, but also in that which is to come"* (Eph. 1:19–21).

In Matthew 13:33 Jesus states, *"The kingdom of heaven is like unto leaven, which a woman took, and hid in three measures of meal, till the whole was leavened."* Adam Clarke, upholding the Church's longstanding belief in victory (until the rise of Dispensationalism), interprets the parable of the leaven thusly:

> As the property of leaven is to change, or assimilate to its own nature, the meal or dough with which it is mixed, so the property of the grace of Christ is to change the whole soul into its own likeness; and God intends that this principle should continue in the soul till all is leavened—till the whole bear the image of the heavenly, as it before bore the image of the earthly. Both these parables are prophetic, and were intended to show, principally, how, from very small beginnings, the Gospel of Christ should pervade all the nations of the world, and fill them with righteousness and true holiness.[8]

The theme of dominion (and the fervent belief this world will become the kingdom of our Lord) is all through the Bible. *"But this man, after he had offered one sacrifice for sins for ever, sat down on the right hand of God; From henceforth expecting till his enemies be made his footstool"* (Heb. 10:12–13). *"The LORD said unto my LORD, Sit thou on my right hand, Until I make thy foes thy footstool"* (Acts 2:34–35). *"And he shall reign over the house of Jacob for ever; and of his kingdom there shall be no end"* (Luke 1:33; see also Matt. 13:24–32)

DISPENSATIONALISM IS A PESSIMISTIC FAITH

There are many who believe Dispensationalism is a pessimistic, not a victorious faith. O. T. Allis says:

> (M)y own studies in this and related fields have convinced me that the most serious error in much of the current 'prophetic' teaching of today is the claim that the future of Christendom is to be read not in terms of Revival and Victory, but of growing impotence and apostasy, and that the only hope of the world is that the Lord will by His visible coming and reign complete the task which He has so plainly entrusted to the church. This claim ... is pessimistic and defeatist. I hold it to be unscriptural. The language of the Great Commission is world-embracing; and it has back of it the authority and power of One who said: "All power is given unto Me in heaven and in earth. Go ye therefore and make disciples of all nations." The duty of the church is to address herself to the achieving of this task in anticipation of the Lord's coming, and not to expect Him to call her away to glory before her task is accomplished.[9]

For Dispensationalist Joe, the world is burning down, victory is nowhere in sight, and escape is the only hope. It is akin to him living in remote woodland. One morning, Joe wakes up and smells smoke. He checks to see if it is from the fireplace in his log cabin. No, the fire is out. However, when he looks through the window, off in the distance, he sees fire and smoke heading in his direction. Nevertheless, Joe does not panic because it is still some distance off. While he makes a phone call to a friend (who conveniently owns a rather large helicopter), he sees on the TV that all hell is breaking loose as the fire starts to rage out of control, consuming everything and everyone in its path. As it gets even nearer (why is *someone* not fighting that darn fire, or at least cutting a firebreak?), Joe checks that everyone in his cabin (the Church) is present and presentable—so that when his buddy in the chopper arrives everyone who has been calmly (and idly) standing round can be winched aboard. It's gonna be close. But Joe's buddy is on his way again ... just like he was back in 1988, 1990, 2000, 2011, and on numerous other scary call-outs that were big news at the time.

At this point, Dispensationalist Joe is not thinking about building an extension to his log cabin. He is certainly not thinking about mulching the garden, planting some vegetables, tidying and decorating his home, starting a Christian school, or applying to become a firefighter, much less cutting a firebreak. His future life on his woodland ranch (the world) is not what he is focused on. All he is thinking about is the "heaven-sent helicopter." Everything he has been working for on the ranch is about to become toast; so he is looking skywards, happy to be getting a free ride out ... any moment now.

That is how it is with not just Joe, but with all Dispensationalists. Planning for the future, working to change our school systems into establishments of godly instruction and true education, building Christian hospitals, having God-fearing great, great, grandchildren 100, 200, or even 1,000 years from now ... none of these would ever enter a Dispensationalist's mind. Why not? Because such futurist thoughts are inconsistent with his doctrine that very soon, in *this* generation, all will be going up in smoke. Just ask Joe! What a brilliantly devilish deception to fool Christians into being utterly ineffective in this world.

Dispensationalists believe the Church is surrounded by an invincible enemy and will have to be evacuated like the Allied troops at Dunkirk, France, in May 1940. The evacuation was successful, though it followed a major defeat, not a victory. At least it was a real, historic event—, which the Rapture will never and can never be.

In the 2001 movie, *Enemy at the Gates*, which describes the events surrounding the Battle of Stalingrad in the winter of 1942 and 1943, Nikita Khrushchev, a commissar who served as an intermediary between Stalin and his generals, took charge of a Russian army that had lost hope and courage in defense of Stalingrad. The scene we will look at begins when Khrushchev walks into the office of the General in charge:

> **Red Army General:** I carried out my orders. I sent in all of my boys. But the Germans engulfed us. They have artillery, aircraft, tanks. And me? What did I have?!

Khrushchev: Sacred duty to resist! I have to report back to the boss. [*hands him a pistol*] Perhaps you'd prefer to avoid the red tape. [*Khrushchev walks out of the room to address political officers. There is a gunshot, then he begins*] My name ... is Nikita ... Sergeyevich ... Khrushchev. I've come to take things in hand here. This city is not Kursk, nor is it Kiev nor Minsk. This city is Stalingrad. **Stalin**-grad! The city bears the name of the boss. It's more than a city, it's a symbol. If the Germans capture this city, the *entire* country will collapse. Now, I want our boys to raise their heads. I want them to act like they have BALLS! I want them to stop SHITTING THEIR PANTS! [*briefly pauses*] That's your job. As political officers, I'm counting on you. You, what's your suggestion?

Officer #1: Shoot all the other generals who have retreated. And their chiefs of staff, too.

Officer #2: M-make s-some examples. D-d-d-d-d-de-port the families of the d-d-deserters.

Khrushchev: [*Bored*] Yes, yes, that's all been done.

Danilov: Give them hope! [*Khrushchev walks over, pushes an officer out of the way to stand face to face to Danilov*] Here the men's only choices is between German bullets and ours. But there's another way, a way of courage, a way of love of the Motherland. We must publish the army newspaper again. We must tell magnificent stories, stories that extol sacrifice, bravery, courage. We must give them hope, pride, a desire to fight. We must make them believe in the victory. Yes, we need to make examples, yes, but examples to follow. What we need are heroes.

Khrushchev: [*skeptical*] Do *you* know any heroes around *here*?

Danilov: Yes, comrade. I know one.

Although an evil man, there is something to be said about Khrushchev's spirit, disposition, and stance. When he heard Danilov speak the words, "Give them hope," he immediately recognized the truthfulness of his words. Without hope, the Russian army could not holdout; much less defeat the mighty forces the Germans had arrayed against them.

The Church in America is going down in flames; the pastors have a

"Sacred duty to resist!" However, what do they give their troops, hope for victory in the land? No, just escape (the Rapture), for they preach things are getting worse and worse.

To use Danilov's words, we must publish magnificent stories, stories that extol sacrifice, bravery, courage (and there are many such true stories). We must give the Church hope, pride, a desire to fight. We must make them believe in the victory. We need heroes (a few have been mentioned in this book), and we do not have but just one hero, there is a multitude of them.

Dispensationalism is not the doctrine the Church has held through the ages. There is no victory in the great escape (the Rapture). Dispensational teaching robs our children of hope for a better world. Believers claim that even after Christ comes back the "third" time, after the tribulation, and rules the earth for the prescribed millennium, Jesus will still fail because the nations will rebel at the end of those 1,000 golden years.

When a Dispensationalist says Jesus is coming "very soon," or "we are running out of time," it is very different from saying Jesus could come at any time. If I said the city of Milwaukee could have a devastating earthquake at any moment, that may be true at some point. However, I have not given any time frame or time limit when the quake would happen. On the other hand, when a Dispensationalist says Jesus is coming soon, he is absolutely predicting that within the generation that saw Israel become a nation, the Lord will return once more. That all but pinpoints the event.

We are not running out of time. We have as much time as we need to accomplish God's plan for our world. Our children, their grandchildren, and their great-grandchildren can work for God, on and on, until this world is no longer in rebellion against its loving Creator and Lord. In addition, these future generations can build on what we accomplish in our lifetime. His coming is not soon, and whether we live 30 years or 120 years, the only thing that *is* certain to occur will be our deaths. From the look of things, it could be a long time before God's Church wakes up and throws off the pessimistic Dispensational teaching that has blighted its mission for 100 years or more. Only when this misdirected belief system is gone will the Church rouse itself and again become the salt and light of this world, with a glorious vision of victory.

In America alone, the Supreme Court is now conservative—with

Ruth B. Ginsburg, Associate Justice of the Supreme Court at death's door with a banana peel underfoot. Roe vs Wade is beginning to lose ground. France, Venezuela, and Hong Kong are under attack by pro-democratic movements. These are wins that favor God and His kingdom. Everything does not always have to be about the Church. God works in all forms and shapes to accomplish His will—to remove evil to bring about His good.

Oh, what a joy to know that my Redeemer lives and He has the power to not only change this world, but to conquer, rule, and reign over this earth in fulfillment of His promise!

For real-life examples of what a vision of victory will accomplish versus a vision of defeat, see Appendix C.

THE LOFTY ONE

Michael Earl Riemer

He was wounded in the battle, blood flowed from His side.
He never was defeated, but He winced, bent low, and cried.
The price was very great, much glory put aside.
He was also torn and bruised, but joy was still inside.

His shame was oh so great, crushing pain and agony.
Kneeling in the garden, a place called Gethsemane.
Betrayed by a friend, forsaken by the rest;
Assailed by His accusers, He withstood their cruelest test.

Laid inside a tomb, a cold and barren place.
A light was there that darkness just could not erase.
The glory that burst forth that morn so long ago
Has rippled down through time and can rapture any soul.

The high and lofty One, the God of eternity,
Looks down through the ages in thought of you and me.

FOOTNOTES

1. Dr. Kenneth L. Gentry, Jr., *He Shall Have Dominion* (Institute for Christian Economics, P. O. Box 8000, Tyler, Texas 75711, 1992) p. 80.

2. Gentry, *He Shall Have Dominion*, p. 89.

3. John Eidsmoe, *Christianity and the Constitution* (Baker Book House, Grand Rapids, Michigan 49516, 1987) p. 32.

4. Eidsmoe, *Christianity and the Constitution,* p. 31.

5. Eidsmoe, *Christianity and the Constitution,* p. 31.

6. Philip Schaff, *History of the Christian Church* (Grand Rapids, Michigan: WM. B. Eerdmans Publishing Company, 1978) Vol. 1, p. 4, 5.

7. Schaff, p. 91.

8. Adam Clarke, *Clarke's Commentary combined edition* (Nashville: Abingdon, volume v. Matthew-Revelation) p. 148.

9. Gentry, *He Shall Have Dominion*, p. 26.

CHAPTER SIX

DANIEL'S SEVENTY WEEKS

Daniel 9:24–27

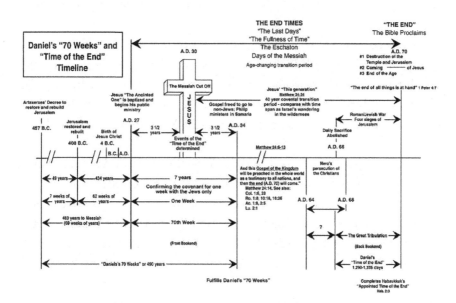

Timeline-John Noē, International Preterist Association

BACKGROUND

The Coming of the Messiah was an event that was looked-for and longed-for since that day in the Garden of Eden when the Lord told the serpent, *"And I will put enmity between thee and the woman, and between thy seed and her seed; it shall bruise thy head, and thou shalt bruise his heel"* (Gen. 3:15). This veiled promise of a redeemer (Jesus) would become clearer as history unfolded.

We next read about the promised One when God called Abram to leave his father's house. Abram, whose name was changed by God to Abraham, was told that the Messiah would come from his line (Gen. 12:3, 17:19, 22:18). This promise was passed on to Abraham's son, Isaac (Gen. 26:4). Then it passed to the son of Isaac, Jacob (Gen. 28:4, 14). Jacob, who also had his name changed by God to Israel, told his son, Judah, that the Messiah would come from his descendants, from the tribe of Judah (Gen. 49:10).

As we continue to read through the Old Testament, we find the details concerning the Messiah become more and more precise. We learn from which family He would come (II Sam. 7:13, 16; Isa. 11:1; Psalm 131:11); His place of birth (Micah 5:2); and even the circumstances of His birth (Isa. 7:14). Finally, Scripture tells us when the Messiah would come (Dan. 9:25).

The Prophecy of Seventy Weeks is a foretelling that God gave to Daniel during the Hebrews' captivity. This prophecy is of enormous significance, for it revealed the time when the Messiah would arrive. The twelve tribes, the descendants of Israel, had at one time been a unified nation. But, because of God's judgment, at the time of Daniel, there were two nations: Israel and Judah. When both nations rebelled against the Lord, God sent prophets to His people, but they were cruelly mocked. Inevitably, *"the wrath of the LORD arose against his people, till there was no remedy"* (II Chron. 36:16).

Daniel was from the southern kingdom of Judah. The northern kingdom of Israel had been conquered and dispersed many years earlier. And now, because of Judah's sin, God allowed the Chaldeans to subdue them and carry the people into captivity. Thus begins our exploration of the last years of the nation of Judah.

In the third year of the reign of Jehoiakim, king of Judah (about 607 BC), Nebuchadnezzar, King of Babylon, came and besieged Jerusalem. Many Jews from the land of Judah and the city of Jerusalem were captured and taken to the city of Babylon. Daniel and his three friends—Hananiah, Mishael, and Azariah (Shadrach, Meshach, and Abednego)—were also taken captive and carried to the city of Babylon. These four were chosen from among their fellow captives to be schooled in the knowledge, wisdom, and language of the Chaldeans. Each of them had already been endowed by God with great knowledge and wisdom, but God further blessed Daniel (Belteshazzar) with the gift of understanding all visions and dreams.

After their three years of schooling were completed, they were tested and found to be ten times better than all the other magicians and astrologers in the realm of the kingdom of Babylon. After Daniel interpreted a dream of Nebuchadnezzar's, Daniel was made the chief ruler over all the wise men and governors of Babylon, and his three friends were promoted to places of trust and authority.

The captivity of God's people in Babylon was to last for seventy years (Jer. 25:11–12, 27:22, 29:10). God said after this period of captivity (known as Jacob's trouble, Jer. 30:7), He would cause Israel and Judah to return to their land (Jer. 30:3), gathering them from *"all the nations and all the places whither He had caused them to be carried away"* (Jer. 29:14; see also Lev. 26:34, Jer. 30:3, 11, 32:37, 33:7,14; Ezek. 37:21–25, 39:25). And as prophesied, the regathering of all Israel was wonderfully fulfilled; see II Chronicles 36:21, Ezra 1:1–4 and the Book of Nehemiah. When Jesus walked this sod, Israel was no longer divided into two nations, Israel and Judah, but just one, the nation of Israel. The twelve tribes were still in existence years after Christ left this earth, as stated in James 1:1.

In the first year of Darius, King of Babylon (about 538 BC), Daniel was reading the Book of Jeremiah when he realized Israel's promised deliverance was at hand. However, he saw nothing about him that indicated an imminent end to their oppression. So, he *"set his face unto the LORD"* to pray and fast in sackcloth and ashes. Daniel earnestly offered up the kind of prayer prescribed by Moses—and later by King Solomon when he dedicated the temple (Lev. 26:40; I Kings 8:47–48). Daniel also remembered the words of Jeremiah: *"ye shall seek me, and find me, when ye shall search for me with all your heart"* (Jer. 29:13).

Responding to Daniel's urgent yet humble prayer, God sent the angel Gabriel (Chapter 9). However, Gabriel answered Daniel's prayer in an unexpected way. The angel told of a different kind of captivity lasting another seventy weeks that would require of Israel a further redemption. Gabriel gave Daniel a glimpse into the future when the Messiah (the Prince) would come. He also told Daniel of the future destruction of Jerusalem, the abolition of the Jewish sacrifices, and the end of the nation of Israel.

The seventy-week interregnum is almost universally accepted by Bible scholars as representing "weeks of years." Thus, one week equals seven years, and 70 weeks amounts to 490 years (7 x 70 = 490). This is the same principle God used in other instances (Num. 14:34; II Chron. 36:21; Ezek. 4:6). The seventy weeks of Daniel constitute a single, complete unit of time with no gaps, interruptions, or extra time added. Some try to separate the last week from the other sixty-nine weeks in this prophecy. How suspect. There is no Scriptural warrant, precedent, or reason to do so. Altering the seventy weeks of Daniel would defeat the whole purpose of the prophecy and render it unscriptural.

John MacArthur deals with the prophecy of Daniel's seventy weeks in his book *The Second Coming*. Because MacArthur's opinion represents the view of most Dispensational teachers, I will be quoting from his book and comparing what the Scriptures actually record versus what Dispensationalists generally teach.

THE PROPHECY AS GIVEN TO DANIEL

Daniel Chapter 9

24. *Seventy weeks are determined upon thy people and upon thy holy city, to finish the transgression, and to make an end of sins, and to make reconciliation for iniquity, and to bring in everlasting righteousness, and to seal up the vision and prophecy, and to anoint the most Holy.*

25. *Know therefore and understand, that from the going forth of the commandment to restore and to build Jerusalem unto the Messiah the Prince shall be seven weeks, and threescore and two weeks: the street shall be built again, and the wall, even in troublous times.*

26. *And after threescore and two weeks shall Messiah be cut off, but not for himself: and the people of the prince that shall come shall destroy the city and the sanctuary; and the end thereof shall be with a flood, and unto the end of the war desolations are determined.*

27. *And he shall confirm the covenant with many for one week: and in the midst of the week he shall cause the sacrifice and the oblation to cease, and for the overspreading of abominations he shall make it desolate, even until the consummation, and that determined shall be poured upon the desolate.*

THE SEVENTY WEEKS ARE
DIVIDED INTO THREE PARTS

7	weeks	49 years
62	weeks	434 years
1	week	7 years
Total: 70 weeks		Total: 490 years

1st part   7 weeks   The restoration and repairing of the city of
            (49 years) Jerusalem and the temple of God.

2nd part   62 weeks   Restoration of the Jewish state until the public
            (434 years) entrance of the Messiah who will be cut off after
                        the sixty-ninth week.

3rd part   1 week   Messiah is cut off in midst of the seventieth week,
            (7 years)   and ritual sacrifices will cease in the midst of
                        the week. The covenant to be *confirmed* by the
                        Messiah for one week.

Although part of the prophecy—the destruction of Jerusalem and the temple (in the year AD 70)—are not included in the time frame of the 490 years (70 weeks).

The seventy weeks deal with just one person—the Prince, Jesus, the Messiah—and what He will accomplish. It seems some commentators hold to the opinion the prince that would destroy the city and sanctuary was Titus, the son of Vespasian with his roman armies. Matthew Henry's Commentary states it this way: "The people of the prince that shall come are considered to refer to Titus and his Roman army. *Wintle* observes, if we refer them to Christ, destroying Jerusalem through the immediate agency of Cesar, the sense is the same."[1] [This is the sense the author observes.] Scripture refers to only one prince;—not a righteous prince and a wicked prince. There is but one Jesus: "*The Prince of Peace*" (Isaiah 9:6); "*the Prince of life*" (Acts 3:15); "*a Prince and a Savior*" (Acts 5:5); and "*the prince of the kings of the earth*" (Revelation 1:5). Many Dispensational authors do not understand this. Instead, they turn Jesus the Messiah into an antichrist when interpreting this prophecy. MacArthur even appears to revile the Messiah: "In the seventieth week, an evil 'prince who is to come' makes a covenant, then interrupts the week with an act of abomination."[2] But Jesus was the one and only prince who was to come.

There is confusion on the part of some people concerning the phrase in verse 26, "*… and the people of the prince that shall come shall destroy the city and the sanctuary…*" They say that cannot mean the people of Christ, the Prince, destroy the city and the sanctuary. However, that is just what it does mean! Jesus gave His people almost forty years to repent, and when they refused, He sent His armies, the Romans, to visit judgment and punishment upon the wicked generation that rejected and crucified their Lord. The Romans were not godly men, but since they were the ones Jesus used to execute His purposes, they were His armies sent to avenge the great wrong.

Much of the Book of Revelation is about Jesus' judgment poured out upon a wicked and reprobate people. "*Alleluia; Salvation, and glory, and honour, and power, unto the Lord our God: For true and righteous are his judgments: for he hath judged the great whore, which did corrupt the earth with her fornication, and hath avenged the blood of his servants at her hand. … And I saw heaven opened, and behold a white horse; and he that sat upon him was called Faithful and True, and in righteousness he doth judge and make war. His eyes were as a flame of fire, and on his head were many crowns; and he had a name written, that no man knew, but he himself. And he was clothed with a vesture dipped in blood: and his name is called The Word of God. And the armies which were in heaven followed him upon white horses, clothed in fine linen, white and clean. And out of his mouth goeth a* sharp sword, that with it he should smite the nations: and he shall rule them with a rod of iron: and he treadeth the winepress of the fierceness and wrath of Almighty God. And he hath on his vesture and on his thigh a name written, KING OF KINGS AND LORD OF LORDS" (Rev. 19: 1–2, 11–16).

In Daniel 9:24–27, six events are mentioned that describe the incarnation of our Lord:

1. **"To finish** (to restrain) **the transgression**."* Jesus is the One who redeems us from our transgressions. *"Therefore he is the mediator of a new covenant, so that those who are called may receive the promised eternal inheritance since a death has occurred which redeems them from the transgressions under the first covenant"* (Heb. 9:15 R.S.V.).

2. **"To make an end of sins** (sin-offerings)."* Jesus made an end of sins. *"Who needeth not daily, as those high priests, to offer up sacrifice, first for his own sins, and then for the people's: for this he did once, when he offered up himself"* (Heb. 7:27). *"[B]ut now once in the end of the world hath he appeared to put away sin by the sacrifice of himself"* (Heb. 9:26). *"And every priest standeth daily ministering and offering oftentimes the same sacrifices, which can never take away sins: But this man, after he had offered one sacrifice for sins forever, sat down on the right hand of God"* (Heb. 10:11–12).

3. **"To make reconciliation for iniquity**."* Jesus made an atonement for our sins when he offered Himself up. *"Who needeth not daily, as those high priests, to offer up sacrifice, first for his own sins, and then for the people's for this he did once, when he offered up himself"* (Heb. 7:27). *"God was in Christ, reconciling the world unto himself"* (II Cor. 5:19). *"For if, when we were enemies, we were reconciled to God by the death of his Son, much more, being reconciled, we shall be saved by his life"* (Rom. 5:10). *"And that he might reconcile both unto God in one body by the cross, having slain the enmity thereby"* (Isa. 53:12; Eph. 2:16).

4. **"To bring in everlasting righteousness**."* Jesus alone brought in everlasting righteousness. Jesus is the subject and object of faith of all the prophets through all the ages of the world (Gen. 49:10). *"Of which salvation the prophets have inquired and searched diligently, who prophesied of the grace that should come unto you"* (I Peter 1:10).

"*For Christ is the end of the law for righteousness to every one that believeth*" (Rom. 10:4). "*Yea, and all the prophets from Samuel and those that follow after, as many as have spoken, have likewise foretold of these days*" (Acts 3:24).

5. "**To seal up the vision and prophecy.**" Adam Clarke explicates: To seal up ... "to finish or complete" the vision and prophecy; that is, to put an end to the necessity of any further revelations, by completing the canon of Scripture, and fulfilling the prophecies which related to his person, sacrifice, and the glory that should follow"[3] (Matt. 11:13; Luke 24:25–26; John 19:28).

6. "**To anoint the most Holy.**" The most Holy was not the city of Jerusalem or the temple in Jerusalem. There was One who was more holy than both of those sites. "*But I say unto you, That in this place is one greater than the temple*" (Matt. 12:6). In the Book of Hebrews, the writer explains that the area behind the temple veil was called the Holiest of all. But it was just "*a figure for the time then present, in which were offered both gifts and sacrifices, that could not make him that did the service perfect ... until the time of reformation. But Christ being come an high priest of good things to come, by a greater and more perfect tabernacle, not made with hands*" (Heb. 9:9–11). "*Jesus answered and said unto them, Destroy this temple, and in three days I will raise it up. Then said the Jews, Forty and six years was this temple in building, and wilt thou rear it up in three days? But he spake of the temple of his body*" (John 2:19–21). Jesus is the one who was anointed. "*God anointed Jesus of Nazareth with the Holy Ghost and with power*" (Acts 10:38). "*The Spirit of the LORD is upon me, because he hath anointed me to preach the gospel*" (Luke 4:18).

THE COMMAND TO RESTORE JERUSALEM

Chapter 9, verse 25 of Daniel gives us the starting point of the seventy weeks: the going forth of the commandment to restore and rebuild Jerusalem. Scripture (II Chron. 36:22–23; Ezra 1:1–2) references this decree in marked detail: "*Now in the first year of Cyrus king of Persia ... he made a proclamation throughout all his kingdom, and put it also in writing, saying, Thus saith Cyrus king of Persia, The LORD God of heaven hath given me all the kingdoms of the earth; and he hath charged me to build him an house at Jerusalem, which is in Judah."*

Some say this is not the proper starting point because the king's decree deals only with the temple. Furthermore, Cyrus's command says nothing about the rebuilding of Jerusalem. It is true this portion of Scripture says nothing about rebuilding the city. However, in Ezra 4:12, the Jews were accused of rebuilding the city. *"Be it known unto the king that the Jews which came up from thee to us are come unto Jerusalem, building the rebellious and the bad city, and have set up the walls thereof, and joined the foundations."* Isaiah prophesied that Cyrus would be the one to command the city to be rebuilt: *"That saith of Cyrus, He is my shepherd, and shall perform all my pleasure: even saying to Jerusalem, Thou shalt be built; and to the temple, Thy foundation shall be laid"* (Isa. 44:28). Isaiah also foretold that Cyrus would *"build my city, and he shall let go my captives, not for price nor reward, saith the LORD of hosts"* (Isa. 45:13).

MacArthur states, "The command to restore and build Jerusalem' most likely refers to Artaxerxes' decree recorded in Nehemiah 2:1–8, which occurred in the month of Nisan in the twentieth year of Artaxerxes' reign" (Neh. 2:1).[4] The fact some authors use a different starting point really does not matter, as the Bible clearly says Cyrus would be the one to direct that Jerusalem and the temple be rebuilt. That is good enough for me. And it should be good enough for MacArthur.

From the commandment to restore and rebuild Jerusalem to the coming of the Messiah would require sixty-nine weeks or 483 years. The sixty-nine weeks ended in AD 26—precisely when Jesus was baptized by John the Baptist and started his public ministry. John was *"the voice of one crying in the wilderness,"* saying, *"Make straight the way of the Lord"* (John 1:23). It was John who prepared the way for our Savior before He started His ministry.

THE CONFIRMING OF THE COVENANT

Jesus said, *"the time is fulfilled"* (Mark 1:15). In Matthew 11:12–14, Jesus, speaking of John the Baptist, told the multitudes John was the Elijah prophesied to arrive before the day of judgment, which judgment was to occur after the completion of the seventy weeks. Paul, writing to the churches in Galatia, said, "*But when the fulness* [completeness: Thayer's] *of the time was come, God sent forth his Son, made of a woman, made under the law*" (Gal. 4:4). These arrival points pertain to the completion of the sixty-ninth week and the start of the seventieth week of Daniel. From Jesus' first public preaching of the kingdom of God, the seven-year confirmation of the covenant with Israel began.

As the covenant with Israel would take seven years to fulfill (Dan. 9:27), Jesus told His disciples, "*Go not into the way of the Gentiles ... But go rather to the lost sheep of the house of Israel*" (Matt. 10:5). Moreover, Jesus Himself said, "*I am not sent but unto the lost sheep of the house of Israel*" (Matt. 15:24). After Jesus' three and a half years[5] of ministry to Israel and His resurrection, He then gave His disciples the "Great Commission" (Matt. 28:19; Mark 16:15; Luke 24:47). That done, Jesus told His disciples to preach the Gospel to all nations, with Jerusalem as the starting point: "*And that repentance, and remission of sins should be preached in his name among all nations, beginning at Jerusalem*" (Luke 24:47).

The Church followed His command and preached the Gospel in Jerusalem. Then, because of persecution, the Christians were scattered beyond Jerusalem into other cities, and continued to preach the Gospel— but only to the Jews (Acts 8:1, 11:19). Why did the Church not expound to the Gentiles when Jesus told them to "preach to all nations"? There are two reasons. First, the covenant still had to be confirmed with Israel for the remaining three and a half years. As Paul and Barnabas said, "*It was necessary that the word of God should first have been spoken to you,* (the Jews) *but seeing ye put it from you ... we turn to the Gentiles*" (Acts 13:46).

The second reason is the Church at that time was totally Jewish. And a Jew, even though he believed in Jesus, would not even eat with a Gentile. It took a revelation from God to show the Jewish believers that "*God also to the Gentiles granted repentance unto life*" (Acts 11:18). The Gospel was always intended for the Jew first, to confirm the covenant with Israel for the three and a half years remaining after Christ's ascension. After confirmation was completed, the Gospel was then preached to all nations (Acts 11:19; Rom. 1:16).

JESUS'S TRIUMPHAL ENTRANCE
INTO JERUSALEM

Some believe Jesus' triumphant arrival in Jerusalem on the first day of Passover was His coming. John MacArthur says, "So the sixty-nine prophetic weeks–483 years–may actually have been a precise figure that signified the exact day and year when Christ would enter Jerusalem in triumph."[6]

Jesus spent three and a half years teaching; healing the blind, the dumb, the lame; raising the dead; feeding the multitudes; and casting out devils. Despite this, MacArthur claims the few days before Jesus's crucifixion, resurrection, and ascension represent His true coming. However, five days after His triumphal entrance in Jerusalem, John says *"Jesus knew that his hour was come that he should depart out of this world"* (John 13:1). Jesus' entry into Jerusalem was not His *coming;* He was getting ready to leave. It was, in fact, the commencement of His *going*!

JESUS WAS CRUCIFIED IN THE MIDST
OF THE SEVENTIETH WEEK

The sixty-nine weeks were to measure *unto* the Messiah and the start of His public ministry. He was then to be "cut off" (murdered) after the sixty-ninth week. MacArthur ignores the word "after" in Daniel 9:26, stating instead, "In the sixty-ninth week, Messiah is cut off (v. 26)."[7] With this omission, MacArthur effectively distorts the rest of the prophecy. Scripture does not say He was cut off "in" the sixty-ninth week, it says "after" the sixty-ninth week. There is a big difference between *in* the sixty-ninth week and *after*! We will now see how big.

Tim LaHaye and Jerry B. Jenkins, in their book, *Are We Living in the End Times?*, state after 483 years (69 weeks) "the divine 'counter' stopped just before the death of Jesus, with seven years still left to go. The remaining seven-year period is what we call the Tribulation."[8] But the "divine counter" could not stop until the seventy weeks prophesied were completed. When 490 years elapsed, then and only then would the divine counter stop running!

There is no hiatus between the sixty-ninth and the seventieth week.

Even MacArthur acknowledges this: "Daniel recounts all seventy weeks without mentioning any gap between the sixty-ninth and seventieth weeks."[9] Some Dispensationalists grudgingly acknowledge the word "after," yet still say Jesus is cut off before the seventieth week. However, that would be like saying, "I am coming to your house after Tuesday but before Wednesday." There are no gaps between the days of the week or between the weeks in Daniel's prophecy. Thus it follows, if I come to your house immediately after Tuesday, I am coming on Wednesday. And if Jesus was cut off *after* the sixty-ninth week, He was most certainly crucified *during* the seventieth week.

UNBELIEVERS–THE SERVANTS OF GOD

The next portion of Daniel's prophecy (Dan. 9:26) does not seem to apply to the Messiah: *"and the people of the prince that shall come shall destroy the city and the sanctuary ..."* We know that the temple, along with the entire city of Jerusalem, were destroyed by the armies of Rome and their allies in the year AD 70. So, in what way can we call the heathen forces of the Roman Empire, *"the people of the prince"*?

Remember how the King of Egypt, Pharaoh, would not let the children of Israel leave Egypt. God hardened Pharaoh's heart so *"that I may lay my hand upon Egypt, and bring forth mine armies, and my people the children of Israel, out of the land of Egypt by great judgments"* (Ex. 7:4). God can, and at times does, intervene to control the lives of people. God controlled the events in the life of Pharaoh, who then did God's will, and thus became the servant of God, even though he did not know he was in full compliance with the LORD.

The King of Babylon, Nebuchadnezzar, the man God used to judge and destroy the city of Jerusalem and God's people, Israel, was called God's "servant" more than once:

> Because ye have not heard my words, Behold, I will send and take
> all the families of the North, saith the Lord, and Nebuchadnezzar the
> king of Babylon, <u>my servant</u>, and will bring them against this land
> (Jer. 25:9).

And now have I given all these lands into the hand of Nebuchadnezzar the king of Babylon, my servant (Jer. 27:6).

Thus saith the LORD of hosts, the God of Israel; Behold, I will send and take Nebuchadnezzar the king of Babylon, my servant (Jer. 43:10). (emphasis added)

Nebuchadnezzar was indeed God's servant, not that he loved or followed God, but because he did the will of God—even though he did not know it.

The kingdom of Assyria also became the servant of God: "*O Assyrian, the rod of mine anger, and the staff in their hand is mine indignation*" (Isa. 10:5). King Nebuchadnezzar's last recorded words show that anyone can become the servant of God, with or without consent: "*And all the inhabitants of the earth are reputed as nothing: and he doeth according to his will in the army of heaven, and among the inhabitants of the earth: and none can stay his hand, or say unto him, What doest thou?*" (Dan. 4:35).

God appointed Jehu as the next King in Israel, and used him to execute His judgment on King Ahab: "*And the LORD said unto Jehu, Because thou hast done well in executing that which is right in mine eyes, and hast done unto the house of Ahab according to all that was in mine heart, thy children of the fourth generation shall sit on the throne of Israel. But Jehu took no heed to walk in the law of the LORD God of Israel with all his heart for he departed not from the sins of Jeroboam*" (II Kings 10:30–31). Jehu was God's servant, even though he did not walk in God's ways.

ABOMINATION OF DESOLATION: THE ROMAN ARMIES

Jesus wept over the city of Jerusalem (Luke 19:14). He often tried to win the love of its inhabitants, but they would not change or repent (Matt. 23:37). He wept for He knew He would soon send armies to visit judgment and then destruction on Jerusalem and on the Jewish people because of their rejection of Him. There is a note in the margin on the portion of Scripture that reads, "*and the people of the prince that shall come.*" The note says, "and the prince's [Messiah's, ver. 25] future people." The Roman armies were the armies (servants) of the Lord Jesus, the prince who was to come.

The Roman armies that destroyed the temple and the city of Jerusalem were the fulfillment of the abomination of desolation stated in the rest of Daniel's prophecy (v. 26–27): "*and the people of the prince that shall come shall destroy the city and the sanctuary; and the end thereof shall be with a flood, and unto the end of the war desolations are determined ... and for the overspreading of abominations he shall make it desolate, even until the consummation, and that determined shall be poured upon the desolate*" (Dan. 9:26–27). The Roman armies were the abomination that made Jerusalem, a desolation.

Philip Schaff, in his eight-volume set of books, *History of the Christian Church*, powerfully depicts the abomination of desolation: "The Romans planted their eagles on the shapeless ruins, over against the eastern gate, offered their sacrifices to them, and proclaimed Titus Imperator with the greatest acclamations of joy. Thus was fulfilled the prophecy concerning the abomination of desolation standing in the holy place."[10]

Jesus, in His Olivet Discourse, was mindful of Daniel's abomination of desolation prophecy. The Olivet Discourse is given in the Gospels of Matthew, Mark, and Luke. It is important to compare all three accounts because Luke includes details that are not in the other two Gospels. Consider these four verses:

> When ye therefore shall see the abomination of desolation, spoken of by Daniel the prophet, stand in the holy place, (whoso readeth, let him understand:) Then let them which be in Judaea flee into the mountains (Matt. 24:15–16).
>
> But when ye shall see the abomination of desolation, spoken of by Daniel the prophet, standing where it ought not, (let him that readeth understand,) then let them that be in Judaea flee to the mountains (Mark 13:14).
>
> For the days shall come upon thee, that thine enemies shall cast a trench about thee, and compass thee round, and keep thee in on every side, And shall lay thee even with the ground, and thy children within thee; and they shall not leave in thee one stone upon another (Luke 19:43–44).

> *And when ye shall see Jerusalem compassed with armies, then
> know that the desolation thereof is nigh. Then let them which are in
> Judaea flee to the mountains* (Luke 21:20–21).

In the Gospel of Luke, Jesus tells us the abomination begins *"When
ye shall see Jerusalem compassed with armies, then know that the desolation
thereof is nigh"* (Luke 21:20). What armies are encompassing Jerusalem?
The armies of Rome. What would Rome's armies (the abomination of
desolation) bring about? *"They shall not leave in thee one stone upon another"*
(Luke 19:44, 21:6). When did the Judaeans see Jerusalem surrounded with
armies? In AD 70. When was *"not one stone left upon another"*? In AD 70.

MacArthur is correct when he states, "And on the wing of abominations
shall be one who makes desolate" (v. 27). That quite clearly describes the
very same "abomination of desolation" Jesus cites in Matthew 24:15.[11]
Because Jesus never mentioned two abominations of desolation in His
Olivet Discourse, all three Gospels inarguably refer to Daniel 9:27. Now
we know what the abomination of desolation was, and when it happened.

However, for the sake of argument, let us allow *"the people of the
prince that shall come"* (v. 26) to mean "the Antichrist." That would imply
the Roman armies that destroyed Jerusalem were the Antichrist's armies;
however, their leader, prince, and general (the Antichrist) still has not
come. Imagine that, the Roman army with no general. What nonsense!

MAKING, BREAKING, AND
CONFIRMING THE COVENANT

We now come to the last portion of the prophecy in verse 27: *"And
he shall confirm the covenant with many for one week."* As is apparent, this
quotation does not say anything about *making* a covenant or *breaking* a
covenant. However, it does say something about *confirming* a covenant.
The word "confirm" means, "to make strong, firm."[12]

MacArthur says "In the seventieth week, an evil 'prince who is to come'
makes a covenant, then interrupts the week with an act of abomination."[13]
He further states, "The Antichrist, following the same pattern as Antiochus
Epiphanes, will evidently pretend peace with Israel. Although Scripture
does not expressly identify the nature of the "covenant" he confirms (cf.

Dan. 9:27), some have speculated the Antichrist will work out a peace treaty ..."[14]

We have already seen God uses covenants in His dealings with His people. Of course, Scripture does not expressly identify the nature of the Antichrist's covenant—because there is no Antichrist covenant! Moreover, we surely do not have to speculate about the confirmation process ... Scripture tells us who confirmed the covenant and when!

As we compare Scripture with Scripture—as MacArthur says we should, and I believe we must—we see Jesus Christ confirmed the covenant. As Paul says when writing to the Galatians, *"Now to Abraham and his seed were the promises made. He saith not, And to seeds as of many; but as of one, And to thy seed, which is Christ. And this I say, that the covenant, that was confirmed before of God in Christ"* (Gal. 3:16, 17). Paul also told the Romans that it was Jesus who confirmed the covenant: *"Now I say that Jesus Christ was a minister of the circumcision for the truth of God, to confirm the promises made unto the fathers"* (Rom. 15:8). The Book of Hebrews says it was Jesus who used signs, wonders, miracles, and gifts of the Holy Spirit to confirm the covenant (Heb. 2:3–4).

Nowhere does Scripture talk about an "Antichrist" making or breaking any kind of covenant. But Scripture certainly does talk about Jesus breaking a covenant with His people:

> And I took my staff, even Beauty, and cut it asunder, that I might break my covenant which I had made with all the people. And it was broken in that day: and so the poor of the flock that waited upon me knew that it was the word of the LORD. And I said, unto them, If ye think good, give me my price; and if not, forbear. So they weighed for my price thirty pieces of silver. And the LORD said unto me, Cast it unto the potter: a goodly price that I was prised at of them to the potter in the house of the LORD. Then I cut asunder mine other staff, even Bands, that I might break the brotherhood between Judah and Israel (Zech. 11:10–14).

The fulfillment of this prophecy is in Matthew 26:15, 27:3–10. The sequence of events in the seventy weeks prophecy is as follows:

1. The building and restoration of the city of Jerusalem and the temple.
2. The Messiah's coming and confirming the covenant after the sixty-ninth week.
3. The death of the Messiah in the seventieth week.
4. The destruction of the city of Jerusalem and the temple within a generation after the seventy weeks are completed.

Jesus the Messiah was to come on the scene before Jerusalem was destroyed. Even though its destruction occurred after the seventy weeks had elapsed, it was still part of the prophecy and events to transpire. We also know Jerusalem was destroyed in AD 70. Therefore, even if Jesus was crucified in the sixty-ninth week, the destruction of Jerusalem took place after completion of the seventy weeks. In view of the facts, how can Dispensationalists like MacArthur take the seventieth week and place it 2,000 years in the future, when the seventieth week occurred before the destruction of Jerusalem?

It was Jesus who would end the practice of animal sacrifice: "*he shall cause the sacrifice and the oblation to cease*" (Dan. 9:27). Once Jesus had died, any animal sacrifice or offering denies the finished work of Calvary (I Cor. 5:7–8; Heb. 9:26, 10:10, 12). Thus, if any animal was sacrificed for sins after the crucifixion, it became an abomination, reproach, and loathing to the Lord. The writer of the Book of Hebrews put it this way: "*Of how much sorer punishment, suppose ye, shall he be thought worthy, who hath trodden under foot the Son of God, and hath counted the blood of the covenant, wherewith he was sanctified, an unholy thing*" (Heb. 10:29). Therefore, because animal sacrifices for sin continued (*overspreading of abominations*, ver. 27), God made Jerusalem "*desolate, even until the consummation*" (ver. 27) (complete destruction).

A REBUILT TEMPLE AND ANIMAL SACRIFICES

The temple in Jerusalem was God's temple. It was commissioned by God and built to His specifications. Even after Christ's death and the continual offering of animal sacrifices by the Christ-rejecting Jews, it was still God's temple. No other temple is commanded to be built, is prophesied to be built, or will ever need to be built again. Since Christ was the final sacrifice, no other manmade temple will ever be called the temple of God because His people—the Church—are now the temple of God (I Cor. 3:16–17, 6:19; II Cor. 6:16; Eph. 2:21; Heb. 3:6).

Dispensationalists have some very bizarre ideas about a supposed Antichrist, a future rebuilt Jewish temple, and the seventieth week of Daniel. We read in II Thessalonians 2:4, "*Who opposeth and exalteth himself above all that is called God, or that is worshipped; so that he as God sitteth in the temple of God, shewing himself that he is God.*" Dispensationalists believe this verse means the Antichrist will appear in a rebuilt Jewish temple and proclaim that he is God. LaHaye anticipates the dreadful moment "When the Antichrist commits the ultimate blasphemy by appearing in the temple to declare that he is God.…"[15]

However, the above quote from Thessalonians has nothing to do with a supposed rebuilt Jewish temple during the tribulation period (seventieth week of Daniel). To effectively show this verse genuinely alludes to an Antichrist, or a rebuilt temple, Dispensationalists need to explain how a temple built by unbelieving, Christ-rejecting people could be called "the temple of God." They need to explain how a place of worship that willfully practiced animal sacrifices, thereby trampling underfoot the blood of Jesus, could be called "the temple of God." They also need to explain why the reinstatement of such an odious pagan ritual (a primary reason why the LORD destroyed His temple in the first place) could be at all pleasing to God.

When God ordained the tabernacle in the wilderness, it was the only way He could reside among a sinful people. "*And let them make me a sanctuary; that I may dwell among them*" (Ex. 25:8). Its construction would follow God's design (v. 9), and it was from this tabernacle that God would commune with Israel. "*And there I will meet with thee, and I will commune with thee from above the mercy seat*" (Ex. 25:22; Lev. 1:1).

Years later, God told King David his son, Solomon, would build a house for the LORD (I Chron. 22:7–10). (Because David had been a man of war and had shed much blood, he was not allowed to build the temple.) Nevertheless, to ensure its opulence, David had prepared abundantly for the temple. Much gold, silver, brass, and cedar were amassed for the project, and skilled workmen were gathered and stood ready.

The temple was commissioned by God to be built by Solomon and was modeled after the tabernacle built in the wilderness. It was ordained and consecrated by the LORD. But the tabernacle and the temple were merely representative of the "true tabernacle" (Heb. 8:1–2) and were only meant to exist until Jesus came and offered Himself as the final sacrifice for sins (Heb. 10:12).

No other temple was commanded to be built, and no other temple was prophesied. The Book of Hebrews tells us very plainly why God would never commission another temple (Heb. 9, 10). Indeed, even if the Jews had built another temple, it would not be God's temple. For now, and always, God will dwell in His temple, which is His people, the Church (I Cor. 3:16–17, 6:19; II Cor. 6:16).

Some Dispensationalists teach the Antichrist's stopping of Jewish sacrifices will be the abomination of desolation. "Then in the middle of this seven-year period, the Anti-Christ refuses to allow the Jews to offer sacrifices in the temple, which is the abomination of desolation spoken of by Daniel the prophet ..."[16]

MacArthur has a different view. He believes an idol placed in a rebuilt Jewish temple will be the abomination of desolation. "In the middle of the week, the Antichrist will commit an act of abomination, probably by defiling the rebuilt temple with an idol of himself."[17]

Neither of these two explanations is based on Scripture, for there is not one verse in the Old or the New Testament that says any such thing. In addition, if either of those explanations were true, we would expect to find them in the Book of Revelation. However, not even a hint of such an idea appears there—or anywhere else!

In *Are We Living in the End Times?* by LaHaye and Jenkins, Chapter 10 is entitled *The Temple Rebuilt*.[18] A rebuilt temple is very important to the Dispensationalist. The chapter is nine pages long, but not one verse of Scripture is cited that says anything about the Jews rebuilding a temple. Why is that? Because there is no Scriptural basis for a temple to be rebuilt! Might the reason be so the Antichrist could defile this rebuilt temple? Certainly not, for how could the Antichrist defile something that was already a Christ-denying abomination in the sight of God?

What would happen if Jews built a temple and offered animal sacrifices today or at some future date during the supposed great tribulation? What would happen if the Antichrist stopped them from sacrificing? Preventing abominations (animal sacrifices) from taking place would not be typical of an antichrist! If anything, it would be pleasing to Christ; there would surely be joy in heaven, for the blood of Christ would no longer be trampled underfoot by wicked people. Biblically, any rebuilt temple where animal sacrifices are offered would be a *temple of abomination*! And nothing placed inside it, such as an idol, could make it more detestable to God than it already would be.

Don Koenig believes Israel will eventually rebuild the temple and resume the ritual of animal sacrifice:

> When Israel rebuilds its third temple it will also have to sacrifice animals as offerings to the Lord. The world will find this practice obnoxious. Animal rights people will wage war against what they will see as an abominable practice. Today we see eating meat coming into disfavor among many. Within one or two decades it is likely that sacrificing animals and eating meat might be more than just frowned upon. It might even be outlawed by the world government. Some of the fuel to instigate more intense hatred of the Jews might just come from the sacrificial fires of their third temple.[19]

If the Jews actually rebuilt a third temple and reverted to animal sacrifice, their real concern would not be the anger from animal rights folks or the repercussions of breaking of the law, but rather the intense holy wrath of an Almighty God pouring out His vengeance as flaming fire for not obeying the Gospel of our Lord Jesus Christ! How dare some Christians teach God has ordained that wicked, reprobate Jews would once again offer such obnoxious abominations as offerings to Him!

Dispensational (especially Pentecostal) believers have an unscriptural fascination with and belief in a rebuilt Jewish temple with its restored animal sacrifices. Clyde Lott, a United Pentecostal Church preacher and cattle breeder from Canton, Mississippi, has been trying to breed red heifers that would conform to the rigid set of Biblical laws from the Book of Numbers.[20] These heifers would be used to "purify" the Jews so they can enter the temple Dispensationalists believe will be reconstructed in the near future.

The "Frontline (Readings)" website posts an article by Lawrence Wright about Clyde Lott titled "Forcing the End: Why does a Pentecostal cattle breeder from Mississippi and an Orthodox Rabbi from Jerusalem believe a red heifer can bring change?"

In explaining Lott's rationale, Wright states:

> As Lott read the Bible that day, he realized that the Second Coming and the fate of humankind now depended on the red heifer. In order for the Jews to rebuild the Temple and prepare the way for the return of the Messiah they must be purified with the ashes of a red heifer.

Does the fate of humankind depend on the ashes of a singular, pristine red heifer? Can these ashes truly purify someone from sin? No, for only the precious blood of Jesus—God's Blood—can perform that task. It is really a shame Lott does not believe and teach that. The old hymn asks, "What can wash away my sin? What can make me whole again?" Its scriptural answer is "Nothing but the blood of Jesus."

Pastor and former president of Dallas Theological Seminary Dr. John F. Walvoord said, "The fascination of the Pentecostal Apostolics with the heifer is that they see the Jewish people as a critical element in fulfilling the Biblical promise of the return of Christ."[21] Many have criticized Lott, and to the credit of United Pentecostals, his ministerial license was suspended. Lott and his friend, Rabbi Chaim Richman, were publicly criticized because of their attempts to reintroduce the sacrificing of red heifers as an aspect of Jewish worship. Many think Lott and Richman are even trying to force God's hand for their own self-serving reasons.

Clyde Lott is just one of many Dispensationalists who have been deceived by the "rebuilt temple" heresy. Gershon Salomon, of the Temple Mount Faithful, has toured the United States to promote, raise money, gather materials, and advance the temple rebuilding project. During his tour, he was a guest on Pat Robertson's *700 Club* and was interviewed on many Christian radio stations throughout the country.

I, too, would have liked to chat with Pat Robertson and been granted such widespread media exposure. Had I the opportunity, I would have asked each interviewer these questions: "Do you believe Jesus shed his blood for our sins? Do you realize because the Jews rejected Christ, the nation of Israel was destroyed? Do you realize, through their continued animal sacrifices for sin, the Jews 'counted the blood of the covenant, wherewith he was sanctified, an unholy thing,' and Jerusalem was destroyed as a result? Do you believe 'the offering of the body of Jesus' was once for all? Do you agree it is wicked and evil to trample underfoot the precious blood of Christ? Do you realize by having Gershon Salomon on your show you are helping to promote wicked people who want to trample underfoot the precious blood of Christ?"

As to Salomon, I would have also asked: "Do you know Jesus died for your sins? Do you know the blood of red heifers can never take away your sins? Do you know Jesus is greater than any temple? Do you know Jesus is the Holy One, your Messiah? Do you know you need to repent of this great wickedness, the desire to rebuild the temple? Do you know you need to believe what Moses wrote because, if you did, you would believe in the Lord Jesus? Do you know you need to repent and be converted?" Apparently, none of the interviewers asked Salomon even one of these questions.

It is simple heresy and plain blasphemy to breed red heifers for sacrifice. It is also heretical to believe and teach God has ordained a rebuilt temple with animal sacrifices. God speaks very clearly about this issue. After the death of Christ and His sacrifice for all humanity, any ceremonial or animal sacrifice became an abomination. In Isaiah 66:3–4, Isaiah prophesied of the time when animal sacrifices would be a sin. God says:

> *He that killeth an ox is as if he slew a man; he that sacrificeth a lamb, as if he cut off a dog's neck; he that offereth an oblation, as if he offered swine's blood; he that burneth incense, as if he blessed an idol. Yea, they have chosen their own ways, and their soul delighteth in their abominations. I also will choose their delusions, and will bring their fears upon them; because when I called, none did answer; when I spake, they did not hear: but they did evil before mine eyes, and chose that in which I delighted not.*

Matthew Henry, in his great *Commentary* on the Bible, had this to say about Isaiah 66:3–4:

> The sacrifice of the wicked is not only unacceptable, but an abomination to the Lord, Prov. 15:8; this is shown here. The carnal Jews after their return out of captivity, though they relapsed not to idolatry, grew very careless in the service of God, Mal. 1:8, 13; therefore, how could they think God should regard them? The unbelieving Jews, after the gospel was preached, and in it notice given of the offering up the great Sacrifice, which put an end to all the ceremonial services, continued to offer sacrifices, as if the law of Moses had been still in force, and could make the comers thereunto perfect: this was an abomination. He that kills for his own table, is welcome to do it; but he that now kills a sacrifice for God's altar, is as if he committed murder, profanation, or idolatry. It is a great offense to God. He that does it, does in effect set aside Christ's sacrifice, treads under foot the blood of the covenant, and makes himself accessary to the guilt of the body and blood of the Lord; setting up what Christ died to abolish. He that burns incense, and so puts contempt upon the incense of Christ's intercession, is as if he blessed an idol; it was as great an affront to God as if they paid their devotions to a false god. In so doing, they chose their proud and rebellious ways, delighted in their abominations and showed their contempt of Jehovah, who would choose their delusions as the means of bringing judgments upon them.[22]

Apostles Paul and Barnabas were on their first missionary journey when they came to the city of Lystra to preach the Gospel. It was there a crippled man was healed. The men of the city who witnessed the healing thought Paul and Barnabas were gods. The priest of Jupiter then brought oxen and garlands to the city gate and were in the process of offering a sacrifice to the apostles. However, when Barnabas and Paul found out, *"they rent their clothes, and ran in among the people, crying out, and saying, Sirs, why do ye these things? We also are men of like passions with you, and preach unto you that ye should turn from these vanities unto the living God,* which made heaven, and earth, and the sea, and all things that are therein" (Acts 14:14–15).

The Gospel message taught by the Jewish believers Barnabas, Paul, and Peter still needs to be preached today. Clyde Lott needs to teach Rabbi Richman and all Jews to *"turn from these vanities* (worthless things, animal sacrifices) *unto the living God."* Richman needs to hear what Peter told the Jews on the day of Pentecost: *"Repent, and be baptized every one of you in the name of Jesus Christ for the remission of sins, and ye shall receive the gift of the Holy Ghost. For the promise is unto you, and to your children, and to all that are afar off, even as many as the Lord our God shall call"* (Acts 2:38–39). Rabbi Richman needs to accept the message of Peter, just like the first Christians (all Jews) who *"gladly received his word and were baptized."*

The problem with Clyde Lott and all Dispensationalists is not only are they trying to "force God's hand," but more importantly, they are simply missing the whole point: never again will any kind of animal sacrifice be pleasing to God. Nor does any element of Scripture indicate there will ever be any restored animal sacrifice or restored temple.

MISSING BELIEFS

Numerous other belief points are also missing from Scripture, particularly from the Book of Revelation. For example, the word "week" and the phrase "the middle of the week" are not found in the Book of Revelation. The only time periods mentioned are *"three days and an half"* (11:9); *"ten days"* (2:10); *"five months"* (9:5); *"forty and two months"* 11:2, 13:5; *"a thousand two hundred and three-score days"* (11:3, 12:6); *"a time, and times and half a time"* (three and a half years) (12:14); and *"a thousand years"* (20:2–7). What happened to the "seventieth week"?

The Antichrist is not found in the Book of Revelation. The word "sacrifice" only appears in regard to the churches in Pergamos and Thyatira (Rev. 2:14, 20), not to any supposed Antichrist halting a Jewish sacrifice. If the Antichrist's stopping of Jewish sacrifices in the middle of the seventieth week is a central theme of the Book of Revelation, then why is there no mention of this seminal event? Moreover, for those who consider the Antichrist the key player in Revelation, where did he go? The "beast" mentioned is surely not the same person or being as the Antichrist.

Also absent is the final disposition of the nation of Israel. MacArthur states, "Christ's coming was to usher in the final salvation of Israel, not the end of national Israel as the people of God."[23] Paul spoke much about the Jews, the promises God made, and Abraham, but he did not mention anything about any earthly blessing of the Jews concerning the future land of Israel. The only future Jesus foresaw concerning Israel was its destruction, not its regathering (Matt. 21:43). In fact, not only did He strip the kingdom from them, but He also divorced them (Isaiah 50:1; Jeremiah 3:8)—thereby having nothing more to do with them.

These are the principal Dispensational doctrines that fail to appear anywhere in Scripture:

- There is not one verse about an Antichrist stopping Jews from making sacrifices.
- There is not one verse that prophesies a rebuilt Jewish temple— only the destruction of the one then standing.
- Paul's concern for Israel was not that Jews should possess the land of Israel and have their own kingdom, but that they might be *saved* (Rom. 10:1).
- There is nothing about Jews offering animal sacrifices after the destruction of the temple in Jerusalem.
- There is not one verse about an Antichrist making or breaking a covenant with anyone.

When the Seventy Weeks sequence of events are properly expounded and fully understood, they give glory and honor to Jesus. They harmonize with the Olivet Discourse and with history. They detail the wonderful confirmation of the promises made by God to Israel. They foretell the time of the Messiah's coming and of His death on the cross for the redemption of all mankind. Above all, any proper interpretation of the Seventy Weeks of Daniel does not blaspheme the Prince, Jesus Christ the Messiah by turning Him into the Antichrist!

FOOTNOTES

1. Matthew Henry, *Matthew Henry's Commentary on the Holy Bible, With the Comments of Thomas Scott* (Nashville, Tennessee: Royal Publishers, 1979) Job-Malachi, p. 390.

2. John F. MacArthur, *The Second Coming* (Crossway Books, A Division of Good News Publishers, 1300 Crescent Street, Wheaton, Illinois 60187, 1999) p. 85.

3. Adam Clarke, *Clarke's Commentary*, Combined Edition, Job-Malachi, Vol. IV, p. 602.

4. MacArthur, *The Second Coming*, p. 85.

5. Got Questions Ministries, "What was the length of Jesus' public ministry?" https://www.compellingtruth.org/length-Jesus-ministry.html.

6. ...scholars note that if Jesus began His public ministry between mid to late AD 26 and died in the spring of AD 30, His ministry would have been a total of 3½ years (including His resurrection, 40 days of appearances, and ascension). Others who argue for the crucifixion taking place in AD 33 argue Jesus did not begin His ministry until AD 29, calculating the starting date of Tiberius Caesar's reign based upon the death of his predecessor Augustus Caesar in AD 14, meaning that the ministry of John the Baptist began in AD 29. In either case, a public ministry of about 3½ years is still the conclusion.

7. MacArthur, *The Second Coming*, p. 85.

8. MacArthur, *The Second Coming*, p. 85.

9. Tim LaHaye, Jerry B. Jenkins, *Are We Living in the End Times?* (Tyndale House Publishers, Inc., Wheaton, Illinois) p. 153.

10. MacArthur, *The Second Coming*, p. 85.

11. Philip Schaff, *History of the Christian Church* (Grand Rapids, Michigan: WM. B. Eerdmans Publishing Company, 1978) Vol. 1, p. 398.

12. MacArthur, p. 86.

13. *Gesenius' Hebrew-Chaldee Lexicon to the Old Testament*, #1396 (Baker Book House, Grand Rapids, Michigan).

14. MacArthur, *The Second Coming*, p. 85.

15. MacArthur, *The Second Coming*, p. 112.

16. LaHaye, Jenkins, *Are We Living in the End Times?*, p. 123.

17. Teachers' Manual, *Search for Truth* (Search for Truth Publications, 10929 Almeda-Genoa Rd., Houston, Texas, 77034, 1965) p. 113.

18. MacArthur, *The Second Coming*, p. 112.

19. LaHaye, Jenkins, *Are We Living in the End Times?*, p. 121.

20. The Prophetic Years, Bible Prophecy–Christian worldviews– Christian Commentary–web-site Article: "Israel the third temple and the coming Jewish holocaust" by Don Koenig.

21. *Wisconsin District News*, "Quest for the Red Heifer," United Pentecostal Church, September 1997, p. 4.

22. *Wisconsin District News*, United Pentecostal Church, September 1997, p. 5.

23. *Matthew Henry's Commentary*, p. 150.

24. MacArthur, *The Second Coming*, p. 124.

CHAPTER SEVEN

IS MODERN-DAY ISRAEL GOD'S CHOSEN PEOPLE?

—⊸∞⊶—

WHO IS A JEW?

The primary question for those who insist the people who inhabit modern Israel are the Jews of Biblical promise is this: What exactly is a Jew? Being Jewish is not an ethnic identity, any more than being an American (or a Christian) is an ethnic identity.

Even if someone were a remnant ethnic Jew, descended from the loins of Abraham, whose bloodline had been kept pure and undiluted all these thousands of years, the Bible says faith is the only ingredient in determining who is a true Jew and who is not.

To become a Jew, one would need to study Jewish theology, culture, customs, rituals, and history preparatory to incorporating Jewish practices into their life. If they do, and faithfully follow all the rites and duties required of Judaism, they are rightly deemed Jewish. Any children born to them after their conversion will be Jews, and their progeny will be Jewish, too—albeit with a very short Jewish heritage and ancestry.

Hence, anyone who wishes can become a Jew and follow the teachings of Judaism. In Uganda, there are the Black Abayudaya (People of Judah) who have relatively recently embraced Judaism—only since 1917. There are also the Black Jews of Rusape, from Zimbabwe. Their active practice of Judaism dates back to only 1903.

Wikipedia carries an article titled "Who is a Jew?" which states:

> According to the Mishnah, the oldest codified normative definition used by Jews for self-identification, a person is matrilineally a Jew by birth, or becomes one through conversion to Judaism... In general, Orthodox Judaism considers a person born of a Jewish mother to be Jewish, even if they convert to another religion.

On the website "Judaism 101," an article titled "What Is Judaism?" states:

> But setting aside the emotional issues, Jews are clearly not a race. Race is a genetic distinction, and refers to people with shared ancestry and shared genetic traits. You can't change your race; it's in your DNA. I could never become black or Asian no matter how much I might want to.
>
> Common ancestry is not required to be a Jew. Many Jews worldwide share common ancestry, as shown by genetic research; however, you can be a Jew without sharing this common ancestry, for example, by converting. Thus, although I could never become black or Asian, blacks and Asians have become Jews (Sammy Davis Jr. and Connie Chung).

The confusing of those who follow the teachings of Judaism—whose ancestors have converted to Judaism decades or even centuries ago—with those who are genetically connected to Abraham in the Old Testament is part of the problem. The other part is the realization that, biblically, faith in the one true God was the key definition of a true Jew (a son of Abraham) and who was not—the key to who was a member of God's covenant body the Church, or a member of the "synagogue of Satan. *"I know the blasphemy of them which say they are Jews, and are not, but are the synagogue of Satan"* (Rev. 2:9).

Many Christians who support the modern-day nation of Israel are unaware of the fact that most—if not all—the Jews that now inhabit the land where Jesus walked are not genetically related to Abraham, Isaac, or

Jacob. These contemporary Jews may have been practicing the teachings of Judaism for a long time, but it is still a spurious and deceptive belief system.

Dispensationalists are very confused on this issue. Many ancestors of Israel's current Jewish population converted to Judaism eons ago. Nevertheless, Dispensationalists insist we must support modern Israel simply because its citizens (except for its atheists!) practice a Gospel-denying religion. Dispensationalists insist God is now obligated to Jews—and that they are his "chosen people"—precisely because they faithfully practice an erroneous religion which is roundly condemned in Scripture! They also insist Jews are deserving of God's blessings by remaining committed to error and false teaching, which at times causes pain and suffering.

It is also a fact that no modern Jews hold to the Biblical faith of Abraham; instead, they reject the teachings of Moses concerning the Messiah and hate the idea of Jesus being the Son of God and their Messiah.

Peter and John, as they were about to go into the temple, stopped and took a bit of time to heal a lame man. When those gathered saw that man now whole—leaping, walking, and praising God—all were filled with amazement. Peter then preached to those assembled—the Jews, the seed of Abraham, the literal children of the prophets and of the covenant—a message of their guilt, their denial, rejection, and participation in the murder of the Prince of Life, Jesus Christ. He told them they needed to *"Repent ye therefore and be converted"* (Acts 3:19).

He finished his short message with a reminder of what Moses had said and the dire consequences if his decrees were not followed: *"And it shall come to pass, that every soul, which will not hear that prophet, shall be destroyed from among the people"* (Acts 3:23).

Still, just because someone calls himself a "Jew" and practices a specious faith, Dispensationalists say Christians must support them. Modern Israel is a melting pot of nationalities and ethnic groups. Moreover, the religious Jews among them all rejected God and the words of Moses when they converted to Judaism instead of turning to Jesus.

However, unless the reasons behind Christ's rejecting the notion of Jews being God's "chosen people" is fully understood, what follows will be, to some who are reading this, anathema or abhorrent.

WAS THE ORIGINAL NATION OF ISRAEL
RE-ESTABLISHED IN 1948?

As God's covenant people, the Jews have not been "regathered" in modern Israel as prescribed in Scripture. For this regathering to have taken place, there needed to be a prior time when *their* ancestors—with a tangible connection to Abraham and his descendants—were inhabitants of that land. In addition, their ancestors must have been present at the foot of Mt. Sinai where Moses received the Law. However, the forebears of the people who inhabit modern Israel never had residence in the land promised to Abraham.

After the death of Christ, there was no Mosaic law to follow because a new covenant/testament had been established by the blood of the Lamb of God. Repentance and faith in Christ are the way to enter a relationship with God. Only those who are covenanted together with Christ and have the faith of Abraham are Jews. Jews living in the modern state of Israel have neither the faith of Abraham nor are they related by blood to Abraham.

The followers of Judaism are not God's people. However, if they repent and turn from that fallacious dogma, they can become part of God's family. In addition, once they repent, they become part of the assembly (church) in the wilderness (Acts 7:38), which is the Church, the Bride of Christ. God's people are now called Christians. (See Appendix B.) Never again will there be a reason or a need for a restored nation-state called Israel. There is no New Testament Scripture dealing with a restoration of the nation of Israel, only its destruction (Matt. 21:43, 24:2; Mark 13:2; Luke 19:42–44, 21:20–24). If there was to be a restoration of the nation of Israel, why didn't the greatest prophet of all, Jesus, say a single word about it?

Many believe the Bible teaches the eventual restoration of the nation of Israel. Just a short search on the internet turns up many websites with articles such as "The Rebirth of Israel," which proclaims:

> The rebirth of Israel as an independent nation in 1948 is one of the most significant events in world history ... Those who study the Word of God recognize the restoration of Israel as the primary sign of the end of the age. Jesus promised the generation

that witnessed this event would also witness His return. Matthew 24:34 (NLT)[1]

On the *Biblicist* website, another article titled "Bible Prophecy Sequence of Events" states:

1948 marked an important date in Bible Prophecy. The restoration of the Jewish state is a fulfillment of those prophecies that spoke of a regathering in unbelief in preparation for judgment. This is another event leading up to the Tribulation and sets the stage for other Pre-Tribulation events.[2]

Religion author Ken Marineau, in an article featured on the *Bible Probe* website, had this to say:

One essential ingredient for the fulfillment of Bible prophecies in the last days that was not present until May 14th, 1948, is the nation of Israel. Without the existence of Israel, the presence of the other signs would mean very little. The end time events revolve around this little country, which seems to be constantly in the news. It is important to understand that the rebirth of Israel was a prophetic event, predicted in the Bible, and brought forth by the direct will of God ... To summarize, Israel is the key to God's prophetic calendar. We have been privileged to be present during this time in history. With this key part of the prophetic puzzle in place, and all the other signs are occurring simultaneously, we more than any other generation can wait with anticipation for the fulfillment of all things, and the return of our Lord and Savior, Jesus Christ.[3]

For those who believe Israel becoming a nation in 1948 was the fulfillment of Bible prophecy, I have a few questions. What kind of nation would God have re-established? A nation filled with those who hate Christ and thus reject Him? A nation that does not share the same faith as Abraham? Are we to believe God established a covenant with those who are not even the blood descendants of Abraham, Isaac, or Jacob? Would God maintain a covenant relationship with unbelievers and those who trample underfoot the blood of Christ?

Despite what many affirm, ever since Israel's destruction in AD 70 it has been completely impossible to "re-establish Israel" as a covenant nation under God's blessings and protection, for the only true Jews that now exist are Christians. It is only they who believe what Moses wrote and who follow God's commandments: *"This is the work of God, that ye believe on him whom he hath sent"* (John 6:29). The only true Jews that exist are those who hold to the faith of their father, Abraham. As Jesus told the Jewish sons of the devil, *"If ye were Abraham's children, ye would do the works of Abraham"* (John 8:39).

The only covenant people God recognizes today are those whose sins have been washed away by the blood of the Lamb. The only true Jews to whom any promises of God apply are Christians. They alone have a holy priesthood, are the true and holy nation—the chosen generation. God's only true possession is constituted by those who once were not a people or nation of God, but the ones whom Jesus has called into His marvelous light: Christians (I Peter 2:5–10).

The Lord Jesus took away from the unbelieving nation of Israel their place in the kingdom of God. Jesus told them, *"Therefore say I unto you, The kingdom of God shall be taken from you and given to a nation bringing forth the fruits thereof"* (Matt. 21:43). Who comprises that nation? The Church of God.

God will not consider any relationship with those who hate Him; He never has and He never will! Moreover, a foundation that God has destroyed and done away with can never be re-established. The Old Testament has been replaced and fulfilled by the New Testament. *"Drink ye all of it; For this is my blood of the new testament, which is shed for many for the remission of sins"* (Matt. 26:27–28).

The Israel of old consisted of those who shared a covenantal relationship with God, not just the descendants of Abraham, Isaac, and Jacob. Today, the only certain way for a people to share fellowship with God, to be redeemed, is through belief in the shed, precious blood of the Lamb.

Judaism is now, at best, a moribund belief system that can never flourish as it once did. It is an obsolete, archaic, and false religion. Judaism, with its adherence to the Torah/Talmud, has been replaced, for the old covenant has been superseded by the New Covenant: *"He taketh away the first, that he may establish the second. By the which will we are sanctified through the offering of the body of Jesus Christ once for all"* (Heb. 10:9–10). Only those who continue in God's New Covenant are true Jews.

Some believe the Book of Romans talks about a Jewish restoration. In Rom. 11:25–27, Paul writes:

> *For I would not, brethren, that ye should be ignorant of this mystery, lest ye should be wise in your own conceits; that blindness in part is happened to Israel, until the fulness of the Gentiles be come in. And so all Israel shall be saved: as it is written, There shall come out of si-on the Deliverer, and shall turn away ungodliness from Jacob: For this is my covenant unto them, when I shall take away their sins.*

Note these verses say nothing about a restoration or regathering of the nation of Israel. Those ideas have to be read into the text. The apostle was referencing Old Testament Scripture whose fulfillment was still in the future but now refers to events in the past: the coming of Jesus and the redemption He brought by His death on the cross.

Paul was alluding to Isaiah 59:20 and the Book of Psalms 14:7. These verses refer to what the Deliverer, Christ, would do. We have already seen in Chapter 6 the important things the incarnation of the Lord would accomplish (Dan. 9:24)—and were accomplished on Calvary and through the empty tomb. Christ ushered in the New Covenant to take away the Jews' sins, and ours. And *all Israel* was saved. But Dispensationalists do not believe all Israel will be saved, just a remnant.[4] MacArthur writes, "As many as two-thirds will die ..."[5] Just remember this: *"they are not all Israel that are of Israel"* (Rom. 9:6).

No prophecy concerning the nation of Israel remains to be fulfilled. Everything that was prophesied concerning God's promise to Abraham (Deut. 1:10) and Israel's conquest of Canaan has been fulfilled (Josh. 21:43–45, 23:14; I Kings 8:56). Everything that was prophesied concerning the restoration of Israel to their land after the seventy years in exile has been fulfilled (Jer. 30:3,11, 32:37, 33:7,14; Ezek. 37:21–25, 39:25). All these verses tear the Dispensational doctrine apart.

WHY MODERN-DAY ISRAEL
IS NOT GOD'S PEOPLE

The nation of Israel today is not the nation of God. Thus, the Jews living there are not true Jews. "*[H]e is not a Jew, which is one outwardly, neither is that circumcision, which is outward in the flesh: But he is a Jew which is one inwardly; and circumcision is that of the heart*" (Rom. 2:28–29, 8:17, 9:7; Gal. 3:7, 29). When those gathered about him asked the Lord how He defined a "true" Jew, "*Jesus answered and said unto them, This is the work of God, that ye believe on him whom he hath sent*" (John 6:29). A "true" Jew believes in Jesus. Remember what He told the Jews of His day—the ones who really could trace their lineage back to Abraham—that they were of their father, "*the devil!*" (John 8:44). Why? Simply because they did not believe Jesus was the Messiah. Therefore, according to Jesus, they were not the sons of Abraham! Moreover, what has changed since then? Nothing.

Even if a Jew could still trace his lineage back to Abraham, that would not mean he was a son of Abraham. He might be a son in the flesh; but, if he is not a believer in Christ, he is cut off from the blessings of the covenant. He is then no longer a son, but a covenant-breaker who is thereby disinherited (Gen. 17:14; Ex. 4:24; Num. 15:31; Jer. 31:32). Nonetheless, when a Jew confesses Jesus, what does he become? A Christian, part of the Bride of Christ, just as the Apostle Paul and the three thousand Jews on the day of Pentecost, and every one of the first converts—who were all Jews!

When Gentiles believe in the Lord Jesus, they too become the children of Abraham and "*are blessed with faithful Abraham*" (Gal. 3:7–8). "*And if ye be Christ's, then are ye Abraham's seed, and heirs according to the promise*" (Gal. 3:29). All believers, including Gentiles, are grafted into the lineage of Abraham as true sons and "*receive the adoption of sons*" (Gal. 4:5). In Christ, there is no need for a distinct and separate Jewish people, nor is there a need for a separate Jewish nation. For in Christ, "*There is neither Jew nor Greek, there is neither bond nor free, there is neither male nor female: for ye are all one in Christ Jesus*" (Gal. 3:28).

In Christ, there is just one body, which is made up of Jews and Gentiles (Eph. 2:16). Christ, "*who hath made both one, and hath broken down the middle wall of partition between us ... for to make in himself of twain one new man, so making peace, and that he might reconcile both unto God in one body by the cross*" (Eph. 2:14–16). Christ destroyed the *wall of partition* between us (Jew and Gentile), never to be rebuilt again. When a Jew becomes a Christian, he becomes part of a holy, separate, and distinct group of people—the Church, the Bride of Christ—who believe in the God of Abraham, the father of the faithful.

In his "postmillennial eschatology" *He Shall Have Dominion*, Kenneth Gentry, Th.D., explores the concept of Covenantalism:

> One God, one covenant law: through time and across borders. The successive covenants of Scripture really record for us a gradual historical unfolding of *one overarching covenant*, rather than the successive, compartmental establishing of distinctively different capsule covenants. This is clearly expected in the initial covenant directive of God for history that flows out of the Genesis 3:15 curse, which mentions only one basic struggle between two seeds, the Satanic and the Messianic. This also is clearly asserted in Paul's argument in Ephesians, chapter 2. In this passage, Paul speaks not of the establishing of a new and distinct community separate from Israel, but of *God's annexing of additional people*–the Gentiles–into His one people. He speaks in verse 12 of "the covenants of the promise" (Greek), which defined His singular purpose. In verses 14–16, he speaks of the removal of the dividing wall between Jew and Gentile, so that the Gentiles might be included in God's one redemptive purpose. In verses 19–22, he speaks of *the merging of these two peoples into one, indivisible temple.*[6] (emphasis his)

Jewish people need to be grafted into the "olive tree," which has long symbolized the true faith of Father Abraham and the one faith in the one true God. Christians compose a large part of the olive tree; Jesus and His disciples ensured that the Gentiles were also grafted into that one tree, one faith, and one body (Rom. 11:20–23). Our Lord does not have two trees or separate bodies of believers. He has one group of people, His Church. Unbelievers, whether Jews or Gentiles, can become part of this one body whenever they choose. (see Appendix A.)

There are—and always have been—just two groups of people in this world. On the one hand, you have the saved, the believers, the Bride (the

Church) of Christ; and on the other, those that belong to Satan. The Bible clearly teaches there is only one body, the Church, made up of both Jew and Gentile (Eph. 2:13–22). It was the Church that sustained the covenant and fulfilled the promises God gave to Israel. (see Appendix B.)

The Church is not identical to (or a replacement for) Israel. Nor does the Church represent a different entity, faith, or belief. Believers in Christ have simply embraced the same faith as Noah, Abraham, Moses, David, and all the other prophets and patriarchs of old. The Church of Jesus Christ holds to the same beliefs, prays to the same God, and is heir to the same blessings bestowed by God upon Abraham.

Just as Jews need to believe in the one of whom Moses spoke to remain connected to the true faith, so, too, the Gentiles must believe in the Christ to be grafted into the true faith (Rom. 11:24).

Until a Jew becomes a believer in Jesus, he is excluded from His grace. Even if the modern nation of Israel consisted solely of the descendants of Abraham, it would still have nothing to do with Bible prophecy. God said through Jeremiah, *"And ye shall seek me, and find me, when ye shall search for me with all your heart"* (Jer. 29:12–13). In other words, repentance leads to finding God. Have the entirety of Jews in Israel or anywhere else repented? No! For if they had, they would then be believers—Christians.

Jerusalem and all Israel were destroyed in AD 70 because of their unbelief. They rejected their Redeemer, Jesus; therefore, judgment came upon them. Has God changed His mind about people rejecting Christ? He removed the entire Jewish population out of their land precisely because of unbelief. Is He now going to relent and bring them back to their land, even though they are still unbelievers and refuse to repent, still reject and hate Jesus, despise His name, and would advocate crucifying Him again if they could? Of course not! God is not double-minded on this issue.

Alex Awad was director of Hope Secondary School, a Christian institution in the West Bank until Israeli authorities deported him in September 1987. When interviewed by author James Byron Huggins, Awad said this about life in modern Israel: "If we were to begin evangelizing in Israel, the Jewish community would not tolerate it at all ... if we tried to evangelize the Jews, we would probably be beaten and harassed. In fact, if you convert to Christianity a Jew who is younger than 17 years old, you could go to prison."

Huggins also asked: "What position has Israel adopted toward missionary work? Awad replied: "To say 'missionary' in Israel is like saying 'Nazi.' The Jews do not like missionaries because when a Jew becomes a Christian, he loses his ethnic as well as his religious identity. It is more a political issue than a religious one. If all Jews became Christians, that would be the end of Israel as a state."[7] (Israel ultimately reconsidered Awad's deportation, for he is currently pastor of East Jerusalem Baptist Church and professor at Bethlehem Bible College.)

The Jews hated the first Christians and regularly harassed, beat, stoned, and killed them (Acts 4:1–21, 5:17–41, 6:9–14, 7:54–60, 8:1–3, 9:1–2, 9:23–24, 12:1–3, 13:6–8, 45, 14:2,5,19, 17:5–9, 18:5–6, 23:12–14; II Cor. 11:23–26). Nothing has changed in the unregenerate Jewish heart since God judged the Jews for their unbelief in AD 70. Until they repent, the same reason still exists for the judgment and dispersion that happened in AD 70.

Dispensationalists forget that God's law concerning marriage applies to Him as much as to us. God is not a polygamist; He does not have two brides, Israel *and* the Church. Nevertheless, according to some Dispensationalists, God has two brides. This premillennial notion teaches when the Bride of Christ, the Church, has been raptured and is in heaven at the Marriage Supper of the Lamb, the other wife (God's "chosen people," the Jews) will be on earth. "Israel will be the restored wife during the period of the great tribulation."[8] But God does not have two seeds, just one: believers in Jesus, who are the Church. In addition, God is not going to remarry His former wife whom He divorced (Isaiah 50:1; Jeremiah 3:8).

THE ORIGIN OF MODERN JEWRY

What does the term "Jew" mean? The word itself was formed from the name of the patriarch, Judah, and originally signified the people from the tribe of Judah. Later it denoted the people of the southern kingdom of Judah, as distinct from the northern kingdom of Israel. The name Jew was eventually used for all the descendants of Abraham.

However, by the time of the Apostle Paul, little distinction separated the terms Hebrew, Jew, and Israel; thus, any of those designations could equally apply to an individual or to the twelve tribes. On various occasions,

Paul related each of those terms to himself, stating, *"I am a man which am a Jew of Tarsus"* (Acts 21:39); *"of the stock of Israel, of the tribe of Benjamin, an Hebrew of Hebrews"* (Phil. 3:5); *"Are they Hebrews? so am I. Are they Israelites? so am I. Are they the seed of Abraham? so am I"* (II Cor. 11:22).

There are many Jews today, but they are a mixed multitude. Few, if any, are from the lineage of Abraham. Theology author John Bray has written about the Jews as a distinct race: "Dr. Camille Honig, a Jewish authority and editor of a Jewish publication, who has studied Jewish types and communities on five continents, said that, 'it is sheer nonsense ... as well as unscientific to speak of a Jewish race' and that 'Jews do not belong to a single homogeneous group.'"[9]

Arthur Koestler, in his meticulously researched and detailed book *The Thirteenth Tribe*, offers compelling evidence that most, if not all, modern Jewry is of Khazar origin. The Khazar Empire embraced the Jewish faith about the year AD 740, and Judaism became the state religion. The Khazar conversion was remarkable, considering the relentless Christian proselytizing by Byzantium in the west and the burgeoning Muslim influence from the East.

The Khazar Empire was a major power in Eastern Europe at the time Charlemagne was Emperor in the west. They ruled from the Black Sea to the Caspian, from the Caucasus to the Volga. Khazaria was finally wiped out by the forces of Genghis Khan, but evidence indicates the Khazars themselves managed to survive.

What emerges from the historical record is the Khazars migrated to the regions of Eastern Europe, mainly Russia and Poland, the cradle of western Jewry—where, at the dawn of the modern age, the greatest concentrations of Jews were found. Koestler writes, "[T]he large majority of surviving Jews in the world is of Eastern European—and thus perhaps mainly of Khazar—origin. If so, this would mean their ancestors came not from the Jordan but from the Volga, not from Canaan but from the Caucasus, once believed to be the cradle of the Aryan race; and genetically they are more closely related to the Hun, Uigur and Magyar tribes than to the seed of Abraham, Isaac, and Jacob."[10]

Koestler continues: "On the evidence quoted in previous chapters, one can easily understand why Polish historians—who are, after all, closest to the sources—are in agreement that 'in earlier times, the main bulk of the Jewish population originated from the Khazar country."[11] Koestler concludes, "The evidence quoted in previous chapters adds up to a strong case in favour of those modern historians—whether Austrian, Israeli or Polish—who, independently from each other, have argued the bulk of modern Jewry is not of Palestinian, but of Caucasian origin."[12]

In examining the origins of Jews from different lands, John Bray describes the following incident:

> A missionary who has lived in Jerusalem for eight years asked me, "Why do the Jews from Syria look like Syrians? And the Jews from Iran and Iraq, like the people of Iran and Iraq? And the Jews from Egypt like the Egyptians? And the Lebanese Jews like the Lebanese? And the Jews from Yemen like the people of Yemen? And so on?" The point is, that the Jews in all these and other countries intermarry with the people of those countries, and become like them. The point is, further, that there are not many full-blooded Jews, if any![13]

There are many examples in Scripture of people who were not the descendants of Abraham who became Jews. In the time of Esther, *"many of the people of the land became Jews; for the fear of the Jews fell upon them"* (Esther 8:17). Moses had married an Ethiopian woman (Num. 12:1). When the children of Israel left Egypt, *"a mixed multitude went up also with them"* (Ex. 12:38). Rahab the Canaanite became the mother of the line from which sprung David and, eventually, Christ. Ruth the Moabite became the mother of Obed, the father of Jesse and grandfather of David. Naamah, an Ammonitess, was the mother of Rehoboam, who was the son of King Solomon and successor to his father's throne. Many Jews were the proselytes down through the centuries. To be a Jew simply means observing the practice of Judaism.

FALLACIES CONCERNING THE NATION OF ISRAEL

There is a place in Jerusalem known as the "Wailing (Western) Wall." It is where Jews go to pray and cry out to their God. They believe this wall is all that remains of the Second Temple since the destruction of the city in AD 70. Yet if this is still part of the temple, the words of the prophet Micah would not have been fulfilled: "*Therefore shall Zion for your sake be plowed as a field, and Jerusalem shall become heaps*" (Micah 3:12). Nor would the words of Jesus have come to pass when He said, "*There shall not be left here one stone upon another, that shall not be thrown down*" (Matt. 24:2). With this in mind, what is the true origin of the Wailing Wall?

One pernicious or destructive error frequently taught by Dispensationalists is that God will specially bless the people and nations that help the "heathen, God-hating" modern nation of Israel.

In the past, I have taught, "The United States has been blessed because it has been helping the nation of Israel." What was my rationale for this belief? God's own words when He said, "*I will bless them that bless thee, and curse him that curseth thee*" (Gen. 12:3). However, the Zionist, unbelieving, Christ-rejecting modern nation of Israel is not the "*thee*" referred to in the Book of Genesis. As a nation, it does not honor the Son; so—according to the Bible—they are anti-Christ and anti-God (John 15:23; I John 2:22).

Furthermore, does it look as though the United States has been blessed by helping the nation of Israel since its formation in 1948? Or does it seem more likely the USA has been cursed and judged by God? Regarding this issue, well-known Baptist evangelist Colonel Jack Mohr shares my thoughts:

> A few years ago Jerry Falwell, noted fundamentalist television preacher and head of the Moral Majority, said: "God has blessed America, because we have been good to the Jews."
>
> This is an obvious, observable lie! An outright falsehood! The time of America's greatest derogation, in every phase of life: militarily; economically; educationally; morally, and spiritually, has come since we recognized that little "bandit" state of the Israelis in 1948. This country can never be blessed when it "helps the ungodly, and loves them that hate the Lord!" It will never be blessed as long as it makes agreements with anti-Christ nations, whether they be Red China, the Soviet Union, the Cannibal Debating Society of the United Nations, or the anti-Christs in

Israel. Think well on this truth, before you approve of another "hand out" to the Israeli.[14]

In the Old Testament, we have an example of the LORD pronouncing wrath upon the upright Jew, Jehoshaphat, King of Judah, for helping the wicked Jew, King Ahab of Israel. God had warned Israel about entering alliances with the heathen nations that bordered them (Ex. 23:32, 34:12, 15; Deut. 7:2). Israel, with Ahab as king, no longer served the Lord and soon devolved into a heathen nation.

As the Bible relates, Jehoshaphat formed an alliance with heathen Ahab, which was cemented by a marriage between Jehoram, the crown prince of Judah, and the princess Athaliah, daughter of Ahab. Jehoshaphat for the most part was a good king. But Ahab was one of the most wicked kings the nation of Israel ever had.

God was displeased when one of His people formed an alliance with a wicked Jew. In response, He sent Jehu the prophet to speak to King Jehoshaphat. Appearing before the king, Jehu said, "*Shouldest thou help the ungodly, and love them that hate the LORD? therefore is wrath upon thee from before the LORD*" (II Chron. 19:2; see also Acts 3:22–23). Imagine that! God declaring a Jew was ungodly and not one of the LORD's people!

Biblically, what is the difference between the nation of Israel today and the ancient nation of Israel under the unbelieving King Ahab? Nothing I can discern. The Israel of old was full of unbelievers; the nation of Israel today is full of unbelieving, Christ-hating people. Could it be God's wrath is upon America for helping an ungodly state whose citizens spurn the Lord Jesus?

At one time it was necessary for Christ to come from the lineage of Abraham to ensure the promises made by God to the Fathers were fulfilled; however, even then it was only the believing Jews who were considered the children of promise (Rom. 9:7–8, 11:20; Gal. 3:22; Heb. 3:9–19). Every Jew who does not confess Jesus as the Christ is not a true worshipper of the Father and is cut off from the olive tree. Jeremiah the prophet said, "*it is an evil thing and bitter, that thou hast forsaken the LORD thy God, and that my fear is not in thee*" (Jer. 2:19). Today there are no promises that need to be fulfilled concerning the nation of Israel or the descendants of Abraham.

How does God redeem lost Jews today? Through repentance and faith in Jesus. God will readily deliver any Jew who rejects the apostate religion of Judaism. And when He does, Jews will be saved the same way all Christ's people have been for the last 1,950 years.

From the day of Pentecost when Peter gave his sermon and the Jews asked, *"Men and brethren what shall we do?"* (Acts 2:37), repentance and faith in Jesus has been the required response. Those who repent, Jew, and Gentile alike, will enter into the one faith, the faith of Abraham, and become Abraham's seed (Gal. 3:7, 26). God does not have a special plan of salvation for any group of apostates, including the Jews. Those who reject Christ, be it Jew or Gentile, are simply cut off from the true religion, Christianity, and have the same fate—eternal punishment.

It follows that not one person who follows Judaism today can rightly be claimed a Jew! As the Scripture teaches: *"For he is not a Jew, which is one outwardly; neither is that circumcision, which is outward in the flesh: But he is a Jew, which is one inwardly"* (Rom. 2:28–29). For in Christ, *"There is neither Jew nor Greek, there is neither bond nor free, there is neither male nor female: for ye are all one in Christ Jesus. And if ye be Christ's then are ye Abraham's seed, and heirs according to the promise"* (Gal. 3:28–29). Those who follow Judaism are of the synagogue of Satan (Rev. 2:9), for they have rejected God and His word.

As Jesus said: *"For had ye believed Moses, ye would have believed me: for he wrote of me"* (John 5:46). *"If ye were Abraham's children, ye would do the works of Abraham"* (John 8:39). Only those who have the faith of Abraham are the children of Abraham. Today, if the Jews wish to be in a covenantal relationship with the Lord, they need to believe in the Messiah, Jesus.

David Chilton states it well in his book *Paradise Restored*:

> It is important to remember that Judaism is *not* Old Testament religion, but rather a rejection of the Biblical faith altogether in favor of the Pharisaical Talmudic heresy. Like Mormons, Jehovah's Witnesses, the Unification Church, and other cults, it claims to be based on the Bible, but its actual authority comes from the traditions of men. Jesus was quite clear: Judaism denies *Christ* because it denies *Moses*. Orthodox Christianity *alone* is the true continuation and fulfillment of Old Testament religion (see Matt. 5:1–9, 15:17; Mark 7:1–13; Luke 16:29–31; John 5:45–47; 8:42–47).[15]

What is the difference between someone who converts to Judaism and someone who has descended from the loins of Abraham? None, for there is no difference. Unless the natural Jew and the convert have the faith of Abraham, each is, as Jesus said, a son of Satan and a member of the synagogue of Satan (John 8:39–44; Rev. 2:9).

Unless those who follow the practices of Judaism repent and turn from their misguided path, God is under no obligation to bless or protect them.

One final problem: if I convert to Judaism, my children become Jews—for by Jewish tradition a child of a Jewish mother whose father is a Gentile is still a Jew. This actually became law in Israel: "In 1970 the Israeli Knesset adopted legislation defining a Jew as one born of a Jewish mother or a convert" (Funk and Wagnall's New Encyclopedia, vol. 14, p. 214).

So, if I become a Jew, does that mean the blessings and promises God gave to Abraham now belong to me, my children, and my grandchildren, because we are all Jews?

If you answer "yes" (God forbid), that would mean I would have to turn my back on Jesus and follow teachings that brought judgment on those who continued in their rebellious ways. However, if you answer I would not be eligible for the blessings and promises God gave to Abraham, how is my conversion to Judaism any different from the conversions of those who became Jews a hundred or a thousand years ago? The only difference between my conversion and those who have been practicing Judaism for generations is the length of time they have been following a spurious, invalid, and rebellious religion. Promoting error and rebellion for an extended length of time does not further endear one to God. Even though the Jews have suffered for their false beliefs, as they did under the oppression of Adolf Hitler, their suffering for a religion that rejects Christ did not entitle them to the promises God made to a man of faith, Abraham, millennia before.

Remember what Christ said to the woman of Samaria: "*The hour cometh, when ye shall neither in this mountain, nor yet at Jerusalem, worship the Father ... the true worshippers shall worship the Father in spirit and in truth*" (John 4:21–23); and to the unbelieving Jews: "*If ye believe not that I am he, ye shall die in your sins*" (John 8:24).

FOOTNOTES

1. "BrittGillette.Com, A Christian examination of bible prophecy and emerging technology ..." website, Article titled: *The Rebirth of Israel*, Posted on April 21ˢᵗ, 2007.
2. The "Biblicist" website, Article titled: *Bible Prophecy Sequence of Events*.
3. Bible Probe website; *Israel: The Greatest Sign* by Ken Marineau.
4. Dr. Jack Van Impe, *Everything you always wanted to know about PROPHECY* (Jack Van Impe Ministries, Box J, Royal Oak, Michigan, 1980) Chart on the last page.
5. John F. MacArthur, *The Second Coming* (Crossway Books, A Division of Good News Publishers, 1300 Crescent Street, Wheaton, Illinois 60187, 1999) p. 114.
6. Dr. Kenneth L. Gentry, Jr., *He Shall Have Dominion* (Institute for Christian Economics, P. O. Box 8000, Tyler, Texas 75711, 1992) p. 128.
7. *Christian Mission*, May/June 1988, p. 6.
8. Teachers' Manual, *Search for Truth* (Search for Truth Publications, 10929 Almeda-Genoa Rd., Houston, Texas, 77034, 1965) p. 118.
9. John L. Bray, *Israel in Bible Prophecy* (John L. Bray Ministry, Inc., P.O. Box 90129, Lakeland, Florida 33804, 1997) p. 44.
10. Arthur Koestler, *The Thirteenth Tribe* (New York: Random House, 1976) p. 17.
11. Koestler, *The Thirteenth Tribe*, p. 169.
12. Koestler, *The Thirteenth Tribe*, p. 180.
13. Bray, *Israel in Bible Prophecy*, p. 45.
14. Colonel Jack Mohr website, *Things Christians Need to Know (About Jews, Judaism and Zionism)* by Lt. Col. Gordon "Jack" Mohr. AUS RET.
15. David Chilton, *Paradise Restored* (Dominion Press 1985) p. 182.

CHAPTER EIGHT

MATTHEW TWENTY-FOUR: THE OLIVET DISCOURSE

—❈—

Before continuing, the reader should review the *Harmony of the Olivet Discourse*, which follows this chapter.

The Olivet Discourse is the most comprehensive answer Christ gave to any question asked of Him. The Bible contains more than 100 verses relating to this one prophecy. The sermon Christ gave to His disciples, there on Mount Olivet, was so important its message resonates throughout most of the epistles written to the early Church.

As strange as it seems, many of those who profess to champion the cause of Christ go to great lengths to obscure the simple truth of Christ's Olivet Discourse. For the sake of a recently invented doctrine— Dispensationalism—they use every means at their disposal to cloud, mask, and repress some of the best evidence Christ was a true prophet while seeking to invalidate the overwhelming evidence for the truth of the Gospel itself.

This book seeks to reaffirm the best and oldest interpretation of Christ's Olivet prophecy is the one that was held by the early Church. By following the Lord's clear instructions, all Christians escaped the destruction of Jerusalem.

This interpretation is far from new. The esteemed British Methodist theologian Adam Clarke (among many others) espoused the preterist view. In his *Commentary* he states:

This chapter contains a prediction of the utter destruction of the city and temple of Jerusalem, and the subversion of the whole political constitution of the Jews; and is one of the most valuable portions of the new covenant Scriptures, with respect to the evidence which it furnishes of the truth of Christianity. Everything which our Lord foretold should come on the temple, city, and people of the Jews, has been fulfilled in the most correct and astonishing manner; and witnessed by a writer who was present during the whole, who was himself a Jew, and is acknowledged to be an historian of indisputable veracity in all those transactions which concern the destruction of Jerusalem. Without having designed it, he has written a commentary on our Lord's words, and shown how every tittle was punctually fulfilled, though he knew nothing of the Scripture which contained this remarkable prophecy.[1]

The historian mentioned by Clarke is Flavius Josephus. He was born into a priestly family in the year AD 37 or 38. At the age of nineteen, he became a Pharisee. He was thrust into prominence when he championed the release of fellow Jews held captive by Felix the Procurator. When he was thirty he was on a mission in Galilee when the Roman General Vespasian advanced against Jewish rebels and captured the fortress at Jotapata. During this military action, Josephus was captured and brought before Vespasian. The general was so impressed with Josephus's unlikely prediction—that Vespasian would shortly become Roman Emperor—he released his captive.

Grateful for his life, Josephus chose to ally with Rome, but still loved his people. He urged them to surrender when the Roman General Titus and his army invaded Israel and besieged Jerusalem. Josephus always considered himself a loyal Jew, though most of his countrymen considered him a traitor.

Josephus was an eyewitness to the besieging of Jerusalem. Much of the confirmation we have today concerning the fulfillment of Christ's prophecy comes from Josephus's writings.

Let us now examine this marvelous prophecy and see if we might gain an understanding of its ancient meaning.

THE DISCIPLES' QUESTIONS

As Jesus departed from the temple, the disciples came to show Him the temple and complex, with its splendid buildings adorned with goodly stones. Impressive and beautiful green and white spotted marble, massive, 50-feet long, 24-feet broad, and 16-feet thick monoliths. What, exactly, was their purpose? It wasn't that Jesus hadn't seen the temple before ... He was just there! Whatever their reasons, Jesus just pointed at the temple and said, "*See ye not all these things? Verily I say unto you, there shall not be left here one stone upon another that shall not be thrown down*" (Matt. 24:2).

This statement of Jesus probably stunned and troubled the disciples. The temple was the focal point of their worship, culture, and way of life. They also knew if the temple were destroyed, it would mean the city of Jerusalem and their entire nation would be left in ruins. How would they worship God without a temple in which to offer sacrifices?

What Jesus said about the temple mirrored the message He had just delivered about the nation of Israel and the city of Jerusalem: "*For the days shall come upon thee, that thine enemies shall cast a trench about thee, and compass thee round, and keep thee in on every side, And shall lay thee even with the ground, and thy children within thee; and they shall not leave in thee one stone upon another; because thou knewest not the time of thy visitation*" (Luke 19:43–44).

They also remembered the woes Jesus pronounced upon the Jewish unbelievers: "*Woe unto you, scribes and Pharisees, hypocrites ... Ye serpents, ye generation of vipers, how can ye escape the damnation of hell? ... That upon you may come all the righteous blood shed upon the earth ... Verily I say unto you, All these things shall come upon this generation*" (Matt. 23:13–39).

Jesus had told the disciples *they* and their generation would still be alive when the judgment of God, with its time of great tribulation, would fall upon Jerusalem. Thus forewarned, they wanted to know what sign would show it was about to happen. Moreover, as Jesus answered their questions in the Olivet Discourse, He told them again they were the ones—*their generation*—who would live to see "*all these things.*"

As Jesus sat upon the Mount of Olives, the disciples came to Him privately to ask about "*these things,*" whereby "*not one stone left upon another shall not be thrown down.*" Many readers of the Scripture misunderstand the answer Jesus gave because they forget what prompted His reply. Let us not forget how precisely Jesus answered the disciples' questions about the destruction of the temple. Here are all three accounts of the disciples' questions:

> *Tell us, when shall these things be? and what shall be the sign of thy coming, and of the end of the world?* (Matt. 24:3)
> *Tell us, when shall these things be? and what shall be the sign when all these things shall be fulfilled?* (Mark 13:4)
> *When shall these things be? and what sign will there be when these things shall come to pass?* (Luke 21:6)

All the disciples wanted to know *"when shall these things be?"* What things? The destruction of the temple and the city of Jerusalem, when not one stone would be left upon another. They also asked what sign they should look for. The answer was: *"And when ye shall see Jerusalem compassed with armies, then know that the desolation thereof is nigh"* (Luke 21:20).

In Matthew's account, *"the sign of thy coming and the end of the world"* are added to the disciples' questions. Were the disciples also asking about something else completely unrelated to the temple? Were they pondering the actual end of the entire world and the end of time as we know it? The answer is no. They were not asking about the end of human history. The Greek word translated as "world" in Matthew 24:3 is *aion*, which actually means "age." The Greek word *Kosmos*, which does mean the entire world (planet) and its inhabitants, is altogether different. Yet in one respect the disciples were asking about the end of the world because, with the city of Jerusalem and the temple destroyed, their way of life—*their* world—would literally end.

The Jewish temple, however, was never intended to stand forever. The Mosaic rites and ordinances for divine service were only *"a figure for the time then present, in which were offered both gifts and sacrifices, that could not make him that did the service perfect"* (Heb. 9:9). The temple was to endure only until Christ came, died, rose, and then entered *"into heaven itself, now to appear in the presence of God for us"* (Heb. 9:24).

The offering up of Jesus as a sacrifice for sins happened at the end of the world: *"but now once in the end of the world hath he appeared to put away sin by the sacrifice of himself*" (Heb. 9:26). Who sacrificed himself and then appeared as the world ended? As Paul declared, it was Jesus! Paul also said, when writing about the time he lived, "*Now all these things happened unto them for ensamples: and they are written for our admonition, upon whom the ends of the world are come*" (I Cor. 10:11). Or, as the Greek version says, "*to whom the ends of the ages has arrived.*"[2] Who, according to Paul, would suffer "*the ends of the world*"? The disciples together with the first Christians!

The destruction of the temple, along with the entire Jewish state, did indeed signal the end of the age. The Biblical "end of the age" is not the same as the era in which we live today or some age in our future. Jesus' death, marked the beginning of the end of the age. And it was so described as such by the New Testament writers. Moreover, that age came to a dramatic and terrible end in AD 70.

Many believe the disciples' questions were about a second coming of Jesus and a future rebuilt temple. However, as John L. Bray points out:

> Our dispensational, pre-tribulation rapture, futuristic friends would have Jesus answering this way: "Hold on, fellows! What is going to happen is that you are asking about *this* Temple, but my reply is to tell you about *another* Temple, which will be rebuilt many years down the road, and then it will be destroyed in *that* generation." Or, "Fellows, before that Temple (the second one, the one which you didn't ask about) is destroyed, there will be an abomination of desolation put in the Temple, which will be an image of the Antichrist. That will be a sign that the end is approaching. When the people (not you to whom I am talking) see this, they are to flee the city." Or, "Fellows, I know what your question is, but I am telling you what is going to happen way on down the road, at least a couple of thousand years from now, so that you can watch and be ready for it ..."[3]

When the disciples asked Jesus about the temple, they did not yet understand how He had to suffer and die for their sins! They did not know He would rise from the dead and ascend into heaven. Thus, how could they possibly be asking about His returning when they did not know He had to die first, come back to life, and ascend into heaven? The following verses nail the matter conclusively:

> *From that time forth began Jesus to shew unto his disciples, how that he must go unto Jerusalem, and suffer many things of the elders and chief priests and scribes, and be killed and be raised again the third day. Then Peter took him, and began to rebuke him, saying, Be it far from thee, Lord: this shall not be unto thee. But he turned, and said unto Peter, Get thee behind me, Satan: thou art an offense unto me: for thou savourest not the things that be of God, but those that be of men* (Matt. 16:21–23).

> *And as they came down from the mountain, he charged them that they should tell no man what things they had seen, till the Son of man were risen from the dead. And they kept that saying with themselves, questioning one with another what the rising from the dead should mean* (Mark 9:9–10).

> *For he taught his disciples, and said unto them, The Son of man is delivered into the hands of men, and they shall kill him; and after that he is killed, he shall rise the third day. But they understood not that saying, and were afraid to ask him* (Mark 9:31–32).

> *Afterward he appeared unto the eleven as they sat at meat, and upbraided them with their unbelief and hardness of heart, because they believed not them which had seen him after he was risen* (Mark 16:14).

> *Afterward he appeared unto the eleven as they sat at meat, and upbraided them with their unbelief and hardness of heart, because they believed not them which had seen him after he was risen* (Mark 16:14; see also Luke 9:44–45, 18:31–34; John 20:8–9

It was not until the Lord rose from the dead that the disciples fully understood the truth of Jesus' words. Then, and only then, did they start to comprehend what Jesus meant by the "*rising from the dead*." The following verses substantiate this:

> *Then he said unto them, O fools, and slow of heart to believe all that the prophets have spoken: Ought not Christ to have suffered these things, and to enter into his glory* (Luke 24:25–26)?

He is not here, but is risen: remember how he spake unto you when he was yet in Galilee, saying, The Son of man must be delivered into the hands of sinful men, and be crucified, and the third day rise again. And they remembered his words (Luke 24:6–8).

Then opened he their understanding, that they might understand the scriptures, And said unto them, Thus it is written, and thus it behooved Christ to suffer, and to rise from the dead the third day (Luke 24:45–46).

Jesus answered and said unto them, Destroy this temple, and in three days I will raise it up. Then said the Jews, Forty and six years was this temple in building, and wilt thou rear it up in three days? But he spake of the temple of his body. When therefore he was risen from the dead, his disciples remembered that he had said this unto them; and they believed the scripture, and the word which Jesus had said (John 2:19–22).

Contrary to what most Christians think, it does not make sense that the disciples would be asking about something (a second coming or returning), of which they knew nothing. If I said I was going on a vacation, you could ask where I was going, and when I would be returning. You might also ask many other questions about my future excursion. But if you do not know I am taking a trip, you would not wonder when I would be returning—or ask about it. You simply would not.

THE PAROUSIA OF CHRIST

The disciples' question in Matthew 24:3 about the *coming* of the Lord is better understood if we read it in the original Greek: "*Tell us, when these things will be, and what the sign of thy **presence** and of (the) completion of the age?*"[4] (emphasis added) The disciples wanted to know what sign would signal His presence, which would then herald the destruction of Jerusalem and the temple. However it was manifested, they knew the sign would be followed by a judgment from the Lord Jesus and they needed the forewarning to prepare for this monumental event.

What did the disciples mean when they asked Jesus about "*the sign of thy coming?*" Were they referring to what many call the "second coming of

Jesus"? Emphatically No! The word transliterated as *parousia* from the Greek is translated as *coming* in the KJV. What does the word parousia mean? The *Baker Encyclopedia of the Bible*[5] states that parousia is a transliteration of a Greek word meaning: "presence," "arrival," "appearance," or coming." Vine's *Expository Dictionary of New Testament Words*[6] states: "3. Parousia, "lit., a presence, *para*, with, and *ousia*, being (from *eimi*, to be), denotes both an arrival and a consequent presence with." And *Strong's Exhaustive Concordance of the Bible*[7] states: "*a being near*, i.e. *advent* (often return; spec. of Christ to punish Jerusalem or finally the wicked); (by impl.) phys. *aspect*: –coming, presence." [Strong's concordance was originally published in 1890. This is significant, for his comment, "often return; spec. of Christ to punish Jerusalem or finally the wicked," shows the dispensational doctrine of the Rapture had not as yet captured most of the evangelical Church.] To sum this up, the Greek *parousia*, which was translated as coming means: arrival, advent, and presence, not "return." Interestingly, *The International Standard Bible Encyclopaedia*[8] states: "the phrase "Second coming" is nowhere used in the Bible." And I would add, nor is any such terminology.

There are descriptive terms used to denote Christ's Parousia: "Day of God," II Peter 3:12; "Day of the Lord," I Thess. 5:2; "Day of the Lord Jesus," and "of Jesus Christ," I Cor. 1:8; Phil. 1: 6, 10; II Peter 3:10; "That Day," II Thess. 1:10; II Tim. 1:12, 18; The Last Day" John 6:39—54; "The Great Day," "The Day of Redemption," "The Day of Wrath," "Day of Judgment," "Day of Revelation," Rom. 2:5; Eph. 4:30; II Peter 2:9; Rev. 6:17. Though some of these verses do not use the word Parousia, they are still referring to that event. Here are the three popular descriptive terms used, in what is described as Christ's "Second Coming."

Apocalypse: *revelation* — I Cor. 1:7; II Thess. 1:7; I Peter 1:7, 13; 4:13

Epiphany: *manifestation, or appearance* — I Tim. 6:14; II Tim. 4:1, 8; Titus 2:13

Parousia: *presence* — Matt. 24:3, 27, 29, 37; I Cor. 15:23, 16:17; II Cor. 7:6, 7, 10:10; Phil. 1:26, 2:12; I Thess. 2:19, 3:13, 4:15, 5:23; II Thess. 2:1, 8, 9; James 5:7, 8; II Peter 1:16, 3:4, 12; I John 2:28

The biggest problem with this teaching (Christ's return or second coming), none of these three words mean return! We learned in Chapter 2 that Dispensational doctrine distorts Scriptural words and terms and replaces them with non-Biblical meanings and explanations. As it happens, the way modern Christendom uses these three terms, they are also guilty of misconstruing and modifying the Scripture; and which words, when altered, are used to build a teaching which is detached from the meaning Jesus intended and what was believed by the early Church. The Church believed (and so does this author) and was taught the Parousia of Christ would happen in their lifetime.

There are a number of proceedings that are connected with Christ's Parousia:

(1.) **The resurrection of all the dead, both good and bad**: Daniel 12:2; John 5:28–29, 6:40, 44, 11:24; I Cor. 15:23; I Thess. 4:16; Rev 20:11–15.

(2.) **The Judgment of all men, the good and the bad**: Matt. 7:21, 23, 13:30–43, 16:27, 25:31–46; Acts 17:31; Rom. 2:5, 16, 14:10; I Cor. 3:12–15, 4:5; II Cor. 5:9–11; II Thess. 1:6–10; II Tim. 4: 1; Jude 15; Rev. 1:7, 20:11, 21:1.

(3.) **The setting up of His kingdom**: Matt. 16:28; Mark 9:1; Luke 9:27; Titus 2:13; II Tim. 4:1.

These events, plus His judgment upon the Nation of Israel, and the city of Jerusalem in particular, comprise the Parousia (coming or "return"), of the Lord. Jesus taught the generation contemporary with Him would live to see this happen. Christ's Parousia was not a vague ill-defined concept that would keep His Church waiting and looking an indeterminate amount of time (as most Christians are still looking and waiting). Jesus plainly stated: "*This generation shall not pass, till all these things be fulfilled*" (Matt. 24:34). The epistles written by Paul and others echo the same message; the time was at hand, they were going to witness that event, for it would happen in their lifetime! What people call the "Second Coming," or as Scriptures puts it, Christ's Parousia, took place almost 2,000 years ago. We will deal with these things in greater detail in the next few chapters.

DECEIVERS, WARS, FAMINES, PESTILENCES, AND EARTHQUAKES

Jesus told the disciples many deceivers and false Christs would arise. Some are mentioned in the Book of Acts (Acts 5:36–37, 13:6, 21:38). He also told them they would hear of wars, and rumors of wars, though they should "*be not troubled: for all these things must come to pass, but the end is not yet*" (v.6). These "things" (wars and rumors of wars) were not the sign, but events leading up to the sign. At the time of Christ, there was a general peace (Pax Romana)[9] throughout the Roman Empire. However, shortly after Jesus spoke these words, rebellion and insurrection broke out in many places across the empire.

Jesus then told the disciples there would be famines, pestilences, earthquakes, and troubles. Famines and pestilence almost always follow wars and earthquakes. The Scriptures mention famines and earthquakes that took place at this time in history (Acts 11:28, 16:26; Rom.15:25–28; I Cor. 16:1–5). Earthquakes were not the sign either; despite their level of destruction, they were just "*the beginning of sorrows*" (Matt. 24:8).

Today, earthquakes are not increasing in frequency,[10] but, even if they were, they would not be a sign of the *last days*. Charles Richter, who devised the globally accepted scale for measuring the magnitude of quakes, posited this expert view:

> Throughout the world, ... earthquakes have not increased in frequency, despite newspaper accounts to the contrary ... We usually have an average of one or two magnitude – 8 quakes, worldwide, per year. Decidedly more major earthquakes occurred from 1896 to 1906 than in any decade since.[10a]

There have always been earthquakes, but in the First Century, they evidently occurred with terrifying regularity. Evangelical minister Ralph Woodrow, writing about this time, says:

> Tacitus mentions earthquakes at Rome, that 'frequent earthquakes occurred, by which many houses were thrown down' and that 'twelve populous cities of Asia fell in ruins from an

earthquake.' Seneca, writing in the year 58 A.D., said: 'How often have cities of Asia and Achaea fallen with one fatal shock! How many cities have been swallowed up in Syria! How many in Macedonia! How often has Cyprus been wasted by this calamity! How often has Paphos become a ruin! News has often been brought us of the demolition of whole cities at once.' He mentions the earthquake at Campania during the reign of Nero. In 60 A.D., Hierapolis, Colosse, and Laodicea were overthrown. Pompeii was greatly damaged by earthquake in 63 A.D. There were earthquakes in Crete, Apamea, Smyrna, Miletus, Chios, Samos, and Judea.[11]

Jesus also told His disciples they would be subject to the harshest punishments, up to and including death. Furthermore, they would be imprisoned and adjudged for their beliefs:

> *Then shall they deliver you up to be afflicted, and shall kill you: and ye shall be hated of all nations for my name's sake* (Matt. 24:9).
> *But take heed to yourselves: for they shall deliver you up to councils; and in the synagogues ye shall be beaten: and ye shall be brought before rulers and kings for my sake, for a testimony against them* (Mark 13:9).
> *They shall lay their hands on you, and persecute you, delivering you up to the synagogues, and into prisons being brought before Kings and rulers for my name's sake* (Luke 21:12).

As Jesus foretold, all these unspeakable horrors were heaped upon the disciples and the first Church. You can read about it in the following Scriptures: Acts 4:1–21, 5:17–41, 6:9–14, 7:54–60, 8:1–3, 9:1–2, 23–24, 12:1–3, 13:6–8, 45, 14:2, 5, 19, 17:5–9, 18:5–6, 23:12–14; II Cor. 11:23–26. Jesus' accounts of the disciples' trials and tribulations do not, and cannot, apply to a far-distant future ordeal for the Jews. First of all, Jesus was answering the disciples' questions not only about the temple but about their fate as well. He was referencing what would happen to *them*, not people 2,000 years hence. If Jesus had meant an entirely different generation, He would have said when *they* see these things, or when *that* generation sees these things.

When was the last time anyone heard of a Christian being delivered up to or beaten in a synagogue? (Though highly improbable, such a thing could happen in Israel today—but as a fulfillment of prophecy? Hardly.) When was the last time a Jewish council or synagogue delivered a Christian to prison or had the authority to do so? When was the last time the leaders of a Jewish synagogue delivered up a Christian to be killed? When did the Jews last produce a "letter of authority" allowing them to bind Christians and bring them in chains to Jerusalem for trial? The last time the Jews perpetrated any of these deeds was more than 1,900 years ago. They are detailed in the Book of Acts. These incidents actually and specifically happened to the Christian generation of which Jesus spoke. Those people are long gone, and the tribulations Jesus warned His disciples about are ancient history.

THE GOSPEL PREACHED IN ALL THE WORLD

The last thing Jesus said would happen before the end was "*[T]his gospel of the kingdom shall be preached in all the world for a witness unto all nations; and then shall the end come*" (Matt. 24:14; Mark 13:10).

We have already seen the end Jesus was talking about was the end of the *age*—the Jewish Covenant age—not the end of the world. But what does it mean the "gospel of the kingdom" would be preached "*in all the world*"? How was this great notion to be fulfilled? And how could the gospel have been preached so widely before AD 70? The fact that Scripture itself says the gospel was preached in "*all the world*" before AD 70 is sufficient proof Jesus' words were amply fulfilled.

Arthur W. Pink, in his book *The Redeemer's Return*, answers those who would object to the suggestion the Gospel could have gone out into the entire world in their day. After quoting the relevant verses (Acts 19:10; Colossians 1:1–6, 23), he states:

> From these passages then it is abundantly clear that no such formidable hindrance ... interposed between the apostles and the hope of the imminent return of the Redeemer. Scripture thus affords positive evidence that the Gospel had been so widely diffused by the apostles themselves that nothing further *necessarily*

and *inevitably* intervened between them and the realization of their hope.[12] (emphasis his)

The key to understanding how this was achieved derives from the Scriptural meaning of *"all the world."* Let us begin with the Book of Daniel. When Babylon became a mighty empire under the reign of king Nebuchadnezzar, its power was so great it wielded influence over much of the Middle East. In chapter 4, Daniel interprets king Nebuchadnezzar's dream. In verse 22, he tells the king his dominion (in Hebrew, "empire") was to the end (in Hebrew, "termination," "conclusion," "hinder part") of the earth. Did Nebuchadnezzar's empire extend south of the Sahara Desert, or reach Australia, or to North and South America? Was its influence felt in China or Japan? Of course not!

We should remember Daniel was not giving the king a lesson in geopolitics. Daniel's use of the words "dominion" and "end" is to make a point. He was emphasizing the greatness of Nebuchadnezzar's empire, not describing its geographical extent. It is the same as when parents make an emphatic point when disciplining their children ... "I've told you a thousand times ..."

As Gary DeMar states: "The interpreter would be making a serious mistake if every time he read "all nations" he concluded that the Biblical writer had every nation around the globe in mind. The following examples will show that "all nations" and "all kingdoms" often have a limited geographical application (Gen. 41:57; I Kings 10:24; I Chron. 14:17; II Chron. 32:23; 36:23; Ezra 1:2; Psalm 118:10; Jer. 27:7; Hab. 1:6; Matt. 24:9; Acts 2:5; I Tim. 3:16)."[13]

Context is always important when reading the Scriptures. The context in this instance involves the whole New Testament world. For example, it says in Luke, *"And it came to pass in those days, that there went out a decree from Caesar Augustus, that all the world should be taxed"* (Luke 2:1). Are we supposed to construe from this that people from North America, South America, Australia, Asia, Europe, and Africa were to be taxed by Caesar Augustus? Of course not! This verse simply refers to the "world" ruled by Caesar—the Roman Empire. We use language in the same way today. In baseball, the playoffs in the United States are called the World Series.

How many nations play in the "World" Series? Just one, the USA (and the Toronto Blue Jays every now and then).

In the Book of Acts a prophet named Agabus *"stood up and signified by the Spirit that there should be great dearth throughout all the world: which came to pass in the days of Claudius Caesar"* (Acts 11:28). Again, "the world" was referring to the entirety of the Roman Empire.

In writing to the saints at Rome, Paul says, *"I thank my God through Jesus Christ for you all that your faith is spoken of throughout the whole world"* (Rom. 1:8). Paul concludes: *"But now is made manifest, and by the scriptures of the prophets, according to the commandment of the everlasting God, made known to all nations for the obedience of faith"* (Rom. 16:26).

Paul wrote to the Church in Colossae, telling them he thanked God for their faith and their love for all the saints. He added, *"For the hope which is laid up for you in heaven, whereof ye heard before in the word of the truth of the gospel; Which is come unto you, as it is in all the world"* (Col. 1:6–7). Paul also told them that the Gospel *"was preached to every creature which is under heaven"* (Col. 1:23). *"But I say, Have they not heard? Yes verily, their sound went into all the earth, and their words unto the ends of the world"* (Rom. 10:18).

In examining the fulfillment of Matt. 24:14, Scripture provides this alternative: On the day of Pentecost, there were in Jerusalem *"Jews ... out of every nation under heaven"* (Acts 2:5). Taking the Gospel with them when they left Jerusalem, they were witnesses of "the Way" *"to every nation under heaven."* (The following Scriptures show how "all nations" is used to describe only those lands within Israel's orbit: I Chron. 14:17; II Chron. 32:23; Jer. 27:7, 28:11; and Psalm 118:10).

Properly understanding Scriptural usage, and comparing Scripture with Scripture, are essential to revealing just how the Gospel was preached to the whole world (i.e., the Roman Empire) and to every creature under heaven–before that world ended in AD 70.

SIGN / THE ABOMINATION OF DESOLATION

None of the incidents discussed to this point was *the sign*. Each was a separate event that came to pass before *the sign*. But what would this so-called sign look like? What would it signify? And what would happen once this sign appeared?

Remember what the disciples so urgently wanted to know when they asked Jesus, "*What shall be the sign when these things shall take place and are fulfilled?*" The answer was the destruction of the temple, an event so irrevocable that "*There shall not be left here one stone upon another, that shall not be thrown down*" (Matt. 24:3).

What were Jesus' words regarding the temple's destruction? Let us compare all four Scriptural accounts, whereby Jesus responds to the disciples' questions about the "*sign of thy coming*":

> *When ye therefore shall see the abomination of desolation spoken of by Daniel the prophet, stand in the holy place, (whoso readeth, let him understand)* (Matt. 24:15).
>
> *But when ye shall see the abomination of desolation, spoken of by Daniel the prophet, standing where it ought not, (let him that readeth understand)* (Mark 13:14).
>
> *For the days shall come upon thee, that thine enemies shall cast a trench about thee and compass thee round, and keep thee in on every side, and shall lay thee even with the ground, and thy children within thee; and they shall not leave in thee one stone upon another* (Luke 19:43–44).
>
> *And when ye shall see Jerusalem compassed with armies, then know that the desolation thereof is nigh* (Luke 21:20).

As Daniel grimly foretold: "*And the people of the prince that shall come shall destroy the city and the sanctuary ... and unto the end of the war desolations are determined ... and for the overspreading of abominations he shall make it desolate*" (Dan 9:26–27).

The sign Jesus gave the Christians was one they could readily comprehend—the abomination of desolation occurred when the Roman armies encompassed Jerusalem, destroying the city and the temple. Cestius Gallus, the Roman general, had actually arrived with his army in AD 66 and proceeded to surround the city. But, for some unknown reason, he lifted the siege of Jerusalem. This occasioned all Christians to do precisely what Jesus had told them: Head for the hills! Every Christian who heeded

Jesus was able to flee Jerusalem; they went to the mountains, to the city of Pella, and safe places across Jordan and beyond.

As to how they would survive the "abomination of desolation," here is the crucial advice Jesus gave to His disciples:

> *Then let them which be in Judaea flee into the mountains: Let him which is on the housetop not come down to take any thing out of his house: Neither let him which is in the field return back to take his clothes* (Matt. 24:16–18).
>
> *Then let them that be in Judaea flee to the mountains: And let him that is on the housetop not go down into the house, neither enter therein, to take any thing out of the house: And let him that is in the field not turn back again for to take up his garment* (Mark 13:14–16).
>
> *Then let them which are in Judaea flee to the mountains; and let them which are in the midst of it depart out; and let not them that are in the countries enter thereinto. For these be the days of vengeance, that all things which are written may be fulfilled* (Luke 21:21–22).

Concerning the siege and destruction of Jerusalem, Adam Clarke writes:

> It is very remarkable not a single Christian perished in the destruction of Jerusalem, though there were many there when Cestius Gallus invaded the city; and, had he persevered in the siege, he would soon have rendered himself master of it; but, when he unexpectedly and unaccountably raised the siege, the Christians took that opportunity to escape.

Commenting on verse 16, Clarke continues:

> "Then let them which be in Judea flee into the mountains." This counsel was remembered and wisely followed by the Christians afterwards ... After Cestius Gallus had raised the siege, and Vespasian was approaching with his army, all who believed in Christ left Jerusalem and fled to Pella, and other places beyond the river Jordan; and so they all marvelously escaped the general shipwreck of their country: not one of them perished.[14]

R. A. Torrey's *Treasury of Scripture Knowledge*, with its five hundred thousand Scripture references and parallel passages, discusses the word *flee* in Luke 21:21:

> Accordingly, when Cestius Gallus came against Jerusalem, and unexpectedly raised the siege, Josephus states that many of the noble Jews departed out of the city, as out of a sinking ship; and when Vespasian afterwards drew towards it, a great multitude fled to the Mountains. And we learn from Eusebius, and Epiphanius, that at this juncture, all who believed in Christ left Jerusalem, and removed to Pella, and other places beyond Jordan; and so escaped the general shipwreck of their country, that we do not read of one who perished in Jerusalem.

MacArthur does not believe the destruction of Jerusalem in AD 70 fulfilled the words of Jesus in the Book of Luke. He writes: "Yet those were not in the words of Luke 21:22, 'the days of vengeance, [when] all things which are written may be fulfilled ...' The opposing armies were not defeated by His presence."[15] Of course the opposing Roman armies were not defeated. They were the instruments of judgment God used to punish the wicked generation that rejected His Son, Jesus. However, the main reason MacArthur argues for nonfulfillment in AD 70 is that throughout the Middle Ages, especially during the Crusades, Jerusalem was frequently surrounded by armies. He states, "Jerusalem was repeatedly attacked, and control of the city changed hands several times from the start of the First Crusade in AD 1095 until the time of Suleiman the Magnificent, the great Ottoman Sultan, in the early 1500s. (The stone walls and battlements encircling the Old City of Jerusalem today are actually fairly late fortifications, built in the early sixteenth century by Suleiman, a visible reminder that Jerusalem has often been 'surrounded by armies.')"[16]

MacArthur then speculates: "So, if the gathering of armies against Jerusalem is supposed to be a sign, as Luke 21:20 suggests, how can this sign be distinguished from all these other times throughout history when the city has been under siege?"[17]

The answer to this question is anything but ambiguous. The sign in dispute (*"Jerusalem compassed with armies"*) is easily discernible from every other siege or attack on the city of Jerusalem. This answer may seem redundant but go back to the statement Jesus made about the temple: *"Seest thou these great buildings? there shall not be left one stone upon another that shall not be thrown down"* (Mark 13:2). This momentous occurrence was not just about an army surrounding and attacking the city of Jerusalem. It was about the complete destruction of the temple (*"these great buildings"*), which we know occurred in AD 70. Once the temple was destroyed, any succeeding hostilities or attacks against Jerusalem would never—*could never*—have anything to do with Jesus' end-time, last-days warnings. Thus, the climactic events of AD 70 inarguably confirmed the onset of the prefigured *sign* that filled the disciples with such dread.

Thus, Jesus' statement, *"this generation shall not pass till all these things be fulfilled"* became a reality for those fortunate few who heeded the Lord's warnings and managed to live through the "great tribulation."

THE TRIBULATION

Many believe the great tribulation is still to come. They take the next few verses of Jesus' discourse out of context and apply them to a future, restored Israel. But the tribulation prophesied by Jesus was only intended for the Jews that rejected their Messiah. As it happened, the early Church was caught in the middle of Israel's total destruction.

> *For then shall be great tribulation, such as was not since the beginning of the world to this time, no, nor ever shall be. And except those days should be shortened, there should no flesh be saved: but for the elect's sake those days shall be shortened* (Matt. 24:21–22).
>
> *For in those days shall be affliction, such as was not from the beginning of the creation which God created unto this time, neither shall be. And except that the Lord had shortened those days, no flesh should be saved: but for the elect's sake, whom he hath chosen, he hath shortened the days* (Mark 13:19–20).
>
> *For these be the days of vengeance, that all things which are written may be fulfilled. But woe unto them that are with child, and to them that give suck in those days: for there shall be great distress*

in the land, and wrath upon this people. And they shall fall by the edge of the sword, and shall be led away captive into all nations; and Jerusalem shall be trodden down of the Gentiles, until the times of the Gentiles be fulfilled (Luke 21:22–24).

The Lord purposed to shorten the time of affliction because of His elect. Who were these "elect" Jesus spoke of? In I Peter 1:2, the Apostle Peter calls the Christians, the Church of God, the *"elect according to the foreknowledge of God the Father, through sanctification of the Spirit, unto obedience"* In Chapter 2:9–10, Peter says the Church is *"a chosen generation, a royal priesthood, an holy nation, a peculiar people ... Which in time past were not a people, but are now the people of God."* Reading through the epistles, we find it was the believers who were the *elect* of God (Rom. 8:33; Col. 3:12; II Tim. 2:10; I Thess. 1:4; Titus 1:1; I Peter 1:2, 5:13; II Peter 1:10).

Dispensationalists teach the second half of the seven-year tribulation deals with the Antichrist and his persecution of the Jews. *Search For Truth*, a Dispensational Bible study used by the United Pentecostal Church, puts it this way: "Then the Antichrist will turn against the Jews and terrible persecutions shall follow, called 'the time of Jacob's trouble,' Jer. 30:5–7, when the Anti-Christ will endeavor to destroy the seed of Abraham from the face of the earth."[18] But the tribulation Jesus depicted in Matt. 24, Luke 21, and Mark 13 refers to how *the Jews then present* were going to deliver up and persecute His elect—the Church. These verses are not about some supposed Antichrist persecuting Christ-hating Jews during the second half of the seventieth week of Daniel. Rather, they concern the Roman army that would invade and destroy the nation of Israel, the Jewish temple, and the city of Jerusalem. Jesus was not referring to Jews living thousands of years in the future, but those who were His contemporaries.

As we have seen, the first Christians never imagined the sign Jesus described was intended for some future generation (or ours, for that matter). They knew the tribulation would befall them and their fellow countrymen, the ones who lived in and around the city of Jerusalem. History confirms that the tribulation did indeed happen in the years immediately preceding and following AD 70.

As Jesus related, after the abomination of desolation a great tribulation would take place. This tribulation was God's wrath upon the unbelieving

Jews of Jesus' day. As Jesus said: "*[Y]e are the children of them which killed the prophets ... That upon you may come all the righteous blood shed upon the earth*" (Matt. 23:31–39). The "ye" that Jesus was talking about were the unbelieving Jews who steadfastly refused to accept Jesus as Messiah. Jesus also told those who followed Him to His crucifixion, "*Daughters of Jerusalem, weep not for me, But weep for yourselves, and for your children. For, behold, the days are coming, in the which they shall say, Blessed are the barren, and the wombs that never bare, and the paps which never gave suck. Then shall they begin to say to the mountains, Fall on us; and to the hills, Cover us*" (Luke 23:28–30). This is the same tribulation that the Apostle John and the seven churches in Asia were already experiencing: "*I John who also am your brother, and companion in tribulation, and in the kingdom and patience of Jesus Christ*" (Rev. 1:9).

In discussing Luke 21:22, Adam Clarke states "These were the days in which all the calamities predicted by Moses, Joel, Daniel, and other prophets, as well as those predicted by our Savior, met in one common centre, and were fulfilled in the most terrible manner on that generation."[19]

Which city was "trodden down" by the Gentiles? Jerusalem. Who were "this people" that God's wrath was upon? Unbelieving Jews. Who was slain by "the edge of the sword and led away captive into all nations"? Unbelieving Jews. When, as related in Luke 19:43–44, did the Jewish enemies (the Romans) cast a trench about Jerusalem and leave not one stone upon another? When did the Christians in Judaea flee for their lives? Finally, when did all this happen? In the year's AD 66–73. History says so.

The tribulation that came upon the Christians shortly before, during, and after Jerusalem fell in AD 70 resembled what befell the Israelites when they were slaves in Egypt. Israel also had to suffer through the first three of the ten plagues God brought upon the Egyptians. Correspondingly, just before the destruction of Jerusalem, the warning signs began to happen: earthquakes, famines, wars, and pestilences. The Christians who lived in Jerusalem and throughout the nation of Israel also went through the same horrors. Thankfully, for the sake of His saints (the Church), God cut that tribulation short.

COSMIC SIGNS AND PROPHECIES

The Bible abounds in the use of symbolism, metaphors, signs, and allegory. These different types of teaching are found throughout the Scriptures. In the Bible we discover:

- Blood talks–Gen. 4:10
- Sun and moon bow down–Gen. 37:9
- Fish and animals talk–Job 12:7–8
- Mountains and hills skip–Psalm 114:4
- Hearts melt–Isa. 13:7
- Trees clap their hands–Isa. 55:12
- Mountains and hills sing–Isa. 55:12
- Men have beams in their eyes–Matt. 7:3
- Camels pass through eyes of needles–Luke 18:25
- Rivers of water flow out of people–John 7:38
- Christians are to wear armor–Eph. 6:11

Of course, none of the images cited above are *literally* true. [Actually, the camel passing through eyes of needles refers to a place in the Jerusalem wall that is very narrow called the "eye of the needle", and while it is not impossible for a camel to pass through it, it is very difficult, especially if one is loaded.] Symbolism is used throughout Scripture to emphasize, clarify—and sometimes even obscure the meaning of God's word (from unbelievers). Jesus used parables to teach deep spiritual truths ... but also to hide that truth from some.

> *The disciples came, and said unto him, Why speakest thou unto them in parables? He answered and said unto them, Because it is given unto you to know the mysteries of the kingdom of heaven, but to them it is not given* (Matt.13:10–11).

In Isaiah 40:3–4, there is a prophecy concerning John the Baptist:

> *The voice of him that crieth in the wilderness, Prepare ye the way of the LORD, make straight in the desert a highway for our God. Every valley shall be exalted, and every mountain and hill shall be*

made low: and the crooked shall be made straight, and the rough places plain.

The Gospel writers tell us John was the fulfillment of Isaiah's prophecy (Matt. 3:3; Mark 1:2; Luke 1:13–17; John 1:19–23). John's was the clarion *"voice of one crying in the wilderness"* (Matt. 3:3). But was every mountain and hill literally going to *"be made low"*? Were the Jews going to see a great army of workers leveling the mountains and hills around Israel? Were all the valleys going to be filled in, or were they to be raised up by some supernatural miracle? No, of course not. This was metaphorical language referring to a literal event and person, the commencement of John's ministry.

In the Book of Malachi, there is another prophecy concerning John the Baptist: *"Behold, I will send you Elijah the prophet before the coming of the great and dreadful day of the LORD"* (Mal. 4:5). If we interpret this verse literally, it would seem to mean the prophet Elijah would be raised from the dead to prophesy once more. In truth, this declaration speaks metaphorically of John the Baptist. For Jesus said, "[T]*here hath not risen a greater than John the Baptist ... For all the prophets and the law prophesied until John. And if ye will receive it, this is Elias* [Elijah], *which was for to come"* (Matt. 11:13–14).

John the Baptist was the Elijah "to come." He laid the foundation for Jesus *"in the spirit and power of Elias, to turn the hearts of the fathers to the children, and the disobedient to the wisdom of the just; to make ready a people prepared for the Lord"* (Luke 1:17). John started his public ministry a few months before Jesus came to him to be baptized. John also appeared 40 years before the great and dreadful day of the LORD that saw the final judgment on the nation of Israel and the city of Jerusalem in AD 70.

There is a key prophecy in the Book of Amos about restoring the temple of David. But does it, as some suppose, refer to a rebuilt Jewish temple in our modern era? As the prophecy foretells:

In that day will I raise up the tabernacle of David that is fallen, and close up the breaches thereof; and I will raise up his ruins, and I will build it as in the days of old (Amos 9:11).

The New Testament explains the fulfillment of Amos's prophecy:

> *Simeon hath declared how God at the first did visit the Gentiles, to take out of them a people for his name. And to this agree the words of the prophets; as it is written, After this I will return, and will build again the tabernacle of David, which is fallen down; and I will build again the ruins thereof, and I will set it up. That the residue of men might seek after the Lord, and all the Gentiles, upon whom my name is called, saith the Lord, who doeth all these things* (Act 15:14–17).

In the Book of Acts, the Apostle James interprets what Amos said metaphorically, not literally. James shows the conversion of the Gentiles fulfilled the declarations made by Amos and the other prophets.

James the Apostle was not a Dispensationalist. Nor was Jesus, for He did not take the prophecy concerning John the Baptist literally. Certainly, Peter was no believer in the Dispensational doctrine because, as we will see, he too realized the prophecy of Joel chapter 2 was not to be taken literally.

Dispensationalists all too frequently violate the rules and principles of interpretation (as made clear in Chapter 2 of this book) when dealing with eschatology. MacArthur violates at least four key rules (usage, context, precedent, and unity) when addressing what he calls the "cosmic signs."

On that seminal subject, MacArthur writes, "Here is another powerful reason to reject the preterist interpretation of the Olivet Discourse: No great cosmic signs like this ever occurred in connection with the destruction of Jerusalem in AD 70." MacArthur says many preterists dismiss Jesus's language as metaphorical. He chides Gary DeMar for saying many of the passages in the Bible (Matt. 24:29, 24:35; Isa. 14:12; Dan. 8:10; Rev. 6:13, 9:1, 12:4) that talk about the darkening of the sun and moon and the falling of the stars were descriptive, not literal.[20]

The apostles' sage interpretation of Old Testament Scripture is itself a "powerful reason" to reject MacArthur's argument, which he furthers by stating:

> DeMar believes that when Jesus says, 'Heaven and earth will pass away' (v.35), He is not speaking of any literal eschatological cosmic judgment that will really destroy the earth. Instead, the

passing away of the heaven and earth, according to DeMar, is merely metaphorical language that speaks of the transition from Old Covenant to New. Similarly, DeMar claims, the darkening of the sun and moon in Matthew 24:29 are merely metaphorical terms that refer to the passing away of the Jewish dispensation.[21]

Quoting from Isaiah 13:9–15 and 34:1–5, MacArthur asserts these verses describe a worldwide judgment of unfathomable magnitude. He also states, "Joel foretold the same cosmic signs. *'And I will show wonders in the heavens and in the earth: Blood and fire and pillars of smoke. The sun shall be turned into darkness, and the moon into blood, before the coming of the great and awesome day of the LORD'* (Joel 2:30–31). *'The sun and moon will grow dark, and the stars will diminish their brightness'* (3:15). Those words are set in the midst of the millennial and end-times prophecies ..."[22]

As it happens, MacArthur is partially right about the prophecy of Joel. It was indeed set in the context of the "end times," just before the Jewish temple was destroyed with its sacrificial religion. However, verses 2:30–31 are not set "in the midst of the millennium" as MacArthur states. Nor is Joel conjuring up cosmic events and signs in the heavens. MacArthur can speculate all he wants about those verses, but Joel was not prophesying about the millennium or the future from *our* perspective.

Joel envisioned a turbulent future when he wrote his prophecy. But those earth-shattering events that would forever change the course of history are now long past. They were, indeed, events of cosmic proportions, but not, literally, cosmic events!

We do not have to be in the dark (no pun intended) about Joel's prognostications; his prophecy was fulfilled almost two thousand years ago as recorded by the New Testament. The Apostle Peter's words are notably descriptive:

> But this is that which was spoken by the prophet Joel. And it shall come to pass in the last days, saith God, I will pour out of my Spirit upon all flesh: and your sons and your daughters shall prophesy, and your young men shall see visions, and your old men shall dream dreams: And on my servants and on my handmaidens I will pour out in those days of my Spirit; and they shall prophesy: And I will shew

wonders in heaven above, and signs in the earth beneath; blood, and
fire, and vapour of smoke: The sun shall be turned into darkness, and
the moon into blood, before that great and notable day of the LORD
come (Acts 2:16–20).

It is highly significant MacArthur still believes all these events are slated to occur in the future. As described in Acts 2:1–14, the disciples of the Lord were all gathered together in one accord on the day of Pentecost. Suddenly, a sound came from heaven like a rushing, mighty wind and filled all the house where they were sitting. Then cloven tongues of fire appeared and sat upon each of them. And as the Spirit gave them utterance they began to speak in languages they did not understand, although others present understood what they were saying. Everyone there wondered what the wind and fire meant, and how the Galileans came to speak in different languages. Some mocked them and said they were drunk.

Peter always seemed to be the first to respond. With the other eleven apostles waiting in stunned silence, Peter stood up, pointed to the ones speaking in tongues, and explained the significance of this bizarre incident. He then quoted the prophecy, stating quite categorically, "*this is that*": all Christ's disciples had just experienced the so-called "cosmic signs" of Joel! So, as we compare Scripture with Scripture, we see the Apostle Peter, inspired by what he saw, knew this singular event at Pentecost was the fulfillment of Joel's prophecy. Proper scriptural interpretation is always preferable to modern-day guessing, no matter by whom. And prophecy is never fulfilled twice.

OLD TESTAMENT USAGE

DARKNESS FOR BABYLON

When Jesus spoke in the Olivet Discourse about the sun and moon becoming dark and the stars of heaven falling, His language followed the words of the Old Testament prophets who foresaw nations collapsing, including Israel. For example, Isaiah 13:9–10, where the prophet Isaiah pronounces judgment on Babylon, states:

> *For the stars of heaven and the constellations thereof shall not give their light: the sun shall be darkened in his going forth, and the moon shall not cause her light to shine.*

Who would Jehovah raise up to judge Babylon? "*Behold, I will stir up the Medes against them*" (Isa. 13:17). These very words foretold the destruction of Babylon by the LORD almighty (13:6). Notice the picturesque expressions of that judgment, as the sun, moon, stars, and constellations grew dark: "*all hands be faint*" (13:7); "*every man's heart shall melt*" (13:7); "*they shall be in pain as a woman that travaileth*" (13:8); "*I will shake the heavens*" (13:13); "*and the earth shall remove out of her place*" (13:13).

Now compare the words of our Lord in the Olivet Discourse to those of Isaiah's pronouncement on Babylon:

> *The sun shall be darkened, and the moon shall not give her light, and the stars of heaven shall fall from heaven, and the powers of the heavens shall be shaken* (Matt. 24:29).

Both passages cited deal with *judgment*. The words of Isaiah were for ancient Babylon. The words of Jesus were for contemporary Israel.

DARKNESS FOR EGYPT

God's judgment on Pharaoh and Egypt closely resembles the Lord's judgment on Babylon:

> *And when I shall put thee out, I will cover the heaven, and make the stars thereof dark; I will cover the sun with a cloud, and the moon shall not give her light. All the bright lights of heaven will I make dark over thee, and set darkness upon thy land, saith the Lord God* (Ezek. 32:7–8).

God used the Medes to judge Babylon, and He told the Egyptians "*the sword of the King of Babylon shall come upon thee ... Pharaoh and all his army slain by the sword*" (Ezek. 32:11–31). These words are comparable to those spoken by Jesus concerning His judgment on Israel. God used the armies of foreign nations to bring down both Babylon and Egypt. Moreover, when God used Roman armies to judge Israel, it truly was a dark day (Luke 19:43–44; 21:20).

DARKNESS FOR EDOM

Even though it appeared to be one kingdom warring against another, it was God who caused these conflicts. In Isaiah's prophecy on Edom, we can see that it was God who orchestrated the final judgment:

> *And all the host of heaven shall be dissolved, and the heavens shall be rolled together as a scroll: and all their host shall fall down, as the leaf falleth off from the vine, and as a falling fig from the fig tree. For my sword shall be bathed in heaven: behold, it shall come down upon Idumea, and upon the people of my curse, to judgment (Isa. 34:4–5).*

God's pronouncement on Idumea (Edom) declared the heavens "would be rolled together as a scroll." Did that literally happen? Did a sword literally descend from the sky? And did all the stars fall down? Of course not! The verse's portrayal of Edom's destruction is metaphorical and probably refers to the general devastation caused by King Nebuchadnezzar of Babylon years later.

DARKNESS FOR ISRAEL

> *Woe unto you that desire the day of the LORD! To what end is it for you? the day of the LORD is darkness, and not light ... Shall not the day of the LORD be darkness, and not light? even very dark, and no brightness in it (Amos 5:18–20).*
>
> *And it shall come to pass in that day, saith the Lord God, that I will cause the sun to go down at noon, and I will darken the earth in the clear day (Amos 8:9).*

Speaking through the prophet Jeremiah, Jehovah said,

It is an evil thing and bitter, that thou hast forsaken the LORD thy God, and that my fear is not in thee, saith the LORD God of Hosts (Jer. 2:19).

God also told Israel that He would reject their solemn assemblies and festivals because of their disdain for the LORD's holy edicts: *"I hate, I despise your feast days ... Though ye offer me burnt offerings and your meat offerings, I will not accept them"* (Amos 5:21–22). Israel's worship practices had become an abomination in the sight of God.

Israel was to be a blessing and a light to the nations (Gen. 12:2–3; Isa. 49:6). But because of their reluctance to suspend their sacrificial rituals, their light—the once exalted and unique theocracy of Israel—was going to be extinguished. Their kingdom would be taken from them and *"given to a nation bringing forth the fruits thereof"* (Matt. 21:43). This ultimate nation, sanctioned by God, is the Church. *"But ye are a chosen generation, a royal priesthood, an holy nation, a peculiar people ... which in time past were not a people, but are now the people of God"* (I Peter 2:9–10).

God sent Jonah to preach to the city of Nineveh. He gave them forty days to repent, which they did. The nation of Israel was given forty years (AD 30 to AD 70) to repent and embrace their Messiah. But their continued rejection brought the promised judgment. And their light went out. Permanently.

THE GATHERING OF THE EAGLES

For as the lightning cometh out of the east, and shineth even unto the west; so shall also the coming of the Son of man be. For wheresoever the carcase is, there will the eagles be gathered together (Matt. 24:27–28).

And they answered and said unto him, Where Lord? And he said unto them, Wheresoever the body (Greek: dead body) *is, thither will the eagles be gathered together* (Luke 17:37).

Matthew's portion of Scripture is part of the Olivet Discourse. Luke's account, while not part of the Olivet Discourse, doubtless describes the same period of time and the same calamities that would soon come upon Israel.

In the Book of Daniel, we read: *"And the fourth kingdom shall be strong as iron: forasmuch as iron breaketh in pieces and subdueth all things; and as iron that breaketh all these, shall it break in pieces and bruise"* (Dan. 2:40). This was the fourth kingdom in Nebuchadnezzar's vision that Daniel interpreted for the king. Daniel had envisioned five kingdoms, the fourth being the Roman Empire. It was this kingdom God used as His instrument of judgment and punishment upon a wicked and reprobate people.

The imperial armies had a standard they carried into battle. Its ensign was venerated as a holy object. When on the march, this standard was placed in the sacellum (shrine) at the center of the legionary encampment.

Each legion's ensign was jealously guarded by the soldiers; each man was willing to risk his own life for the sake of the standard. For this was the Aquila, the legion's Eagle, the symbol of Rome's omnipotence. As such, the ensign was held in awe and fiercely protected. It was also a rallying point in battle. Any legion that had its eagle captured would be considered a total disgrace. And if by chance it were ever lost, the empire would be turned upside down searching for it.

Each Roman legion had one silver eagle carried by a special grade legionary known as an aquilifer. There was a narrow, trapezoidal base upon which was mounted a pole, with the eagle on top. Held aloft, the eagle epitomized the power of the Roman Empire.

It was upon the dead carcass of the city of Jerusalem the Roman eagles feasted. It was there the Roman legions gathered with their eagle deities and looked down upon the ruined and defeated Jewish capital. Its streets were filled with rivers of blood. Its temple was razed and its foundations dug up. A million and a half Jews are believed to have died in the slaughter. Surviving citizens were sold into slavery. Thus, with unimaginable finality, Jesus was proved right: *"Wheresoever the carcass is, there will the eagles be gathered."*

As history showed, the Roman legions vanquished Jerusalem as the Lord foretold. But what do the "lightning" and the "coming of the Son of man" refer to?

Adam Clarke's commentary on this item is particularly insightful:

It is worthy of remark that our Lord, in the most particular manner, points out the very *march* of the Roman army: they entered into Judea on the EAST, and carried on their conquest WESTWARD, as if not only the extensiveness of the ruin, but the very *route* which the army would take, were intended in the comparison of the *lightning issuing from the east, and shining to the west.*[23] (emphasis his)

Christ was certainly accurate in His prediction of the coming judgment of the Son of man upon that wicked generation. He came in the form of implacable Roman legions, bringing doom and destruction upon those who had rejected Him.

AFTER THE TRIBULATION

Immediately after the tribulation of those days shall the sun be darkened, and the moon shall not give her light, and the stars shall fall from the heaven, and the powers of the heavens shall be shaken (Matt. 24:29).

But in those days, after that tribulation, the sun shall be darkened, and the moon shall not give her light, and the stars of heaven shall fall, and the powers that are heaven shall be shaken (Mark 13:24–25).

And there shall be signs in the sun, and in the moon, and in the stars; and upon the earth distress of nations, with perplexity; the sea and the waves roaring; men's hearts failing them for fear, and for looking after those things which are coming on the earth: for the powers of heaven shall be shaken (Luke 21:25–26).

We have now seen when God pronounced judgment on various nations, the language used by the prophets was *always* intermixed with metaphors and cosmic imagery. Jesus applied a similar mode of expression: in myriad situations, the Lord used word pictures, imagery, metaphors, and allegories to teach His disciples and others. In preaching to the multitudes,

He always employed parables. But in private Jesus would fully explain the parables to His disciples (Matt. 13:34–36).

Here is a sampling of the Lord's metaphorical language:

- Matt. 4:19   *Follow me, and I will make you fishers of men*
- Matt. 5:13   *Ye are the salt of the earth*
- Matt. 10:39   *He that findeth his life shall lose it*
- Matt. 11:29   *Take my yoke upon you*
- Matt. 12:34   *O generation of vipers*
- Matt. 16:6   *Take heed and beware of the leaven of the Pharisees and of the Sadducees*
- Matt. 16:24   *Take up his cross*
- Matt. 18:8   *If thy hand or thy foot offend thee, cut them off*
- Luke 9:60   *Let the dead bury their dead*
- Luke 9:62   *No man, having put his hand to the plough, and looking back, is fit for the kingdom of God*
- Luke 10:2   *The harvest truly is great, but the labourers are few, pray ye therefore the Lord of harvest, he would send forth labourers into the harvest*
- John 3:7   *Ye must be born again*
- John 6:51   *I am the living bread*
- John 6:53   *Verily, verily, I say unto you, Except ye eat the flesh of the Son of man, and drink his blood, ye have no life in you*
- John 9:5   *I am the light of the world*
- John 10:7   *I am the door of the sheep*
- John 10:11   *I am the good shepherd*
- John 15:5   *I am the vine, ye are the branches*

The stars and moon did not literally darken on the day of judgment for Edom, Egypt, or Babylon. The mountains did not melt from the blood of the slain when Edom was judged, nor did the heavens roll together like a scroll. And the stars did not dissolve when Idumea was judged by the Lord.

All those events and judgments were past occurrences for Edom, because the nation of Edom, and the Edomite people, no longer existed.

Edom was literally judged and destroyed, but this destruction was foretold through Isaiah. When Jesus spoke of the sun and moon being darkened and the stars falling from heaven, His language was virtually identical to the prophets of old. And as Scripture clearly shows, Jesus purposely used metaphorical language when He pronounced judgment on Israel.

SIGN OF THE SON OF MAN

Keeping in mind the allegorical language in Scripture, we will now look at the words of Jesus in the Olivet Discourse:

> *And then shall appear the sign of the Son of man in the heaven: and then shall all the tribes of the earth mourn, and they shall see the Son of man coming in the clouds of heaven with power and great glory* (Matt. 24:30).
>
> *And then shall they see the Son of man coming in the clouds with great power and glory* (Mark 13:26).
>
> *And then shall they see the Son of man coming in a cloud with power and great glory* (Luke 21:27).

A number of signs appear in the New Testament concerning Jesus. One such sign was given to John the Baptist when he was in prison. Hearing of the works of Christ, John sent two of his disciples to Jesus with the question, *"Art thou he that should come, or do we look for another?"* (Matt. 11:3). Jesus answered their inquiry by giving them a sign so powerful, it would last for all time. He had them observe the blind restored to sight, the lame walking, lepers being cleansed, deaf ears opened, the dead being raised up, and the Gospel preached to the poor. The miracles Jesus performed erased any doubt on John's part that Jesus was the Christ, the promised Savior of Israel. But these preternatural phenomena did not serve to establish Jesus as Lord. The ultimate sign He was Lord *and* Christ was His resurrection from the dead (Acts 2:31–36).

In the Olivet Discourse Jesus envisions two distinct signs impacting the future of Israel. In answering the disciples' question, the first sign describes the onslaught of Rome's armies (the abomination of desolation) coming to destroy the Jewish temple. The second sign presages what Jesus called the "Son of man": *"And then shall appear the sign of the Son of man in heaven: and then shall all the tribes of the earth mourn, and they shall see the Son of man coming in the clouds of heaven with power and great glory"* (Matt 24:30). It is this sign that entails the actual destruction of the city of Jerusalem and the nation of Israel. In addition, it is this sign that provides the unshakable evidence Jesus would come to reign in heaven as the Lord of Lords and King of Kings.

John Bray states well the meaning of the second sign:

> The sign of the Son of man "IN HEAVEN" is the sign or proof that the Son of man is "in heaven" (as it says), in fulfillment of Daniel 7:13–14 which predicted that the Son of man would come "with the clouds of heaven" and "TO THE ANCIENT OF DAYS" (in Heaven), to receive His everlasting kingdom. His appearing in judgment was proof of that.
>
> I am going to repeat this, with emphasis, as this is the crux of this whole section:
>
> THE "SIGN OF THE SON OF MAN IN HEAVEN" IS THE SIGN OR PROOF THAT THE SON OF MAN IS "IN HEAVEN" (AS IT SAYS) IN FULFILLMENT OF DANIEL 7:13–14 WHICH PROPHESIED THAT THE SON OF MAN WOULD COME "WITH THE CLOUDS OF HEAVEN" AND "TO THE ANCIENT OF DAYS" (IN HEAVEN), TO RECEIVE HIS EVERLASTING KINGDOM. HIS APPEARING IN JUDGMENT WAS THE PROOF OF THAT.[24] (emphasis his)

As the capstone of His ministry, the resurrection from the dead was the requested sign Jesus gave the Jews:

> *Then certain of the scribes and of the Pharisees answered, saying, Master, we would see a sign from thee. But he answered and said unto them, An evil and adulterous generation seeketh after a sign, and there shall no sign be given to it, but the sign of the prophet Jonas: For as Jonas was three days and three nights in the whale's belly; so shall the*

Son of man be three days and three nights in the heart of the earth (Matt 12:39–40, 16:4; Luke 11:29).

When the Jews asked Jesus,

> *What sign shewest thou unto us, seeing that thou doest these things? Jesus answered and said unto them, Destroy this temple, and in three days I will raise it up. Then said the Jews, Forty and six years was this temple in building, and wilt thou rear it up in three days? But he spake of the temple of his body* (John 2:18–21).

In attempting to interpret Jesus' Olivet Discourse, MacArthur and other Dispensationalists have drawn stunningly inaccurate conclusions. And yet, surprisingly, MacArthur appears to make a good point when discussing the preterist view of Matthew 24:30: "If the Preterists are right, not only did the whole world completely miss Christ's return on the clouds in glory, but so did virtually everyone in the church. Because with relatively few exceptions, practically every believer in 2,000 years of Christendom has believed Matthew 24:30 speaks of an event yet to happen."[25]

In building his argument, MacArthur uses one of the oldest extra-Biblical treatises known to exist, the *Didache*: "This document proves those who actually lived through the events of AD 70 regarded Matthew 24:29–31—and the entire Olivet Discourse—as yet-unfulfilled prophecy."[26] However, most Christians living in and around Jerusalem would have died at the hands of the Romans if they had held MacArthur's view of Jesus' words. The early Church produced some of the "few exceptions" MacArthur talks about, precisely because they did not believe what many do today. There is a simple reason why most Christians residing in and around Jerusalem lived through the events of AD 70: they rightly believed the signs Jesus described were intended for them, and they cleaved to His instructions when those signs came to pass. Because of their enlightenment, these early Christians did not "miss" Christ's parousia; they embraced it.

Scholars are not quite sure when the *Didache* was composed. But many believe it was probably written near the end of the First Century. *The International Standard Bible Encyclopedia* states: "There is no reliable external testimony to date ... and the expectation of an impending Second

Advent points to an early date. On the other hand it is unlikely a writing which professes to give the Teaching of the Twelve would be issued until all or most apostles had passed away ..." [27]

There are significant issues with certain of MacArthur's assertions, as well as some of the content in the ISBE. First, a portion of the *Didache* was probably written before the events of AD 70. So, of course, the advent of Christ was treated as being in the future. But if that advent still had not occurred by AD 70, the authors of New Testament Scripture were in error, Jesus was a liar, and they gave false hope of a soon coming to those who yearned for Christ's return. If the section on the advent was written only ten or twenty years after AD 70, that is more than enough time for an error to have crept into that document.

Remember, the basis of our faith is not the creeds of the Church, the traditions, or the writings of the church fathers, but Scripture alone. Once doctrine has been written down and taught to others, if some (or all) of it is in error, then that error will be perpetuated generation after generation—just like Dispensational teaching! And just because many Christians may have misinterpreted a portion of Scripture for a very long time does not mean an error cannot be corrected when it is finally exposed!

There is something else Dispensationalists have missed in Matthew 24:30. The verse says, in part, "*and then shall all the tribes of the earth mourn.*" The word "tribe" appears over 350 times in the Scriptures, and each and every time it refers exclusively to the nation of Israel. MacArthur states the signs given in the Olivet Discourse were for the whole world to see: "Christ is predicting cosmic signs of some kind—signs so spectacular no one on earth can possibly miss them." [28] But Jesus's discourse was given specifically to His disciples for the express purpose of warning when the temple in Jerusalem would be destroyed. This judgment was laid upon the environs of Jerusalem. It occurred in *that* land, the land of Israel, and God's wrath targeted a particular people who lived in Israel—the Jews. "*For there shall be great distress in the land, and wrath upon this people. And they shall fall by the edge of the sword, and shall be led away captive into all nations: and Jerusalem shall be trodden down of the Gentiles*" (Luke 21:23–24). This verse plainly speaks of the land of Israel in AD 70 and its time of great tribulation, when all the tribes (nation of Israel) of the earth (land) lamented the decimation of their incomparable city and temple.

COMING ON CLOUDS

We now know the disciples were not asking about the Lord returning from heaven before or after a tribulation. Jesus told the chief priests, elders, scribes, and council that they would see His "coming":

> *Hereafter shall ye see the Son of man sitting on the right hand of power, and coming in the clouds of heaven* (Matt. 26:64).
>
> *Whosoever therefore shall be ashamed of me and of my words in this adulterous and sinful generation; of him also shall the Son of man be ashamed, when he cometh in the glory of his Father with the holy angels* (Mark: 8:38).
>
> *I am: and ye shall see the Son of man sitting on the right hand of power, and coming in the clouds of heaven* (Mark 14:62).

Jesus also told His disciples that they would behold the Son of man coming in His kingdom:

> *For the Son of man shall come in the glory of his Father with his angels; and then he shall reward every man according to his works. Verily I say unto you, There be some standing here which shall not taste of death till they see the Son of man coming in his kingdom* (Matt. 16:27–28).
>
> *Verily I say unto you, That there be some of them that stand here, which shall not taste of death, till they have seen the kingdom of God come with power* (Mark 9:1).
>
> *For whosoever shall be ashamed of me and of my words, of him shall the Son of man be ashamed, when he shall come in his own glory, and in his Father's and of the holy angels. But I tell you of a truth, there be some standing here, which shall not taste of death, till they see the kingdom of God* (Luke 9:26–27).

In His revelation to John, Jesus told the seven Churches in Asia that even his tormentors would witness Him again when *"he cometh with clouds; and every eye shall see him, and they also which pierced him"* (Rev. 1:7). The chief priests, members of the council, the ones who crucified Jesus, and His disciples have all been dead a very long time. But Jesus had told the chief priests as well as His disciples *they* would see Him, His kingdom, and His coming in the clouds of heaven. So, obviously, this must-have happened when *they* were still alive. Or Jesus was profoundly mistaken—worse yet, a liar—which, of course, He was not.

Every Jew, during their time of great tribulation (AD 66–70)—whether or not they realized it—saw the Lion of the tribe of Judah, the Son of man, come in great power and glory, bringing swift and terrible judgment to the Jewish nation. They saw His power as the impregnable walls of Jerusalem (which, at one time, God Himself watched over and protected) yield to the fierce Roman hordes battling for control of the city. They saw His power as fights arose within the city between the various factions of Jews struggling for control, even while the Roman army besieged Jerusalem from without. They saw Christ's judgment in the rivers of blood flowing down the streets, even as Jew killed Jew.

Finally, they saw His wrath poured out upon the temple—the glory of the Jewish nation—where praise and worship had once been offered, but now had become a place of abomination because of the animal sacrifices that continued unabated for almost forty years after the consummate offering of the Lamb of God had been made.

After the flames consumed the temple, the Romans dug up every block of stone to retrieve the molten gold and silver that had flowed into the joints. The Jews who survived saw their friends and fellow countrymen carried away as captives destined for slavery. Yes, every Jewish eye saw all of this. The chief priests, elders and scribes, those who pierced Him, and all the others who survived truly did see *"the Son of man sitting on the right hand of power, and coming in the clouds of heaven"* (Mark 14:62).

Did Jewish leaders in Christ's day perceive a Dispensational outcome when Jesus told them about His coming of the Son of man? When Jesus told them they would see the Son of man coming in the clouds of heaven, the Jews knew exactly what Jesus meant. Clouds symbolized the presence of Jehovah, the Almighty God, with His unapproachable holiness and righteousness.

And it came to pass, as Aaron spake unto the whole congregation of the children of Israel, that they looked toward the wilderness, and, behold, the glory of the LORD appeared in the cloud (Ex. 16:10).

And the LORD descended in the cloud (Ex. 34:5).

And Moses was not able to enter into the tent of the congregation, because the cloud abode thereon, and the glory of the LORD filled the tabernacle (Ex. 40:35).

And the cloud of the LORD was upon them by day, when they went out of the camp (Num. 10:34).

And the LORD came down in a cloud (Num. 11:25).

(See also Gen. 15:17; Ex. 13:21–22, 14:19–20, 19:9, 40:38; Num.10:12, 12:5; Deut. 4:11; I Kings 8:10–11; II Chron. 5:13–14; Job 22:14; Psalms. 18:8, 97:2, 104:3; Isa.19:1; Ezek. 10:3–4, 32:7–8)

When unleashing judgment on nations, the LORD was also represented by a cloud: "*Behold, the LORD rideth upon a swift cloud, and shall come into Egypt*" (Isa.19:1). "*Behold, he shall come up as clouds, and his chariots shall be as a whirlwind*" (Jer. 4:13).

Jesus was telling the Jews and all of Israel that, in a few years, they would have the fullest proof He was the Christ, the promised Messiah. He assured them He was invested with absolute dominion and power, and that He would come in the clouds of heaven to execute judgment upon their wicked nation. The high priests reacted viciously when Jesus said, "*ye shall see the Son of Man sitting on the right hand of power, and coming in the clouds of heaven. Then the high priest rent his clothes, saying He hath spoken blasphemy; what further need have we of witnesses? behold, now ye have heard his blasphemy. What think ye? They answered and said, He is guilty of death*" (Matt. 26:64–65).

In their book *Beyond Creation Science*, Timothy P. Martin and Jeffrey L. Vaughn provide great insight regarding Matt. 26:64:

> The Jewish Sanhedrin condemned Jesus to death not just for claiming to be God, but for another reason as well. They were infuriated when Jesus claimed that they would see him bring judgment upon Jerusalem ... Imagine, just before sentencing, the most extreme act of defiance. Jesus implied that he would return from the dead and kill the high priest and the entire court with God's full fury and glory.[29]

In the Book of Zechariah, the LORD says, *"I am returned unto Zion, and will dwell in the midst of Jerusalem"* (Zech. 8:3). In other words, when God arrived it was in a spiritual way and not in a physical form that could be seen.

We can now see Jesus' declaration was no great mystery to His hearers when He said: "[*T*]*hey shall see the Son of man coming in the clouds of heaven with power and great glory"* (Matt 24:30). It is here where Jesus promised judgment upon the nation of Israel—and He was not to be doubted!

IN LIKE MANNER

How could anyone still not believe the parousia of the Lord would entail anything other than an invisible presence in the clouds of judgment that came upon the wicked generation that rejected Him?

The website for the *Pristine Faith Restoration Society*, in an article titled "Preterism Coming Again in Like Manner," had this to say:

> Preterists avoid the problem of no historical evidence by claiming that Jesus's coming was "spiritual" and "invisible." He therefore did not come "in the flesh," as He did at His first advent. The question is, what kind of "coming" do the Scriptures predict ...?
>
> According to the two angels, Jesus's second coming will be "in like manner" as His ascension into heaven. This begs the question, in what manner did Jesus ascend into heaven? The answer is in our text [Acts 1:1–12]. Jesus was with the Apostles in person, in His resurrected state. Verse 3 says they saw Him for forty days prior to His ascension. Verse 4 says Jesus was "assembled together with them." Verse 9 indicates that the Apostles observed Jesus's ascension into the sky until a cloud obscured Him from their view. From this historical narrative, we know without question that Jesus ascended in full view of His Apostles in person, visibly. The angels told them that *"this same Jesus"* would be coming back *"in like manner as you have seen Him go into heaven."*

John MacArthur, in his book *The Second Coming*, states:

The bodily return of Christ is not a point on which the Scriptures are ambiguous or unclear. As the disciples watched the resurrected Christ ascend into heaven, Scripture tells us, "Two men stood by them in white apparel, who also said, 'Men of Galilee, why do you stand gazing up into heaven? This same Jesus, who was taken up from you into heaven, *will so come in like manner* as you saw Him go into heaven.'" (Acts 1:10–11, emphasis added) **He ascended in a visible, bodily form; he will return from heaven "in like manner." Nothing could be more plain.**[30] (emphasis added)

Along with MacArthur's incantation, I hear a mighty chorus of Dispensational voices, rising as one, shouting, "**AMEN BROTHER, IN LIKE MANNER, SO BE IT**"!

MacArthur's emphatic statements, given with bulldog tenacity, belie the fact there is precious little Scriptural evidence to back up such bold pronouncements.

The men in white apparel (probably angels) said Jesus would return from heaven "*in like manner*"—which, MacArthur believes (along with an innumerable host of other Christians), would be in a visible, bodily form. And "nothing could be more plain." Really?

Ponder this before we dig deeper into this discussion. There was no fanfare included in Jesus' ascension. There were no public announcements. There was no huge crowd of people to witness Him being received up into the clouds. The *manner*—the way, the means, the technique—in which He ascended was *merely witnessed by a few people*—His Disciples only. That was the setting. That was how He was seen as He ascended to heaven. Since the "manner" in which He left was clandestine and unassuming—with not everyone in the entire world looking on and seeing it take place—then the "manner" in which the two men said he would return as such, would likewise be a return that is not seen by everyone in the entire world, nor discerned by all. Thus, the idea THIS coming was to be a universal—every eye will see Him moment—Second Coming is incorrect. Every Jewish tribal eye would see and discern the moment of this coming but not all mankind (Rev. 1:7).

Therefore, this "manner" (mode or way) does not in the slightest refer to Him as being a physical body or spirit returning but rather, the KIND of return He will be making—just as they said, "This same Jesus, who was taken up from you into heaven, *will so come in like manner as you saw Him go* into heaven." They saw Him go quietly—with no trumpet blast or elaboration; and no billions of onlookers—thus, this return of Jesus would likewise be without trumpet blasts and elaboration with not billions looking on—just those in and around Jerusalem. With these thoughts still fresh in your mind, let us continue.

Dispensationalists make a great fuss concerning the ascension of the physical body of Christ. They reason since he was resurrected bodily and ascended bodily, he must literally come back with a physical body. But could an organic being made up of flesh and bone, a literal, corporeal human body, somehow withstand the trip to that heavenly abode, much less affect a return to earth?

We used to sing this chorus:

> We shall be changed,
> We shall be changed,
> Changed from this mortal to immortality,
> In the twinkling of an eye.

There are points of interest to ponder about Christ after His resurrection. Most remarkably, He did things a human being is not able to do (unless trained as a ninja assassin!). For instance, He was able to appear and disappear at will. He could walk through walls and, as it were, teleport Himself wherever He willed to go. He was also able to disguise Himself so others would not recognize him. (See Mark 16:12; Luke 24:31–36; John 20:19, 26; 21:4)

After His resurrection, Jesus did have some degree of physical form, insofar as He was able to eat, and His disciples were able to touch Him. However, His body was very different from what we mortal beings use to move around, as intimated by the Apostle Paul in I Corinthians (15:42–46):

> *So also is the resurrection of the dead. It is sown in corruption; it is raised in incorruption: It is sown in dishonour; it is raised in glory; it is sown in weakness; it is raised in power: It is sown a natural body;*

it is raised a spiritual body. There is a natural body, and there is a spiritual body. And so it is written, The first man Adam was made a living soul; the last Adam was made a quickening spirit. Howbeit that was not first which is spiritual, but that which is natural; and afterward that which is spiritual.

William Edwy (W. E.) Vine was an English Biblical scholar, theologian, and writer. His most famous work, *Vine's Expository Dictionary of New Testament Words*, states the word "spiritual" derives from the Greek word "Pneumatikos," which *"always connotes the ideas of invisibility and power. It does not occur in the Sept. nor in the Gospels; it is in fact an after-Pentecost word."* (emphasis added) The word "spiritual" is also used in the New Testament to contrast the fleshly nature of man with the spiritual nature of God.

It was the spiritual body described by Paul our Lord used to ascend into heaven. While Jesus still maintained a corporeal presence, He was able to be visible one moment and invisible the next. His corruptible flesh was now incorruptible and immortal, just as ours will be at our resurrection.

Preterists do not deny the parousia of Christ. But we do disagree with Dispensationalists on just what *"in like manner"* means. The only descriptions of the Lord's ascension are found in just four verses: Mark 16:19; Luke 24:51; and Acts 1:9–10. In Mark's account, as Jesus spoke to those gathered around, *"[H]e was received up into heaven, and sat on the right hand of God."* That is not a lot of detail on which to base an entire doctrine. The words *received up* are not a literal description of what actually transpired. "Received" in this verse, according to *Bullinger's Critical Lexicon*, means "to take; take hold of, apprehend, to take or receive from another, to take what is given, pointing to objective reception."

Received up does not literally describe a physical ascent through the air or a trip to heaven. Perhaps it describes the event that took place at the throne room in heaven, where God granted Christ his unique position of authority and power: *"But this man after he had offered one sacrifice for sins for ever, sat down on the right hand of God; From henceforth expecting till his enemies be made his footstool"* (Heb. 10:12–13; see also Acts 2:34–35 and Heb. 1:13)

Moving on to the next—and only other—eyewitness account, Luke states: *"And it came to pass, while he blessed them, he was parted from them, and carried up into heaven."* Again, this passage relates very sparse information concerning the ascension of our Lord.

In Luke's verse, the word *carried* translates from the Greek word *anophero*, which, according to *Strong's,* can be taken in a literal or figurative sense. It can mean "to take up," "bear," "bring," or "offer up." *Thayer's* states: *"to carry or bring up, to lead up* men to a higher place."

Are we to construe our Lord was literally "carried up into heaven"? If such indeed occurred, who did the carrying (for you cannot carry yourself)? Maybe He was carried, like we would carry a small child in our arms. Or, perhaps, there were two angels in attendance that day; holding Christ under each arm and using "wing power," they literally carried Him into heaven.

If we look to *Nestle's* Greek text, verse 51 reads very differently from the King James version: *"And it came to pass in the to bless (while he blessed) him them he withdrew from them."* Though the Greek text seems a little chopped up, it still conveys the idea Jesus departed from His disciples, even as the words fail to describe in what manner or way this occurred.

The Revised Standard Version translates verse 51 this way: "While he blessed them, he parted from them." It does add a footnote: "Other ancient authorities add *and was carried up into heaven.*"

The *New English Bible* has a different translation: "[A]nd in the act of blessing he parted from them." But it also includes this footnote: *"Some witnesses add* and was carried up into heaven."

Whichever textual variation of *"was carried up into heaven"* we choose; this portion of Scripture does not convey the idea of a Superman-type flight, a magician's act of levitation, or even a self-propelled flight by our Lord. Consequently, we need to look elsewhere for any stated evidence of a literal bodily ascension into heaven.

We have just examined two accounts of Christ's ascension. We will now look at the two remaining verses of Scripture that contain an eyewitness account of what happened. They are found in Acts 1:9–10.

As it happens, both accounts come from the pen of Doctor Luke—the one that bears his name, and the one found in the Book of Acts. Both these letters were written to a person named Theophilus (Lover of God), of whom we know very little. It is thought he was a Gentile, perhaps someone of rank and influence.

Does the account in Acts literally describe a bodily ascension into heaven? Do we find here the evidence we seek, the evidence MacArthur assures us could not be more *clear, plain,* and *unambiguous?* It must exist in the Book of Acts, for there is nowhere else to look. What follows is the whole eyewitness account:

> *9.* And when he had spoken these things, while they beheld, **he was taken up; and a cloud received him** out of their sight. *10.* And while they looked steadfastly toward heaven as **he went up**, behold, two men stood by them in white apparel; *11.* Which also said, Ye men of Galilee, why stand ye gazing up into heaven? This same Jesus, which is taken up from you into heaven, shall so come in like manner as ye have seen him go into heaven (Acts 1:9–11).

Pay attention to those twelve highlighted words. This portion of Scripture is the only place in the entire Bible that gives a clear, unambiguous, eyewitness account of what actually happened at the ascension. Or does it? Of course, we do have Daniel's narrative in Daniel 7:13. But that was a vision, not an eyewitness report.

How definitive can a doctrine that consists of only twelve sparse words really be? We have already seen the meaning of "clouds" and what they signify in Scripture. So that leaves Dispensationalists with just seven words upon which to base their precepts: "*he was taken up ... he went up.*"

Think of any important Christian belief, such as justification by faith, the six-day creation, the Fall, sin, judgment, the Gospel, baptism, Christ's death and resurrection, or any other major teaching of the Bible. Now summarize, in just seven words, any one of those teachings! It cannot be done—even with all twelve words (allowing for those clouds!).

Yes, it is entirely possible to convey an important point or record a notable event using very few words. "*Jesus wept*" is plain, concise, unambiguous, and full of profound meaning. With that short statement we have a fuller understanding of how Jesus felt, even though much is left out of that pithy verse. Why did our Lord weep? For whom was he weeping?

Didn't He have sufficient power to control outcomes, so He would have no need to weep?

Context is an important consideration, yet the context of the twelve eyewitness words about the ascension provides no specific information about how Jesus actually ascended. To build a whole doctrine upon such a scant account is, as they say, "skating on thin ice."

Consider how out of balance this is. The word "kingdom," pertaining to the kingdom of God/heaven, was used 124 times by Jesus and 28 times by the authors of the New Testament. Christ's gospel on the kingdom of God was a central part of His ministry and the very essence of His worldview. (see Matt. 3:1–2, 16:28; Mark 1:14–15; Acts 1:3; 28:30–31) Yet—even with so much Scripture to study—there is still much disagreement on the "kingdom" teachings of John the Baptist, Christ, and the apostles. Nevertheless, with just twelve words on which to base a doctrine, is it not absurd for MacArthur and others to state so emphatically the meaning of two sparse verses in the Book of Acts is *plain* and *unambiguous*?

Yes, we agree: Christ ascended into heaven. Yes, we agree: there was to be a parousia of Christ. That much is clear. But not so the manner of His ascension, which MacArthur insists is obvious and clear-cut.

Effectively separating fact from fiction depends upon a proper interpretation of Scripture. Ultimately, the mechanics and timing of the parousia hinge upon what the angels meant when they uttered those three words, "*in like manner.*"

Luke states, "*he was taken up; and a cloud received him … he went up*" (Acts 1:9–10). But this does not describe the manner, the way, or how it was done; just that it happened, not how it occurred.

Scripture says: "*he was taken up; and a cloud received him … he went up.*" But what does *taken up* really mean? Who or what took him up? How was this astounding feat accomplished? Then comes, *he went up.* Is this observation literal or is it meant to be taken in a figurative way? If we put all the words describing Christ's ascension together we would read, *he was received, carried, went up,* and *was taken up.* Is this literal or figurative? Are these statements *plain* and *unambiguous* or are they open to interpretation?

ISRAEL: FIG TREE OR OLIVE TREE?

But what about that iconic fig tree?

Now learn a parable of the fig tree; When his branch is yet tender, and putteth forth leaves, ye know that summer is nigh: So likewise ye, when ye shall see all these things, know that it is near, even at the doors (Matt. 24:32–33).

Now learn a parable of the fig tree; When her branch is yet tender, and putteth forth leaves, ye know that summer is near: So ye in like manner, when ye shall see these things come to pass, know that it is nigh, even at the doors (Mark 13:28–29).

Behold the fig tree, and all the trees; When they now shoot forth, ye see and know of your own selves that summer is now nigh at hand. So likewise ye, when ye see these things come to pass, know ye that the kingdom of God is nigh at hand (Luke 21:29–31).

Tim LaHaye, Jerry B. Jenkins, and many other Dispensationalists believe the fig tree is symbolic of Israel and the verses above refer to the nation of Israel. In their book *Are We Living in the End Times?*, LaHaye and Jenkins write:

Many prophecy students interpret this passage to mean that when we see the rise of Israel as a nation (as we did in 1948), we will know that the time of the end is "near-at the doors." They reason that when a fig tree is used symbolically in Scripture, it usually refers to Israel. If that is a valid assumption (and we believe it is), then when Israel officially became a nation in 1948, that was the "sign" of Matthew 24:1–8, the beginning "birth pains"—it meant that the "end of the age" is "near."[31]

It is usually wise to refrain from making assumptions because they often prove false. When studying the Word of God, we need to be especially careful before jumping to conclusions. Even if the fig tree is used elsewhere as a metaphor for Israel, one should not assume when Scripture talks about fig trees it always means the nation of Israel.

In point of fact, the fig tree is *never* used in Scripture to mean Israel.

Not once. There are 64 verses in Scripture that use the word "fig" or "figs." But there is not one verse in the entire Bible that symbolically portrays Israel as any type of fig tree. There are two verses that come close: Hosea 9:10 and Nahum 3:12, the latter stating: *"All thy strong holds shall be like fig trees with the firstripe figs: if they be shaken, they shall even fall into the mouth of the eater."* And even this verse was not referring to the entire nation of Israel, just its strongholds.

In the Book of Jeremiah, chapter 24, God compares Israel to two baskets of figs. One basket was full of good figs while the other was full of bad, evil figs. The good figs were the Jews who were taken captive to the land of the Chaldeans; it was they who would be restored after 70 years of captivity. The evil figs were King Zedekiah, his princes, and the residue of Jews left in Jerusalem by the Babylonians. The fortunate few King Nebuchadnezzar allowed to remain after he had conquered Israel were eventually dispersed to other nations and were not promised a restoration.

Note that these sections compare the Jews to *figs*, not *fig trees*. Well, are not figs and fig trees the same thing? Not at all. Israel is likened to olive trees, not to olives. Moreover, the nation of Israel is often symbolized by the olive tree, never a fig tree (Psalms 52:8, 128:3; Jer.11:16; Hosea 14:6; Rom. 11:17–24).

The Dispensationalist view, espoused by Tim LaHaye, maintains the fig tree in Matthew 24:32 was the symbol for Israel, and as such heralds, the message Israel was to become a nation again. If that is true, then what does it mean when Jesus said, *"Behold the fig tree, and all the trees"* (Luke 21:29)? Did Jesus envision "all the trees" as other nations following the same road as Israel? No. This verse stipulated the tribulation that would soon come upon the Jews in AD 70. The Olivet Discourse was addressed to the disciples, His Church, at which occasion Jesus warned, *"Take heed that no man deceive you."* Only with a preconceived belief in a regathering of Israel could someone conclude that Israel was symbolized by the fig tree, for the Discourse does not mention such a regathering at all.

So, what was Jesus referring to when He said, *"When his branch is yet tender and putteth forth leaves, ye know that summer is nigh ... and that it is near even at the doors"* (Matt. 24:32–33)? What was it that was drawing so "near"? Certainly not the regathering of Israel. Jesus was foreseeing the imminent destruction of the temple, when "*not one stone would be left upon another.*"

Gary DeMar points out another problem with the fig tree representing Israel:

> If the fig tree is a symbol for national Israel, then there is a problem with Matthew 21:19. Jesus saw "a lone fig tree by the road" and He "found nothing on it except leaves only; and He said to it, 'No longer shall there be any fruit from you.' And at once the fig tree withered." This passage is quite clear. If the withered fig tree is Israel, Jesus tells us, '*No longer shall there ever be any fruit from you.*'[32]

Never. That's what Jesus said. So, what does the fig tree represent? It's just a tree Jesus used as an illustration. An illustration, that helped Christians discern when the temple would be destroyed.

THIS GENERATION

Jesus answered His disciples' questions about what would take place before the destruction of Jerusalem and the temple. He also told them it would happen in *their* lifetime:

> *Verily I say unto you, This generation shall not pass till all these things be fulfilled* (Matt. 24:34).
> *Verily I say unto you, that this generation shall not pass, till all these things be done* (Mark 13:30).
> *Verily I say unto you, This generation shall not pass away, till all be fulfilled* (Luke 21:32).

Some say when Jesus said *this generation*, He really meant the generation alive when "all these things" were slated to occur. Consider these points: When was Jerusalem destroyed so completely, there was "*not left one stone upon another, that shall not be thrown down*"? When was the temple ravaged? When was it "*That upon you may come all the righteous blood shed upon the earth*"? When did *all these things* actually and historically befall the Pharisees and scribes and the rest of the unbelieving Jews? In AD 70!

These prophecies cannot be fulfilled again. Even if some modern Jews rebuilt an exact replica of the temple on the same piece of ground where it once stood, it would not be the temple Jesus pointed to and declared, "*there shall not be left here one stone upon another*" (Matt. 24:3). That temple can never be destroyed again! Once destroyed, always *destroyed*.

In the Greek language, the word *generation* has several meanings. But it is the context that defines its particular meaning. In Matt. 24:34, Mark 13:30, and Luke 21:32, *Thayer's Greek-English Lexicon* defines *generation* as "the whole multitude of men living at the same time."

The phrase *this generation* is used fifteen times by Jesus and once by the Apostle Peter (Matt. 11:16, 12:41–42, 23:36, 24:34; Mark 8:12, 13:30; Luke 7:31, 11:30–32, 11:50–51, 17:25, 21:32; Acts 2:40). Every place in Scripture where *this generation* is used, it means those people who were alive at the same time as Jesus and Peter. There is no indication anywhere in Scripture Jesus was using the phrase in a different way when he delivered the Olivet Discourse. To argue otherwise violates the interpretive rules of usage, context, and logic. Nothing in the Olivet Discourse implies a different and far future generation is meant. If that were the case, Jesus would have said, "when *that* generation" witnesses such events. (See, for example, Heb. 3:10)

When Jesus answered the disciples' questions in the Olivet Discourse, they never doubted He was talking about events that would happen to them. How do we know? Because they believed Jesus's pointed response: "[W]hen *ye shall see Jerusalem compassed with armies, then know that the desolation thereof is nigh. Then let them which are in Judaea flee to the mountains and let them which are in the midst of it depart out*" (Luke 21:20–21). When the First Century Christians saw the abomination of desolation (the Roman armies) they fled Judaea and the city of Jerusalem. As far as we know, not one Christian perished in its destruction.

Just imagine if Tim LaHaye, John MacArthur, and other Dispensationalists had been around when the Roman armies approached Jerusalem. What would they have told the Christians? "Chill out, guys! Don't take things so literally! The terrible things Jesus predicted in His

Olivet Discourse won't happen for another 2,000 years. It's not for *this* generation. It's for another generation—way, way in the future."

If the Christians back then had been disciples of LaHaye and MacArthur, rather than of Jesus, they would surely have perished in the siege of Jerusalem along with the Jewish unbelievers. That woeful misjudgment would have defined those First Century Dispensationalists as unbelievers—akin to the Jews who perished because they did not believe the words of Jesus. What a good thing Dispensationalism did not exist in AD 70!

THE HARMONY OF THE OLIVET DISCOURSE

A side-by-side comparison of the Olivet Discourse, as given in the three Gospels, is printed below. It is helpful to study all three accounts because each version contains slightly different details. Consequently, when those details are put together, we get a fuller picture of Jesus' prophecy. It is also helpful to read Luke 17:22–37 and 19:41–44, as these verses also illuminate the Lord's Olivet Discourse.

Matthew Chapter 24	Mark chapter 13	Luke chapter 21
1. And Jesus went out, and departed from the temple: and his disciples came to him for to shew him the buildings of the temple.	1. And as he went out of the temple, one of his disciples saith unto him, Master, see what manner of stones and what buildings are here!	5. And as some spake of the temple, how it was adorned with goodly stones and gifts, he said,
2. And Jesus said unto them, See ye not all these things? verily I say unto you, There shall not be left here one stone upon another, that shall not be thrown down.	2. And Jesus answering said unto him, Seest thou these great buildings? There shall not be left one stone upon another, that shall not be thrown down.	6. As for these things which ye behold, the days will come, in the which there shall not be left one stone upon another that shall not be thrown down.
3. *And as he sat upon the mount of Olives, the disciples came unto him privately, saying, Tell us, when shall these things be? and what shall be the sign of thy coming, and of the end of the world?*	3. *And as he sat upon the mount of Olives over against the temple, Peter and James and John and Andrew asked him privately,*	7. *And they asked him, saying, Master but when shall these things be? And what sign will there be when these things shall come to pass?*
	4. *Tell us, when shall these things be? And what shall be the sign when all these things shall be fulfilled?*	
4. And Jesus answered and said unto them, Take heed that no man deceive you.	5. And Jesus answering them began to say, Take heed lest any man deceive you:	8. And he said, Take heed that ye be not deceived: for many shall come in my name, saying, I am Christ: and the time draweth near: go ye not therefore after them.
5. For many shall come in my name, saying, I am Christ; and shall deceive many.	6. For many shall come in my name saying, I am Christ: and shall deceive many.	
6. *And ye shall hear of wars and rumours of wars: see that ye be not troubled: for all these things must come to pass, but the end is not yet.*	7. *And when ye shall hear of wars and rumours of wars, be ye not troubled: for such things must needs be; but the end shall not be yet.*	9. *But when ye shall hear of wars and commotions, be not terrified: for these things must first come to pass; but the end is not by and by.*

Matthew Chapter 24	Mark chapter 13	Luke chapter 21

7. For nation shall rise against nation, and kingdom against kingdom: and there shall be famines, and pestilences, and earthquakes, in divers places.

8. All these are the beginning of sorrows.

9. Then shall they deliver you up to be afflicted, and shall kill you: and ye shall be hated of all nations for my name's sake.

10. And then shall many be offended, and shall betray one another, and shall hate one another.

11. And many false prophets shall rise, and shall deceive many.

12. And because iniquity shall abound, the love of many shall wax cold.

13. But he that shall endure unto the end, the same shall be saved.

14. And this gospel of the kingdom shall be preached in all the world for a witness unto all nations; and then shall the end come.

8. For nation shall rise against nation, and kingdom against kingdom: and there shall be earthquakes in divers places, and there shall be famines and troubles: these are the beginnings of sorrows.

9. But take heed to yourselves: for they shall deliver you up to councils: and in the synagogues ye shall be beaten: and ye shall be brought before rulers and kings for my sake, for a testimony against them.

10. And the gospel must first be published among all nations.

11. But when they shall lead you and deliver you up, take no thought beforehand what ye shall speak, neither do ye premeditate: but whatsoever shall be given you in that hour, that speak ye: for it is not ye that speak, but the Holy Ghost.

10. Then said he unto them, Nation shall rise against nation, and kingdom against kingdom:

11. And great earthquakes shall be in divers places, and famines, and pestilences; and fearful sights and great signs shall there be from heaven.

12. But before all these, they shall lay their hands on you, and persecute you, delivering you up to the synagogues, and into prisons, being brought before kings and rulers for my name's sake.

13. And it shall turn to you for a testimony.

14. Settle it therefore in your hearts, not to meditate before what ye shall answer.

15. For I will give you a mouth and wisdom, which all your adversaries shall not be able to gainsay nor resist.

16. And ye shall be betrayed both by parents and brethren, and kinsfolks, and friends: and some of you shall they cause to be put to death.

Matthew Chapter 24	Mark chapter 13	Luke chapter 21
	12. Now the brother shall betray the brother to death, and the father the son; and children shall rise up against their parents, and shall cause them to be put to death.	17. And ye shall be hated of all men for my name's sake.
		18. But there shall not an hair of your head perish.
	13. And ye shall be hated of all men for my name's sake: but he that shall endure unto the end, the same shall be saved.	19. In your patience possess ye your souls.
15. *When ye therefore shall see the abomination of desolation, spoken of by Daniel the prophet, stand in the holy place, (whoso readeth, let him understand:)*	14. *But when ye shall see the abomination of desolation, spoken of by Daniel the prophet, standing where it ought not, (let him that readeth understand), then let them that be in Judaea flee to the mountains:*	20. *And when ye shall see Jerusalem compassed with armies, then know that the desolation thereof is nigh.*
16. *Then let them which be in Judaea flee into the mountains:*		21. *Then let them which are in Judaea flee to the mountains;*
17. Let him which is on the housetop not come down to take any thing out of his house:	15. And let him that is on the housetop not go down into the house, neither enter therein, to take anything out of his house:	and let them which are in the midst of it depart out: and let not them that are in the countries enter thereinto.
18. Neither let him which is in the field return back to take his clothes.	16. And let him that is in the field not turn back again for to take up his garment.	22. For these be the days of vengeance, that all things which are written may be fulfilled.
19. *And woe unto them that are with child, and to them that give suck in those days!*	17. *But woe to them that are with child, and to them that give suck in those days!*	23. *But woe unto them that are with child, and to them that give suck, in those days!*

Matthew Chapter 24	Mark chapter 13	Luke chapter 21

20. But pray ye that your flight be not in the winter, neither on the Sabbath day:

21. For then shall be great tribulation, such as was not since the beginning of the world to this time, no, nor ever shall be.

22. And except those days should be shortened, there should no flesh be saved: but for the elect's sake those days shall be shortened.

23. Then if any man shall say unto you, lo, here is Christ, or there; believe it not.

24. For there shall arise false Christs, and false prophets, and shall shew great signs and wonders; insomuch that, if it were possible, they shall deceive the very elect.

25. Behold, I have told you before.

26. Wherefore if they shall say unto you, Behold he is in the desert, go not forth: behold, he is in the secret chambers; believe it not.

27. For as lightning cometh out of the east, and shineth even unto the west; so shall also the coming of the Son of man be.

28. For wheresoever the carcase is, there will the eagles be gathered together.

18. And pray ye that your flight be not in the winter.

19. For in those days shall be affliction, such as was not from the beginning of the creation which God created unto this time, neither shall be.

20. And except that the Lord had shortened those days, no flesh should be saved: but for the elect's sake, whom he hath chosen, he hath shortened the days.

21. And then if any man shall say to you, Lo, here is Christ; or lo, he is there; believe him not:

22. For false Christs and false prophets shall rise, and shall shew signs and wonders, to seduce, if it were possible, even the elect.

23. But take ye heed: Behold, I have foretold you all things.

For there shall be great distress in the land, and wrath upon this people.

24. And they shall fall by the edge of the sword, and shall be led away captive into all nations: and Jerusalem shall be trodden down of the Gentiles, until the times of the Gentiles be fulfilled.

Matthew Chapter 24	Mark chapter 13	Luke chapter 21

29. Immediately after the tribulation of those days shall the sun be darkened, and the moon shall not give her light, and the stars shall fall from heaven, and the powers of the heavens shall be shaken:

30. And then shall appear the sign of the Son of man in heaven: and then shall all the tribes of the earth mourn, and they shall see the Son of man coming in the clouds of heaven with power and great glory.

31. And he shall send his angels with a great sound of a trumpet, and they shall gather together his elect from the four winds, from one end of heaven to the other.

24. But in those days, after that tribulation, the sun shall be darkened, and the moon shall not give her light.

25. And the stars of heaven shall fall, and the powers that are in heaven shall be shaken.

26. And then shall they see the Son of man coming in the clouds with great power glory.

27. And then shall he send his angels, and shall gather together his elect from the four winds, from the uttermost part of the earth to the uttermost part of heaven.

25. And there shall be signs in the sun, and in the moon, and in the stars: and upon the earth distress of nations, with perplexity; the sea and the waves roaring:

26. Men's hearts failing them for fear, and for looking after those things which are coming on the earth: for the powers of heaven shall be shaken.

27. And then shall they see the Son of man coming in a cloud with great power and great glory.

28. And when these things begin to come to pass, then look up, and lift up your heads; for your redemption draweth nigh.

32. *Now learn a parable of the fig tree; When his branch is yet tender, and putteth forth leaves, ye know that summer is nigh:*

33. *So likewise ye, when ye shall see all these things, know that it is near, even at the doors.*

28. *Now learn a parable of the fig tree; When her branch is yet tender, and putteth forth leaves, ye know that summer is near:*

29. *So ye in like manner, when ye shall see these things come to pass, know that it is nigh, even at the doors.*

29. *And he spake to them a parable; Behold the fig tree, and all the trees;*

30. *When they now shoot forth, ye see and know of your own selves that summer is now nigh at hand.*

31. *So likewise ye, when ye see these things come to pass, know ye that the kingdom of God is nigh at hand.*

Matthew Chapter 24	Mark chapter 13	Luke chapter 21
34. Verily I say unto you, This generation shall not pass, till all these things be fulfilled.	30. Verily I say unto you, that this generation shall not pass, till all these things be done.	32. Verily I say unto you, This generation shall not pass away, till all be fulfilled.
35. *Heaven and earth shall pass away; but my words shall not pass away.*	31. *Heaven and earth shall pass away; but my words shall not pass away.*	33. *Heaven and earth shall pass away; but my words shall not pass away.*
36. *But of that day and hour knoweth no man, no, not the angels of heaven, but my Father only.*	32. *But of that day and that hour knoweth no man, no, not the angels which are in heaven, neither the Son, but the Father.*	

FIVE KEYS TO UNDERSTANDING
THE OLIVET DISCOURSE

There are five keys to understanding the Olivet Discourse that continue to elude the Dispensational prophecy experts—requiring them, every few years, to update their books and sermons on end time and last days' prophecy.

When we lose sight of or choose to ignore any one of these keys, we completely misunderstand Jesus's Discourse. If any interpretation leaves out even one of these elements, the result will be an adulteration and misrepresentation of our Lord's words.

For example, when prophecy experts insist that current day earthquakes, famines, and wars are signs of the end times or last days, is there any connection to the abomination of desolation wrought upon Israel in AD 70? No, and there never has been. Why? Because Jesus' prediction of earthquakes, famines, and wars related specifically to just one specific event in history, which happened in AD 70—God's judgment upon the Jewish nation, the city of Jerusalem, and the temple that was then standing.

These keys to understanding our Lord's Discourse have been brushed aside, disregarded, and overlooked by so many of the misdirected for far too long. It is time to reconsider the context of this wonderful sermon, to re-examine its content, and recollect the urgency that prompted Jesus' singular exhortation to His disciples.

Think of these keys as a parabolic mirror which can so concentrate the sun's light it becomes a beam of searing heat. May the light of truth set our lives on fire for the advancement of God's kingdom.

KEY #1.   Knowing the whole Olivet Discourse relates specifically and exclusively to the destruction of the temple in Jerusalem in AD 70.

KEY #2.   The statement by Jesus concerning *that* temple: "*There shall not be left here one stone upon another, that shall not be thrown down*" (Matt. 24:2).

KEY #3.   The questions Jesus' disciples asked Him concerning His statement about *that* temple: "*Tell us, when shall these things be? And what shall be the sign of thy coming, and of the end of the world*" (Matt. 24:30)?

KEY #4.   Jesus' declaration that *those* to whom He was speaking (His disciples and *their* generation) would not pass away until *they* witnessed all the events described in His Discourse. *"Verily I say unto you, This generation shall not pass, till all these things be fulfilled"* (Matt. 24:34).

KEY #5.   The numerous indications of imminence found throughout the New Testament, confirming the authors' belief in Jesus' words (e.g., Matt. 24:34).

SUMMARY

Comparing Scripture with Scripture, we now know how purposefully Jesus answered His disciples' questions and how thoroughly the Olivet Discourse was fulfilled. Modern-day Dispensationalists need to take a lesson from the First-Century Christians. They should believe Jesus wholeheartedly, just as the early Church believed Him. They should interpret the Scripture just as the early Church did. They should passionately *"contend for the faith which was once delivered unto the saints"* (Jude 2). The First-Century Christians wisely believed the plain teaching Jesus gave on the Mount of Olives. Moreover, what they believed saved their lives.

FOOTNOTES

1. Adam Clarke, *Clarke's Commentary combined edition* (Nashville: Abingdon) vol. v. Matthew–Revelation p. 225.

2. *The Greek-English New Testament.* Christianity Today, Washington Building, Washington, D.C. 20005 (The Iversen-Norman Associates, 175 Fifth Avenue, N.Y. 10010) p. 505.

3. John L. Bray Ministry, Inc., (Lakeland, Florida: Newsletter, October 22, 2001) p. 2.

4. Ibid. *The Greek-English New Testament.*

5. *Baker Encyclopedia of the Bible* vol. 2 Edited by Walter A. Elwell, Baker Book House Grand Rapids, Michigan 49516, 1988, page 1616.

6. *Vine's Expository Dictionary of New Testament Words*, W. E. Vine, Fleming H. Revell Company, Old Tappan, New Jersey, 1966, page 208.

7. *Strong's Exhaustive Concordance of the Bible*, James Strong, Abingdon Press, Nashville, New York, 1974.

8. *The International Standard Bible Encyclopaedia*, Wm. B. Eerdmans Publishing Co. 1956, Volume III p. 2249.

9. Pax Romana–A period of international history characterized by an absence of major wars and a general stability of international affairs, usually resulting from the predominance of a specified political authority. *Webster's Third New International Dictionary and Seven Language Dictionary*, 1976 G. & C. MERRIAM CO.

10. In the *Institute for Creation Research* article entitled *EARTHQUAKES AND THE END TIMES: A GEOLOGICAL AND BIBLICAL PERSPECTIVE*, authors Steven A. Austin and Mark L. Strauss state:

    If the popular notion of many prophecy teachers (Lindsey, Missler, Van Impe, Church, Jeffrey, Stearman, Hagee, Lalonde, etc.) is correct, two assertions about twentieth-century earthquakes must be true:

    (1) a noteworthy *deficiency* of big earthquakes existed in the first half of the century, and

(2) an obvious *increase* in the frequency of big earthquakes occurred since 1950.

These two assertions must be made by prophecy teachers so as to support a notion of the unique "earthquake sign" occurring in the 1990s. Both assertions, we maintain, are false. Using the best earthquake catalog data and statements of seismologists, we have concluded exactly the opposite:

(1) a noteworthy *excess* of big earthquakes existed in the first half of the century, and

(2) an obvious *decrease* in the frequency of big earthquakes occurred since 1950.

10a. *Powers of Nature*, prepared by the Special Publications Division of the National Geographic Society, 1978, p.19.

11. Ralph Edward Woodrow, *Great Prophecies of the Bible* (Riverside, CA: Ralph Woodrow Evangelistic Association Inc., 1989) p. 47.

12. Arthur W. Pink, *The Redeemer's Return* (Swengel, Penn: Bible Truth Depot, 1918), 157-181. Quoted in the appendix of John F. MacArthur's book, *The Second Coming, p. 202.*

13. Gary DeMar, *An Incomplete Systematic Theology,* Published March 15, 2011.

14. Clarke, vol. v Matthew–Revelation p. 228–229.

15. John F. MacArthur, *The Second Coming* (Crossway Books, A Division of Good News Publishers, 1300 Crescent Street, Wheaton, Illinois 60187, 1999) p. 104.

16. MacArthur, p. 105.

17. MacArthur, p. 105.

18. Teachers' Manual, *Search for Truth* (Search for Truth Publications, 10929 Almeda-Genoa Rd., Houston, Texas, 77034, 1965) p. 113.

19. Clarke, vol. v Matthew - Revelation p. 230.

20. MacArthur, p. 121.

21. MacArthur, p. 121.

22. MacArthur, p. 126.

23. Clarke, vol. v Matthew–Revelation p. 231.

24. John L. Bray, *Matthew 24 Fulfilled* (John L. Bray Ministry, Inc., P.O. Box 90129, Lakeland, Florida 33804, 2000) p. 142.

25. MacArthur, p. 123.

26. MacArthur, p. 123.

27. *The International Standard Bible Encyclopedia*, (Peabody Massachusetts: Hendrickson Publishers, 1994) vol. III, p. 1898.

28. MacArthur, p. 122.

29. Timothy P. Martin & Jeffrey L. Vaughn, Ph.D., *Beyond Creation Science,* Apocalyptic Vision Press, P.O. Box 99, Whitehall, MT 59759, Third Edition 2007, p. 47.

30. MacArthur, p. 12.

31. Tim LaHaye, Jerry B. Jenkins, *Are We Living in the End Times?* (Tyndale House Publishers, Inc., Wheaton, Illinois) p. 57.

32. Gary DeMar, *Last Days Madness* (Brentwood, Tennessee: Wolgemuth & Hyatt, 1991) Note #30, p. 226.

CHAPTER NINE

IT WAS AT HAND

WHEN WAS REVELATION WRITTEN?

Some Christians believe the Book of Revelation was written in AD 96. (That is what it says in the margin of *my* Bible!) If this is true, then the events it describes have nothing to do with the destruction of Jerusalem in AD 70. However, if Revelation was written before AD 68, as the evidence shows, a good case can be made the book truly is about the Great Tribulation of AD 70, rather than some supposed great Jewish persecution by the "Antichrist" during a seven-year tribulation in the future.

It would take more than a few pages to show the Revelation was written before AD 96. To give convincing proof of its date is beyond the scope of this book. However, for those who want a detailed analysis of this topic, the following books are helpful: *The Beast of Revelation* and *Before Jerusalem Fell: Dating the Book of Revelation* by Dr. Kenneth L. Gentry, Jr.; and *The Days of Vengeance* by David Chilton.

Suffice to say, there is overwhelming evidence that Revelation was written between AD 64 and AD 68—before the Roman General Titus destroyed Jerusalem in AD 70—and not during the last days of Titus Flavius Domitianus (Domitian), who was assassinated on September 18, AD 96.

Dr. Gentry, in *The Beast of Revelation,* discusses the continuing skepticism surrounding the earlier date for Revelation. He writes, "Almost invariably the major reason for the dismissal of the early date for Revelation is due to one statement by an early church father named Irenaeus ... Initially, however, almost all commentators begin with and depend upon Irenaeus's statement in his late second-century work entitled *Against Heresies* p. 82."[1] But to rely solely on the questionable testimony of just one man is not good scholarship. And besides, Irenaeus could be wrong; or, perhaps, his writings have been misinterpreted.

Philip Schaff, the astute Biblical scholar and author of the well-known eight volume set *History of the Christian Church*, ultimately changed his view regarding the date of the writing of the Apocalypse: "[T]he date of the Apocalypse ... I now assign, with the majority of modern critics, to the year 68 or 69 instead of 95, as before."[2]

Many noted experts believe the latter date for Revelation is incorrect. Kenneth Gentry lists over 100 scholars who hold to the earlier date for Revelation,[3] including Adam Clarke, J. B. Lightfoot, Philip Schaff, Jay E. Adams, Greg L. Bahnsen, and Cornelis Van der Waal.

Even if we assume Revelation was written sometime around AD 96, we still cannot push the events of the book way into the future, to our time or beyond, because the timing of the events was slated to be "soon" according to John: "[T]*hings which must shortly come to pass ... the time is at hand*" (Rev. 1:1, 3). The cataclysms of Revelation were about to happen "*unto his servants*" (Rev. 1:1, 3–4) to whom the book was written, not to believers 1,900 or more years later.

Revelation had to be written before Jerusalem was destroyed, for it talks about Jerusalem "*where also our Lord was crucified*" (Rev. 11:8). If my home burns down, I can rebuild it. If I rebuild it in the same spot, it would have the same address, the same neighbors, and be on the same street. I could even build it to look just like the old one. But it would not be the same house. Nowhere in the Book of Revelation does it say anything about a rebuilt city or temple. In fact, the New Testament says nothing at all about any rebuilt temple.

There is no question the Apostle John wrote Revelation as the city of Jerusalem and the temple were still standing. If Revelation were written after AD 70, how could it fail to reference one of the most significant events in history, the complete destruction of Jerusalem and the Jewish temple?

The Book of Revelation was written by John as he received it from the Lord Jesus. It was written to the Seven Churches in Asia after the tribulation had started. *"I John, who am your brother, and companion in tribulation"* (Rev. 1:9). *"the time is at hand"* (v.3). It was written to *"show unto his servants things which must shortly come to pass"* (v.1). For the Book of Revelation to have any relevance to the Seven Churches (other than just dealing with their strengths and weaknesses in chapters two and three), it had to be about their imminent future. The book clearly demonstrates this salient fact.

If we were part of the Church of Ephesus or one of the other six congregations that received the epochal letter (that came to be known as the Book of Revelation) from John the Apostle, what would we conclude from these words ...

> *The Revelation of Jesus Christ, which God gave unto him, to shew unto his servants things which must shortly come to pass* (Rev. 1:1).
> *The time is at hand* (Rev.1:3).
> *Behold, I come quickly* (Rev. 3:11).
> *The things which must shortly be done* (Rev. 22:6).
> *Behold, I come quickly* (Rev. 22:7).
> *Seal not the sayings of the prophecy of this book: for the time is at hand* (Rev. 22:10).
> *And behold, I come quickly* (Rev. 22:12).
> *Surely I come quickly* (Rev. 22:20).

Would anyone of reason deduce that Revelation was intended for people living thousands of years in the future? Surely not. One of the hallmarks of Dispensational teaching is supposed to be its literal interpretation of Scripture. Therefore, if I were to write a letter to a Dispensationalist, saying, "Behold, I come quickly," would he interpret that to mean thousands of years in the future?

Remember, this letter was written specifically for the Seven Churches in Asia—which no longer exist—to apprise God's saints of the stunning afflictions that were about to affect their lives. [The actual churches ceased to flourish in the centuries of Muslim control after the Romans, but the archaeological remains of all seven congregations are located in present-day

Turkey.] They were carefully forewarned to *"keep those things which are written therein: for the time is at hand."* There is simply no way to sensibly construe these prophesied events were going to happen to people living in the 21st Century.

In Revelation 13:18, John tells the churches to *"count the number of the beast: for it is the number of a man; and his number is six hundred threescore and six."* The name of the Beast would have to be someone relevant to the First Century Christians, since they were the people to whom John was writing. They would be able to recognize who this "Beast" was. Down through the centuries, there have been hundreds, and possibly thousands of men whose name added up, one way or another, to the dreaded 666. So far, everyone named since AD 70 as a likely candidate has proven to be just another mortal Joe.

Dr. Gentry lists five principles for determining who the Beast with the number 666 may have been.[4] The final two criteria should cause most people to seriously reconsider their end time beliefs about the Antichrist:

Principle #4:

> The name-number must speak of one of John's *contemporaries.* This is due to the temporal expectation of John. The events of Revelation are to occur "soon"; John insists "the time is at hand" (Rev. 1:1, 3, 19, 22:6ff). This principle alone will eliminate 99.9% of the suggestions by commentators.

Principle #5:

> The name must be that of someone *relevant* to the first-century Christians in the seven churches to whom John wrote (Rev. 1:4, 11). He expected them to give heed to what he wrote (Rev. 1:3) and to calculate the Beast's number (Rev. 13:18). How could they have done so if the Beast were some shadowy figure far removed from their own situation?

The word "saints" appears 47 times in the Gospels and the epistles. Each and every time, it refers to New Testament believers or members of the Body of Christ (the Church of God). All the saved of the New

Testament era are sanctified by virtue of their position "in Christ" (I Cor. 1:2; Rom. 6:3; 8:1; Eph. 1:3).[5]

W. E. Vine defines "saints" this way: "In the plural, as used of believers, it designates all such and is not applied merely to persons of exceptional holiness, or to those who, having died, were characterized by exceptional acts of saintliness."[6] Who are these saints that are mentioned in the Book of Revelation 13 times? Are they a different body of believers outside of the Church? No, it's referring to those first century Christians who would shortly go through great tribulation.

THE ANTICHRIST

The imminent arrival of the vaunted Antichrist is something we hear so much about. Many believe the Scripture presages or foretells an Antichrist that will soon emerge as a world ruler and super persecutor of the Jews. Many link the teaching of an Antichrist to the Jews and the Seventieth Week of Daniel during the Tribulation. But, as we have already seen, the Seventieth Week of Daniel has already been fulfilled.

The word "antichrist" is found only in the epistles of John: I John 2:18, 22; 4:3; and II John 7. The Bible's entire antichrist doctrine is found in only those four verses. The composite being referred to as "the Antichrist" does not exist in Scripture. Others identify the "man of sin" (in II Thess. 2:3) as the beast of Revelation. Be that as it may, just because both passages refer to wicked individuals it does not follow, they are one and the same person.

In fact, the Bible indicates the existence of numerous antichrists: "*[A]s ye have heard that antichrist shall come, even now are there many antichrists; whereby we know that it is the last time*" (I John 2:18). How did John just define the fact his audience and he were living in "the last time?" Because of all the antichrists "*even now.*" How does the Bible identify an antichrist? "*Who is a liar but he that denieth that Jesus is the Christ? He is anti-christ, that denieth the Father and the Son*" (I John 2:22). "*And every spirit that confesseth not that Jesus Christ is come in the flesh is not of God: and this is that spirit of antichrist*" (I John 4:3). "*For many deceivers are entered into the world, who confess not that Jesus Christ is come in the flesh. This is a deceiver and an antichrist*" (II John 7).

Well, there it is, the whole Scriptural doctrine of the antichrist, with all the corresponding references. Seems a little thinner than what we have been led to believe. So, who would be considered an antichrist? Anyone who denies the Son and does not confess Jesus Christ is come in the flesh. He is also anyone who denies the Lord by their actions. *"They profess that they know God; but in works they deny him"* (Titus 1:16; see also Luke 9:16)

As we see from Scripture, there is nothing in John I or II about an all-powerful antichrist being a political world ruler and persecutor of the Jews. As defined by Scripture, unbelieving Jews are considered antichrist. So are Muslims, Hindus, Sikhs, Buddhists, Mormons, and atheists. Take your pick. Plenty to choose from. None of them confess Jesus or believe He is (God) come in the flesh. Many Jews, but not all, rejected their Messiah, Jesus. That is the very reason Jerusalem was leveled in AD 70. Every (unconverted) Jew today hates Jesus Christ by denying He is the Messiah. Jesus said, *"He that hateth me hateth my Father also"* (John 15:23); and *"He that is not with me is against me"* (Matt. 12:30). Because Jesus Christ is also God, unconverted Jews hate, deny, and reject Jesus as God. The end result for all these antichrists is what Jesus told the Pharisee, Nicodemus, *"He that believeth on him is not condemned: but he that believeth not is condemned already, because he hath not believed in the name of the only begotten Son of God"* (John 3:18).

WRATH TO COME

John the Baptist said to the Pharisees and the Sadducees, *"O generation of vipers, who hath warned you to flee from the wrath to come"* (Matt. 3:7; Luke 3:7)? Was John talking about the resurrection and judgment at the end of time? Possibly. It is, however, more likely he was referring to the coming "day of the Lord" destined to affect that generation.

In the chapter listing the "eight woes" (Matt. 23), Jesus warns the Jewish leaders, the scribes, and the Pharisees of the wrath to come not many years in the future: *"That upon you may come all the righteous blood shed upon the earth ... Verily I say unto you, All these things shall come upon this generation"* (Matt. 23:35–36).

Paul warned the Church about the devastation soon to come to the unbelieving nation of Israel: *"[F]or the wrath is come upon them to the uttermost"* (I Thess. 2:16). In addition, Paul told the Thessalonians, God had not appointed them to wrath (I Thess. 5:9) and they would be delivered from the wrath to come (I Thess. 1:10). We have already established Jesus made certain to tell the Christians what to do to avoid the abomination of desolation. And we know from history that they were all delivered from "*the wrath to come.*"

IS AT HAND

The phrases "*is at hand,*" "*nigh at hand,*" and "*was at hand*" are used 21 times in the New Testament. This verbiage always means approach, be nigh, imminent, impending, or soon to come. It never means delay, far, distant, remote, a long wait, or an extended period of time.

Anyone who remains unconvinced should substitute the words *delayed, far, distant,* or *long period of time* for the highlighted words in the Scriptures below. It cannot be done without changing the plain meaning of the text.

> *For the kingdom of heaven* **is at hand** (Matt. 3:2)
> *The time is fulfilled, and the kingdom of God* **is at hand** (Mark 1:15)
> *Lo, he that betrayeth me* **is at hand** (Mark 14:42)
> *The kingdom of God is* **nigh at hand** (Luke 21:31)
> *The feast of tabernacles* **was at hand** (John 7:2)
> *The night is far spent, the day* **is at hand** (Rom. 13:12)
> *The Lord* **is at hand** (Phil. 4:5)
> *The day of Christ* **is at hand** (II Thess. 2:2)
> *The time of my departure* **is at hand** (II Tim. 4:6)
> *But the end of all things* **is at hand** (I Peter 4:7)
> *For the time* **is at hand** (Rev. 1:3)
> *For the time* **is at hand** (Rev 22:10)
> (See also Matt. 4:17; 10:7, 26:18, 45–46; Luke 21:30; John 2:13; 11:55; 19:42)

When Jesus said, "*behold the hour is at hand*" (Matt. 26:45), Judas was approaching Gethsemane with a great multitude of priests and elders. And it was within that "hour" that Jesus was betrayed. In John 2:13 we read: "*And the Jews' passover was at hand, and Jesus went up to Jerusalem.*" In context and in fact, the Passover was obviously a few hours or days away, not thousands of years! We could go through each of these verses the same way, and their meaning will never vary: when Scripture says, "*is at hand*," it means near or soon. So how can Dispensationalists continue to ignore that which is plain and inarguable, while still insisting "*is at hand*" means far off into the future—1,950 years away, and counting?

THE LATTER DAYS

In the Old Testament, the phrase "*in the latter days*" occurs 11 times. We also find "*thy latter end*," "*the last day*," "*in the latter years*," "*in the latter time*," "*the last days*," "*the latter days*," etc. In Daniel the angel Michael says, "*shut up the words, and seal the book, even to the time of the end*" (Dan. 12:4). When God referred to the latter days, He meant many years into the future, as opposed to near at hand or soon:

> *Do to thy people in the latter days* (Num. 24:14)
> *Even in the latter days* (Deut. 4:30)
> *Stand at the latter day upon the earth* (Job 19:25)
> *The Lord blessed the latter end of Job* (Job 42:12)
> *The captivity of Moab in the latter days* (Jer. 48:47)
> *In the latter years thou shalt come into* (Ezek. 38:8)
> *And in the latter time of their kingdom* (Dan. 8:23)
> (See also Deut. 8:16; 31:29; Jer. 23:20; 30:24; 49:39;
> Ezek. 38:16; Dan. 2:28; 10:14)

In the Book of Revelation, an angel told John, "*Seal not the sayings of the prophecy of this book: for the time is at hand*" (Rev. 22:12). In the Book of Daniel, the prophecy was to happen many years into the future (i.e., the latter days). For John, something clearly was about to happen; the prophesied event was near at hand. However, Dispensationalists have changed the meaning of what the angel told John. They argue the angel's words "*the time is at hand*" was a projection long, long into the future—an impossibly distant time that still has not come.

Now, let us review the Dispensationalist notion of time. "The time is at hand" means "a long, long time" into the future, over 1,950 years away (and counting). So too, "the latter days" means a long, long time into the future. By this ersatz logic, a short time means a long time; and a long time means a long time. Isn't that more than a little confusing?

THE LAST DAYS

"The last days" and "end times" are terms that are often thrown out during prophetic conferences and Sunday sermons. Christian broadcast media regularly focus on these themes, and Christian bookstores feature many volumes on the last days and end times.

What exactly do the Scriptures mean when they talk about the *end times* and *last days*? These phrases suggest the conclusion of an age—when that age is finished its last days would be finished, and a new age would begin. But here lies the overarching question: what era ended and what era began? The answer from Scripture is the last days of the Old Covenant and Israel's nationhood were the first days of the New Covenant. The last days marked the end of God's special work with the Jews: "*For this is my blood of the new testament, which is shed for many for the remission of sins*" (Matt. 26:28).

The Book of Jude was not intended for any particular entity, but was written for believers everywhere. Hence, his message has been called a general epistle. Jude recommends that all believers "*earnestly contend for the faith which was once delivered unto the saints*" (v.3). We know much of the Bible applies to Christians in all ages and places, its principles and precepts being timeless and true. But in his epistle, as in other parts of Scripture, Jude spoke to a particular historical moment. Jude was warning the Church of events that were taking place in his day, AD 66, which— taken together—signaled the last days of the age; he was not relating something that would happen thousands of years later. Would it have been at all timely and relevant for Jude to warn his readers of things that would take place thousands of years in the future? "*How that they told you there should be mockers in the last time, who should walk after their own ungodly lusts*" (Jude 18). Note the words "*the last time*." As Adam Clarke puts it, Jude's commentary pointedly addresses "The conclusion of the Jewish polity."[7]

Jude wrote his epistle more than 1,900 years ago. Since that time the ungodly, the mockers, murmurers, and scoffers like those who crept into the early Church—the very ones whom Jude wrote about—have always existed. Yet, something was still standing in Jude's day (the temple) that put these people and the events they experienced in a particular time frame: those few short years before the temple in Jerusalem was leveled.

Jude also reminded them of "*the words which were spoken before of the apostles of our Lord Jesus Christ. How that they told you there should be mockers in the last time*". Other words of warning from the apostles can be read in I Cor. 10:11; I Tim. 4:1; II Tim. 3:1; I Peter 4:7; II Peter 3:2–3; and I John 2:18. These warnings were carefully crafted for those "perilous times" impacting that generation—the people who lived through the destruction of Jerusalem and its temple.

The warnings about mockers, scoffers, doctrines of devils, seducing spirits, traitors, and the covetous can apply to Christians of any age or time. But the following verses do not apply to just any time or any age. The words "the time is come," "the time is short," "these last times," and similar terminology would be entirely fitting if events were imminent. But if the end was thousands of years in the future, any reference to time would ultimately be meaningless.

> But this is that which was spoken by the prophet Joel; And it shall come to pass in the last days (Acts 2:16–17).
>
> And that, knowing the time, that now it is high time to awake out of sleep: for now is our salvation nearer than when we believed. The night is far spent, the day is at hand (Rom. 13:11–12).
>
> But this I say, brethren, the time is short (I Cor. 7:29).
>
> As that the day of Christ is at hand (II Thess. 2:2)
>
> Hath in these last days spoken unto us by his Son (Heb. 1:2)
>
> [B]ut now once in the end of the world hath he appeared to put away sin by the sacrifice of himself (Heb. 9:26).
>
> But was manifest in these last times for you (I Peter 1:20)
>
> But the end of all things is at hand: be ye therefore sober, and watch unto prayer (I Peter 4:7).
>
> Little children, it is the last time ... whereby we know that it is the last time (I John 2:18).
>
> Things which must shortly come to pass (Rev. 1:1)

The time is at hand (Rev. 1:3)

Seal not the sayings of the prophecy of this book, for the time is at hand (Rev. 22:10).

(See also I Cor. 10:11; Phil. 4:5; II Thess. 1:7; 3:5; I Tim. 6:14; II Tim. 3:1; Heb. 10:25; James 5:3; I Peter 1:5; 4:17; II Peter 3:3; Jude 18; Rev. 3:11; 22:6–12, 20)

As validated by Scripture, Christ did come quickly, within a few years after the verses above were written. If this had not occurred, the Lord's Word would have had no value! Which is why the writers saw fit to include these different adjectives of time-span into their narratives—for the time was indeed short. We do not read of Old Testament prophesies as having time-span adjectives attached to them when they are concerning far-away fulfillment.

Once again, if we were the ones these verses addressed, would we conclude they refer to a time in the distant future? Or would we recognize and teach—along with the New Testament Church and most people today—that, in each instance, the word "time" referenced something near, not something years away?

FOOTNOTES

1. Dr. Kenneth L. Gentry, Jr. *The Beast of Revelation* (Institute for Christian Economics, P. O. Box 8000, Tyler, Texas 75711, 1989) p. 82.
2. Gentry, *The Beast of Revelation*, p. 83.
3. Philip Schaff, *History of the Christian Church* (Grand Rapids, Michigan: WM. B. Eerdmans Publishing Company, 1978) Vol. 1, p. vi.
4. Gentry, *The Beast of Revelation*, p. 10.
5. Merrill F. Unger, *Unger's Bible Dictionary* (Chicago: Moody Press, 1966) p. 954.
6. *W. E. Vine, An Expository Dictionary of New Testament Words*, p. 315.
7. Adam Clarke, *Clarke's Commentary combined edition* (Nashville: Abingdon, volume v. Matthew-Revelation) p. 955.

CHAPTER TEN

THE RESURRECTION

———◆◆◆———

THE RESURRECTION

The sun was beginning to set on the small Virginia community. Nestled between the many splendid wooded hills and lush valleys was a small and crowded country chapel. There, the aged preacher, Reverend John, slowly made his way up to the front. He lovingly placed his well-worn Bible down on the pulpit. He bowed his head for a moment, then raised it again to face the congregation. His peaked face was stern and pale. As the preacher's eyes met those who had gathered to hear his parting words for the late (but not lamented) member of his flock, Reverend John extended his arm and pointed a gnarled finger at the casket at the front of the chapel. His voice was clear and strong as he began his message …

"Friends, I am so sorry, for I am sure when old Jock met Christ, his maker, our Lord said unto him: 'Depart from me, ye cursed, into everlasting punishment and eternal fire, prepared for the devil and his angels …' As we all know, our dear departed one was a wicked man, a real scoundrel and rascal. The moment the spirit of life left his miserable carcass, his soul set forth for the realms of suffering. Even as we gather here in less than fond remembrance, old Jock is in the lowest pits of hell, tormented by the devil and his legions of demons. He is forever consigned to these horrors, so justly deserved by his evil deeds perpetrated upon the undeserving during his overly long lifetime …"

I am relatively sure you have never heard that kind of preaching at any funeral you have been to. Nor are you likely to hear such an assessment of the recently departed, even if it were true.

I am confident what you typically heard was something along the lines of a song popular during the late 1950s, sung by the Browns and titled "The Three Bells." It was about the life and death of good old Jimmy Brown. The last stanza grieves Jimmy's passing:

> From the village hidden deep in the valley
> One rainy morning dark and gray
> A soul winged its way to heaven
> Jimmy Brown had passed away

Ah, yes, as soon as Jimmy Brown met his fate and breathed his last, his soul (at the moment of death, not at a future resurrection) found its way into the loving arms of Jesus. The lesson in this song, which is generally preached at funerals, is that at death the Christian soul departs for the realms of Glory, to be ever with the Lord. Since this is what most grieving Christians really want to hear, that is what most ministers are bound to preach.

But how could that be? Isn't there first to be a resurrection and judgment for the dead before reward or punishment is meted out? Did Jimmy Brown and your loved ones miraculously go to be with the Lord before the resurrection and judgment? Moreover, if they are with the Lord before the resurrection, why would there be a need for a future resurrection? If Christians die and go straight to heaven to be with our Lord, there would be no one to resurrect, good or bad, for all would already have found their way to that place of bliss—or, alternatively, divine punishment. In addition, doesn't the Scripture teach that at the rapture the dead in Christ shall rise first? If every Christian who dies goes directly into the arms of the Lord, there will be no dead in Christ to rise to meet Him in the air, for they are already with Him!

One pastor I spoke to about this believes your soul goes to heaven when you die, and you must await the Day of Judgment to be reunited with your body. Thus, after we die, we become conscious disembodied spirits, just floating around for ages until a body is prepared for us? However, if your soul is you, you would have already been resurrected (with a body or without a body), for you were with the Lord.

At death, there is no in-between place such as purgatory, paradise, or limbo, souls go to when they leave the land of the living. At death, there are only two options. First, the dead are "sleeping" in their grave until the resurrection when, if righteous, they are resurrected to eternal life. However, if wicked, they wait for their final judgment, which would be eternal damnation. Or, at death, the dead are immediately judged and sent to their final disposition, be it hell or heaven. There is no third alternative.

But what about the thief on the cross next to our Lord; didn't Christ tell him he would be in paradise? Christ ascended into heaven, and that is where the thief would be—with Christ, in heaven, which is paradise. *"And he said Jesus remember me when thou comest into the kingdom of thee. And he said to him. Truly thee I tell to-day with me thou wilt be in the paradise"* (Luke 23:43, Nestle's Greek Interlinear).

Now we are confronted by opposing conclusions. Conclusion number one holds that the resurrection of the just and unjust has already occurred. (This means when a person dies he is judged, then and there, at his time of death. If righteous, he goes to his place of reward with the Lord; if unrighteous, to his place of punishment.)

In contrast, conclusion number two contends all the dead are still in their graves, unaware of anything (soul sleep), and will not come forth until the resurrection. (There are those who fervently believe the dead are asleep until called forth by the Lord at the resurrection, which is expected to occur sometime in the future.)

If the dead have not yet been resurrected (did not Christ say, *"no man hath ascended up to heaven"*?) (John 3:13); and as Peter preached to the Jews on the day of Pentecost, *"For David is not ascended into the heavens"* (Acts 2:34–35), then who is currently in heaven?

If the resurrection has not yet happened, as some Scripture seems to teach, then it must follow no one is presently in heaven. And all dead Christians are still asleep in their graves as indicated by Jesus and Peter (John 3:13; Acts 2:34–35). But—and it is a big "but"—this was the very concept that was taught before the judgment fell upon the city of Jerusalem in AD 70!

These statements by Jesus and Peter may qualify as generalities, but they still apply to the age *before* judgment day in AD 70. There might be a few exceptions, but none powerful enough to invalidate the truths Jesus and Peter taught. For example, there was a man named Enoch, of whom the Scripture says: "*Enoch walked with God: and he was not; for God took him*" (Gen. 5:24). The writer of Hebrews puts it this way: "*By faith Enoch was translated that he should not see death; and was not found, because God had translated him*" (Heb.11:5). Enoch, it seems, did go to a place of bliss, without dying, but whether that place was what we call heaven is open to discussion as, according to Jesus: "*no man hath ascended up to heaven.*"

In another instance, the prophet Elijah was taken up into heaven. As Scripture says: "*And it came to pass, as they still went on, and talked, that behold, there appeared a chariot of fire, and horses of fire, and parted them both asunder; and Elijah went up by a whirlwind into heaven*" (II Kings 2:11). Notice a "whirlwind" conveyed Elijah to heaven, not the chariot and horses of fire. Now, is this the same heaven all Christians, the redeemed of the Lord, go to at their resurrection? It seems this point is open to debate.

An interesting side note about Elijah: thirteen years after his translation (which took place during the reign of Jehoshaphat), a letter ascribed to him was sent to Jehoram, Jehoshaphat's son. This letter pronounced judgment upon the kingdom of Judah because of their wickedness. It also foretold the judgment (in the form of a horrible sickness) that would befall Jehoram because of his abominations.

It appears Elijah had already been residing in heaven for thirteen years by the time the letter arrived. So how could he have written a letter to anyone? Various opinions have been put forth to explain this apparent disconnect.

Some believe Elijah may not have been translated into heaven in a literal sense, but was still in his body, hidden away by the Lord. Some believe, since he was a prophet, the Lord had told him in a vision what would transpire, and Elijah then wrote his prophetic letter before his translation, and gave it to a trusted ally who delivered it when the time was right. To date, because all this is pure conjecture, the mystery remains unsolved. But the possibility exists Elijah did not ascend to heaven and did, in fact, die.

There is no question Moses actually died (Deut. 34:5). However, Moses may be the only other person who ever made it to heaven before the resurrection. For it was Moses, along with Elijah the prophet who appeared at the mount of transfiguration. However, Matthew says this event, the transfiguration of Christ, was a vision witnessed only by the apostles Peter, James, and John. It was not necessarily an actual conversation between Jesus, Moses, and Elijah. *"And as they came down from the mountain, Jesus charged them, saying, Tell the vision to no man, until the Son of man be risen again from the dead"* (Matt. 17:9).

This line of reasoning would also support the argument of the apostle Paul when he said: *"And as it is appointed unto men once to die, but after this the judgment"* (Heb. 9:27). However, the Bible contains certain inconsistencies with some persons dying more than once. Surely, Paul knew about the dead man being buried by the Moabites. As he was being let down into the sepulcher of the prophet Elisha, his remains brushed against the bones of the prophet and came back to life (II Kings 13:21). Paul would also have known about the Shunammite's son (whom the prophet Elisha also brought back to life (II Kings 4:32–36), as well as Jairus's daughter and Lazarus, whom Christ raised from the dead. For Paul to prove his point in Hebrews 9:27, he did not need to list every exception to the standard notion of death and judgment; it would have confused his message. The truth of Paul's statement is still unassailable, despite the possibility of Moses, Enoch, and Elijah securing their heavenly reward before the resurrection.

So, for the sake of argument, let us allow those three are in heaven with the Lord right now. But for David and the rest of God's people, what Jesus and Peter taught is still true: *"No man has ascended into Heaven."* Unless, of course, the resurrection is an event that has occurred sometime in the past.

However, for those who contend souls shall continue to sleep until the resurrection, that line of reasoning reveals an inconsistency. The verses of Scripture that deal with resurrection and judgment all seem to place that event within the lifetimes of those to whom the Scripture was written. This provides yet more proof the resurrection must have happened in the past, and is not a future event.

That the resurrection of the just and unjust is eons in the past (around AD 70) is the position of this book. Now, when a person dies, they are resurrected at their moment of death—the righteous to their place in glory, and the wicked to their place of punishment. When Christians die, their souls, (like Jimmy Brown's), "wing" their way to heaven where they are ushered into the arms of Jesus, to be with Him forevermore.

What does the Scripture teach on the matter of resurrection? Is the resurrection of the dead still in our future, or has it already occurred in the past? Is the resurrection something that will happen at the end of time (assuming time ever ends)? Does it, perhaps, take place at the start of the millennium or maybe at the end? Does the resurrection of the dead, encompassing all the just and all the unjust, take place at the so-called second coming or at the Rapture? Does the resurrection of the righteous and wicked happen at the same time or is there a hiatus between their respective resurrections?

If the resurrection is still a future event, then all the dead–the just and unjust that ever lived (save for the three already mentioned)—are still asleep in their graves waiting to hear the voice of their creator.

And yet, didn't the authors of the New Testament, together with our Lord, teach the judgment and resurrection were to happen within their lifetime. It was precisely what the early Christians so ardently hoped for: the final judgment of those persecuting the Church, along with the resurrection of those who died in Christ.

The doctrine of the resurrection may not seem worthy of the time spent in study and thought. When a Christian dies, does it really matter if their resurrection happens at the moment of death, sometime in the near future, or at the end of time? The point is, whenever their resurrection occurs they will spend eternity with the Lord, regardless of the time it transpired.

What many still fail to comprehend is the New Testament Scriptures teach the resurrection and judgment were going to happen within the lifetimes of those who walked with our Lord. The New Testament authors wrote about the event with every expectation it would occur before their generation passed away.

The timing of the judgment and resurrection is all-important for the following reason: if these events are still to occur, then Jesus was wrong. For Christ said, "*This generation shall not pass till all these things be fulfilled*"—"all things" being the resurrection, Christ's presence (parousia), and the judgment (Matt. 24:34). The timing of the resurrection is tightly bound to the Olivet Discourse, which deals with the events surrounding the Great Tribulation the Jews experienced during the years AD 66–70.

This teaching of a "soon-coming" judgment and resurrection is securely communicated by the authors of the New Testament and is found throughout the epistles. One primary example is Paul writing to the Thessalonians about the Lord emerging from heaven and bringing judgment upon the wicked:

> *And to you who are troubled rest with us, when the Lord Jesus shall be revealed from heaven with his mighty angels, In flaming fire taking vengeance on them that know not God, and that obey not the gospel of our Lord Jesus Christ: Who shall be punished with everlasting destruction from the presence of the Lord, and from the glory of his power; When he shall come to be glorified in his saints, and to be admired in all them that believe* (II Thess. 1:7–10).

In this portion of Scripture, Paul appears to inform the Church at Thessalonica they would witness God's day of vengeance upon the ungodly. Paul's words were a message of comfort and hope to those Christians going through troubling times. His was a fervent desire that the persecution perpetrated by the Jews would soon be ended by the coming judgment of Christ in their generation.

This hope of a "soon-coming" is also brought forth in the first epistle of Paul to the Thessalonians. Paul included himself in that group of believers who might possibly survive that day of judgment soon to be wrought upon the wicked Jews. Notice what Paul says, *"we* which are alive" not, "when *they* who are alive" thus indicating Paul expected this Resurrection to take place within his and his Thessalonian audience's lifetime:

> *For if we believe that Jesus died and rose again, even so them also which sleep in Jesus will God bring with him. For this we say unto you by the word of the Lord, that we which are alive and remain unto the coming of the Lord shall not prevent them which are asleep. For the Lord himself shall descend from heaven with a shout, with the voice of the archangel, and with the trump of God: and the dead in Christ shall rise first: Then we which are alive and remain shall be caught up together with them in the clouds, to meet the Lord in the air: and so shall we ever be with the Lord* (I Thess. 4:13–17).

In our discussion of resurrection and judgment, we have not addressed the popular notion, espoused and championed by so many during the last hundred years or so—the Rapture. We will, like Adam Clarke, continue to assert Paul's teachings that the resurrection and judgment were not just for Christians, but for all those who have ever lived:

> 4. When all the dead in Christ are raised, then the trumpet shall sound, as the signal for them all to flock together to the throne of Christ ... 8. We may suppose that the judgment will now be set, and the books opened, and the dead judged out of the things written in those books. 9. The eternal states of quick and dead being thus determined ...[1]

There was going to be just one resurrection and one judgment, not a series of resurrections and judgments. Further, Clarke dismisses the notion these verses promised an escape (by rapture) from the earth before the time of judgment.

However, Clarke suggests a divergent opinion in declaring Paul did not think the resurrection was near:

> "We which are alive, and remain." By the pronoun *we* the apostle does not intend *himself,* and the *Thessalonians* to whom he was then writing ... But it is impossible that a man, under so direct an influence of the Holy Spirit, should be permitted to make such a mistake; nay, no man in the exercise of his sober reason could have formed such an opinion, there was nothing to warrant the supposition; no premises from which it could be fairly deduced ...[2] (emphasis his)

I could accept what Clarke says concerning Paul's use of the word *we* if this was the only time Paul stated the resurrection was imminent and he might take part in it.

Let us deviate from Adam Clarke and many of our Christian fathers on this matter. Though we agree there was to be just one future resurrection of all the dead, we disagree on the timing of that event and what occurred after.

Paul's epistles to the Thessalonians were written around AD 54. A few years later (AD 60), Paul was in Jerusalem, in the temple, with four companions. Jews in the area had noticed Paul earlier that day accompanied by a cadre of Greeks and accused him of "polluting" the temple. An uproar ensued as Paul was about to be killed. However, tidings came to Claudius Lysias, the chief Roman captain, who rescued Paul—for the captain thought Paul might be a Roman. However, compelled to face the authorities, Paul was sent to Felix the governor, who would be overseeing the case. A few days later, standing before the governor, Paul made his defense against Ananias the high priest, the elders, and the Sanhedrin's "orator" Tertullus.

Rebutting the charges brought against him by the reprobate Jewish leaders, and in answer to Governor Felix, Paul still held to the teaching he gave a few years earlier to the congregation at Thessalonica:

> *But this I confess unto thee that after the way which they call heresy, so worship I the God of my fathers, believing all things which are written in the law and in the prophets: And have hope toward God, which they themselves also allow, that there shall be a resurrection of the dead, both of the just and unjust* (Acts 24:14–15).

Paul spoke of just one resurrection that would unfold within his generation. He also made an observation that often translates loosely from the original Greek, which Nestle's Greek text expresses as:

> *Hope having toward–God, which also (them)selves these expect,* **a resurrection to be about to be** *both of just and of unjust* (Acts 24:15). (emphasis added)

Paul knew the resurrection had not occurred but would transpire soon; he stated this in II Timothy 2:17–18. Paul believed in one future resurrection; but more than that, he was certain it would happen not in a century or a millennium, but within his lifetime.

Paul wrote to Titus sometime during AD 65 and told him how eagerly he anticipated the Parousia of Christ: "*Looking for that blessed hope, and the glorious appearing of the great God and our Savior Jesus Christ*" (Titus 2:13).

In his writings to Timothy, Paul tied the judgment, Christ's' kingdom, and the resurrection together as a single event: "*I charge thee therefore before God, and the Lord Jesus Christ, who shall judge the quick and the dead at his appearing and his kingdom*" (II Tim. 4:1).

Jude 14–15 states: "*And Enoch also, the seventh from Adam, prophesied of these, saying, Behold the Lord cometh with ten thousands of his saints* [angels - Thayer's and Bullinger's lexicons], *To execute judgment upon all.*" This verse seems to imply one all-encompassing judgment to include the just and unjust.

Jesus told the Jews that those who believed in Him would be raised up on the day of judgment, which was the last day. He repeated this three times in John, Chapter 6: "*And this is the will of him that sent me, that every one which seeth the Son, and believeth on him, may have everlasting life: and I will raise him up at the last day ... No man can come to me, except the Father which hath sent me draw him: and I will raise him up at the last day ... and I will raise him up at the last day*" (John 6:40, 44, 54). Those three words—"the last day"—certainly point to the final judgment as a singular event.

Peter, writing to unnamed Christians, states he and they should be looking for that great judgment day, when the Lord will come as a thief in the night: "*Looking for and hasting unto the coming ... Nevertheless we, according to his promise, look for ... Wherefore, beloved, seeing that ye look for these things, be diligent that ye may be found of him in peace and without spot and blameless*" (II Peter 3:12–14). Anyone who believes these verses refer to a future (from our perspective) judgment in which everything will be irrevocably destroyed overlooks the fact that Peter pointedly told his (then) readers to "*look for*" that day, as he certainly believed it was near—or, as Paul taught, it was "*about to be.*"

Let us look at one more example of Scripture, wherein Christ teaches about the resurrection:

> *Verily, verily, I say unto you, The hour is coming and now is, when the dead shall hear the voice of the Son of God; and they that hear shall live ... Marvel not at this; for the hour is coming, in the which all that are in the graves shall hear his voice, and shall come forth; they that have done good unto the resurrection of life; and*

they that have done evil, unto the resurrection of damnation (John 5:25–29).

Here Christ clarifies important facts. First, there was to be *one* resurrection—the only event of its kind in history—of all the just and unjust at once.

Secondly, Christ enunciates that this day of judgment and resurrection was drawing close. Twice He warns, *"The hour is coming and now is ..."* Verse 25 in Nestle's Greek New Testament reads:

> *Truly truly I say to you Comes an hour and now is when the dead will hear the voice of the Son of God and the ones hearing will live.*

The New International Version translates that verse:

> *I tell you the truth, a time is coming and has now come when the dead will hear the voice of the Son of God and those who hear will live.*

In The New English Bible, the verse reads:

> *In truth, in very truth I tell you, a time is coming, indeed it is already here, when the dead shall hear the voice of the Son of God, and all who hear shall come to life.*

By any interpretation, the time for God's judgment and resurrection of the dead was drawing near. Since Paul received his teaching as a revelation directly from the Lord (Galatians 1:12), it is no wonder he taught a judgment and a resurrection would happen in his generation.

Some object to this line of reasoning, arguing there is no physical evidence of a resurrection taking place in AD 70 or within that generation. R.C. Sproul states:

> To maintain that these events [the Olivet teaching] were indeed fulfilled in the first century, one must interpret the relevant passages in a way that makes early fulfillment possible. The most severe obstacle [to that] is the absence of any historical record

that the rapture of the living and the resurrection of the dead occurred.[3]

Though there may be no physical evidence the resurrection of the just and unjust took place, we do have good, solid testimony it did: the words of the apostles stating it was to be soon; and the inarguable very words of our Lord Himself that it was going to happen before that generation had passed away. What better confirmation could one ask for?

We have one more piece of irrefutable evidence the resurrection and judgment did in fact take place before the apostles' generation passed away. This evidence comes from an unlikely source—Dispensational believers themselves. John F. MacArthur, in his book *The Second Coming*, states:

> Some argue that Christ's coming could not possibly have been imminent for the early church, given the obvious fact that 2,000 years later He has still not returned. Skeptics often ridicule Christianity or challenge the inerrancy of Scripture on that very ground. *After all, the verses cited at the beginning of this chapter do prove* that James, Peter, John, Paul, and the writer of Hebrews *all believed Christ's return was very near*—"at the door" (James 5:9); "at hand" (Phil. 4:5; I Pet. 4:7); "approaching" (Heb. 10:25); "coming quickly" (Rev. 3:11; 22:7) ...[4] (emphasis added)

I agree with MacArthur; the verses he cited effectively prove the parousia of Christ was near and about to happen. And there are scores of other verses that unquestioningly teach the parousia of Christ was to be within that generation. That is about the only truth MacArthur's book brings forth. The day of judgment was about to happen and did happen when Christ and the apostles said it would, during that generation.

Sadly, however, the rest of MacArthur's book seeks to deny that truth! In various attempts to explain it away, he states, "I suppose it is *also* possible that Christ could delay His coming another 2,000 years or longer ... He could still delay His coming ... the real reason for the Lord's delay ... the long delay before Christ's appearing ... "[5]

MacArthur also asks this question: "Could the apostles have been in error about the timing?" and continues with "This is precisely what some skeptics claim."[6] But that is precisely what MacArthur claims—that Christ and the apostles were wrong about the timing! Doesn't that make MacArthur just another skeptic? As Scripture shows, all the apostles clearly state the day of judgment was near. Christ said it would happen in His generation, but MacArthur says it hasn't happened yet. Who are we to believe?

In answer to MacArthur's question about the apostles' timing, the answer must be, NO, they were not wrong! The apostles were writing Scripture, and all Scripture is inspired. There are no errors. *"All scripture is given by inspiration of God, and is profitable for doctrine, for reproof, for correction, for instruction in righteousness"* (II Tim. 3:16). Jesus also said: *"Howbeit when he, the Spirit of truth is come, he will guide you into all truth"* (John 16:13). No, the Spirit-guided apostles were not wrong!

I have cataloged a list of over seventy verses that, as MacArthur states, "[D]o prove that Christ's return was at the door."

The question that needs to be asked again is why Paul and all the other authors of Scripture believed so thoroughly that Christ's parousia was soon to occur? Because Christ Himself clearly taught His parousia would be made manifest before that generation passed away!

Just as a Christian has faith that, in the words of Jesus, he will be resurrected someday, we need to have faith in Jesus' statement as to when the resurrection and judgment were going to happen. What evidence do we have that all believers will be resurrected to be with the Lord? Only this— our faith in the words of Christ and His faithfulness. What evidence do we have the parousia of Christ did happen within the promised generation? The confirmation of history; and the sacrosanct words of Christ and His apostles.

FOOTNOTES

1. Adam Clarke, *Clarke's Commentary, combined edition* (Nashville: Abingdon) Matthew—Revelation vol. III, p. 551.
2. Clarke, *Clarke's Commentary*, p. 550.
3. R. C. Sproul, *The Last Days According to Jesus*, Baker Books, 1998, p. 161.
4. John F. MacArthur, *The Second Coming* (Crossway Books, A Division of Good News Publishers, 1300 Crescent Street, Wheaton, Illinois 60187, 1999) p. 56.
5. MacArthur, *The Second Coming*, p. 57–58.
6. MacArthur, *The Second Coming*, p. 57–58.

CHAPTER ELEVEN

IT'S SIMPLY UNBELIEF

TWO EXCUSES

There are two disastrous reasons why those who hold Dispensational beliefs reject positive, kingdom-building postmillennialism and Preterism. The first is they watch too much TV—and, much like having cheese just before you go to bed, it gives you terrible nightmares! Fortunately, most cheese-induced nightmares last only until you wake up. Unfortunately, the nightmare of Dispensationalism does not go away until you get it completely out of your system—which is the fundamental purpose of this book!

The second disastrous reason for hanging on to the failed doctrine of Dispensationalism is a faulty view of end times prophecy—which is like looking through a telescope without realizing it is a microscope. When Dispensationalists peer into the Book of Revelation, they think they are getting a 2,000-year-old prophetic view into the far distant future where they now live. But in reality, they are seeing, in incredible detail, the amazing events, struggles, and triumphs of the Gospel and the early Church in the years running up to AD 70. Wow!

First, let us deal with our nightmarish overload of current events. As Dispensationalists view their world unfolding, all they see is a relentless conveyor-belt of terrifying and cataclysmic events happening at a bewildering pace. Yet they pay little or no attention to world-changing historical events—such as the conversion of the pagan Roman Empire to a largely Christian society rooted in a Christian worldview. For the sake of enlightenment, some historical perspective is in order.

By the end of the Roman imperial persecutions (AD 313), Christians numbered about half the population of the Roman Empire. This Christian society had successfully abolished the myriad barbaric spectacles (e.g., gladiatorial fights) that took place in the colosseum, as well as slavery, the killing of unwanted children, and crucifixion as a form of execution. It had also secured liberty for those who professed the Christian faith and allowed others to follow whatever religion they chose. In D. James Kennedy's book, *What if Jesus Had Never Been Born?* he writes:

> Today, in the Colosseum, in the very amphitheatre where tens of thousands of Christians were sacrificed for sport, there stands a large cross—a silent testimony to the victory of Christianity over the brutality of the ancient world.

> Eminent historian Will Durant, who has written a definitive, multi-volume survey of world history, comments on the conquering of the cross over the Roman Empire:

> There is no greater drama in human record than the sight of a few Christians, scorned or oppressed by a succession of emperors, bearing all trials with a fiery tenacity, multiplying quietly, building order while their enemies generated chaos, fighting the sword with the word, brutality with hope, and at last defeating the strongest state that history has ever known. Caesar and Christ had met in the arena, and Christ had won.[1]

The civilizing advances of the Reformation more than a millennium later also come to mind, along with wondrous developments in the arts and sciences brought into human experience by the Bible-based Christian faith. These monumental accomplishments of countless Christian men and women barely seem to cross the minds of pretribulation believers. They are too focused on the horrors of the present to recognize either past triumphs or future kingdom possibilities.

George Whitefield (1714–1770) preached more than eighteen thousand sermons between 1736 and 1770 to crowds that frequently numbered 30,000 and more. During his lifetime, his audiences numbered in the millions. It is estimated up to 80 percent of those living in the New World personally heard him speak. His influence was also greatly felt through the many printed versions of his sermons, newspapers, letters, magazines, and journals. His remarkable ministry was divided between Great Britain, Northern Europe, and the American colonies.

The series of revivals associated with his preaching in the colonies during 1740 have become known as the "Great Awakening." His staunch Calvinist theology, ethical habits, and godly principles helped shape the Christian foundations of the American Revolution—and contributed mightily to the birth of liberty that blazed so brightly in our new nation.

Oh, how the Gospel has spread! Oh, how the world has been blessed by America, which has sent out more missionaries to the rest of the world than any other nation (so far!). Consider how God's kingdom has grown and what glorious change has come to this world because of godly, Bible-believing, optimistic, Christian men like George Whitefield.

Thanks in large part to missionaries such as John Gibson Paton (whom we will discuss shortly), cannibals no longer inhabit the South Pacific. Other society-changing missionaries include William Carey, English missionary to India; Mary Slessor, Scottish missionary to Calabar (Nigeria); and David Livingstone, legendary missionary and explorer of Africa. All were instrumental in the advancement and enlightenment of millions through faith in Christ Jesus our Lord. Once again, thoughts of these great strides brought about by Christianity—of whole nations being converted—seldom cross the minds of Dispensationalists. Such historic triumphs have little or no place in their thinking. However, if they did, it might challenge their pessimistic, doom-and-destruction mindset that sees no point whatsoever in striving to build Christ's kingdom here on earth … because the Antichrist is about to take charge!

The *Rapture Ready* website illustrates the typical mindset of those who are locked into a belief in the pretribulation rapture. In an article titled "Preterism! I Can't Believe It," Todd Strandberg writes:

> I just cannot understand how anyone can follow a preterist line of thinking in light of current world events.[2]

On the same website, Terry James's article "The Rapture—Answering the Critics," echoes the same incredulity:

> [T]he world isn't getting better and better as the "kingdom-now" people believe (that the Church will make the world better until Christ can return to set up His throne) ... Which do we see happening today? The world getting better and better—or are things looking worse and worse for Planet Earth? Read the daily headlines, or watch the hourly news, and you will have your answer.[3]

The seemingly unbroken chain of diabolical world events has been used by Dispensationalists as their mainstay argument against the victorious outlook of Preterism for the last 100 years. What a waste of a century! The Church could and should have vigorously been advancing Gospel influence for the last four generations. Alas, it has not; and now look where we are!

However, when we examine history with a "God's-eye-view," a very different picture emerges. Slavery, cannibalism, sati, (immolation of widows), human sacrifice, and many other social, political, and moral depredations have been eradicated. (Sadly, some of these horrors are creeping back to plague society, filling the void left by rapture-ready Christians.) Against all odds, the Christian Gospel has enabled countless great and marvelous changes, making our world a much better place. Everything cannot always be walk-on-the-water or Red Sea moments. Usually, it is just the baby-steps making the most difference in an impatient world (of usually believers).

It is also true many of these hard-won gains have been squandered, surrendered, and frittered away with barely a fight. During the last few decades, godless forces have been offered an open door by those professing a pessimistic eschatology. The preaching of assured defeat for the Church has disheartened evangelical Christians and largely quenched the burning passion to advance God's kingdom, which glowed so brightly in ages past. This entrenched pessimism has convinced Christian soldiers to lay down their arms and forfeit their gains to the enemy. Nevertheless, all surrendered territory can be recaptured, but not without a Biblical vision of victory.

LITERALISM RUN AMOK

The second bulwark of the defeatist worldview so tightly held by Dispensationalists is their belief certain prophecies in the Book of Revelation and in Jesus' Olivet Discourse have yet to occur. In "Preterism! I Can't Believe It," Strandberg examines this line of reasoning:

> The heart of this error is based on Jesus's statement that "this generation shall not pass, till all things be fulfilled" (Mat 24:34). It seems easy enough to claim Jesus was speaking about a first-century generation; however, logic ends there when one contemplates the fulfillment of all Bible prophecy.
>
> In order to make 70 AD the magic year, we would have to delete dozens of prophecies that were never fulfilled. When was the Gospel preached to all the nations? When was the Mark of the Beast implemented? What about China's 200-million-man army? When did 100-pound hailstones fall from the sky? And what date was it when the Euphrates River dried up?
>
> The questions are endless. Why did we have the rebirth of Israel? If Jerusalem was forever removed from being the burdensome stone, why has it now returned to that status? When did all the Jews shout, "Blessed is he who comes in the name of the Lord," as Jesus said they would?[4]

Hal Lindsey, in his book *Satan Is Alive and Well on Planet Earth*, reinforces the Dispensational view:

> We are living in a time when history is racing toward a climax ... In the Orient there is a great power that can field an army of 200,000,000 men-Red China.[5]

Irvin Baxter's EndTime Ministries promotes the same doomsday scenario in their tract "Why I Believe Jesus Will Return in My Lifetime":

> **China War—200 million man army...** the prophecy says that an army of 200 million will trigger a war that will kill one-third of the world's population—two billion people....[6]

Occasionally, Dispensationalists pose valid questions that deserve a Scriptural response. Some of these questions (such as, "When was the Gospel preached to all the nations?") have already been considered. Chapter 8 effectively demonstrates Scripture's remarkable capacity for providing the appropriate answer.

The problem confronting Strandberg and his fellow Dispensationalists is they seek to derive their truths through a literal interpretation of symbolic language, especially in regard to the Book of Revelation. In the following pages, we will explore the absurdity of this approach.

From start to finish, the Revelation is filled with ambiguous, misty, metaphorical language, though difficult for modern readers to comprehend, was readily understood by our 1st century brethren, for whom the book was primarily written. Revelation contains a heady mix of symbols, imagery, hyperbole, and prophetic language that must be handled soberly and with care. It should never be construed carelessly or blithely interpreted through the lens of a nightly news report.

The revelation as given to John by Jesus must be understood as a symbolic pronouncement based upon images and verbiage found in the Old Testament. Using current world events to decode the Book of Revelation is a pointless exercise leading nowhere.

Before we can answer the Dispensationalists' questions, we will need to pose a few questions of our own. What do they believe the Mark of the Beast is? Do they really believe 100-pound hailstones will fall from the sky? Will the weight be exactly100 pounds or is there a margin of error?

The Bible does not mention by name the nation of China. So why do Strandberg, Baxter, and Lindsey insist Scripture pinpoints China as the sole nation with a 200-million-man army?

According to GlobalFirepower.com, the Chinese People's Liberation Army currently has a total of 3,712,500 personnel available for combat. This includes its active, reserve, and paramilitary troops. Using these figures, it appears China falls radically short (about 196 million) of the 200 million required to wage the apocalyptic world war projected by the Dispensationalists. How could China possibly reach this staggering number of combat ready soldiers? How long would it take to recruit, train, equip, and deploy them? The Dispensationalists know! They just won't tell us.

According to the International Institute for Strategic Studies, as of 2014 there were approximately 65 million troops worldwide (regular, reserve, and paramilitary) comprising 171 countries. So, even with the combined number of troops from this entire earth, from every nation and state, we would still come up way short of the 200 million China will need to destroy the world. Anyone seen 200 million troops camped anywhere?

It must cost an enormous amount of money and resources to house, equip, train, and feed the many millions of troops already in the world today. How could one nation, or even a union of nations, possibly afford to keep an army the size of the one China is supposed to field in the very near future? God can do amazing things; however, unless it suits Gods' purposes and plans, He is not on the side of this decidedly evil army.

This is only the start of the literalist problem. The 200-million-man army the Scripture mentions is an army of *horsemen*—not foot soldiers, sailors, or jet fighter pilots. *"And the number of the army of the horsemen were two hundred thousand thousand"* (Rev. 9:16). Whoops! Even if China, by some miracle, were able to field an army of 200 million men, much less horsemen, that would only complete half of the prophecy. If Rev. 9:16 were taken literally, logic would dictate 200 million horsemen would need 200 million horses. Does China have 200 million horses today? Are there 200 million horses in the entire world? According to the website horsetalk. co.nz, as of September 12, 2007, the world horse population was estimated at 58 million. Oh dear! According to a 2006 report, compiled by the Food and Agriculture Organization of the United Nations (FAOSTAT), there were 58,372,106 horses in the world. Of that number, China had a mere 7,402,450.

That is not all. The horses China's soldiery would be riding are clearly supernatural, possessing heads like lions, belching brimstone and fire, and "tails like unto serpents." These unearthly beasts are certainly not in the realm of normal horses, but must be some kind of Chinese genetic experiment involving horses, lions, reptiles, and napalm that cannot help but go awry.

Further enriching the imagery, Scripture states, *"By these three was the third part of men killed, by the fire, and by the smoke, and by the brimstone, which issued out of their mouths"* (Rev. 9:18). Those men doomed to die (would that include women?) would not be killed by nuclear bombs, ships, poison gas, airplanes, helicopters, tanks, guns, swords, or any other manmade instrument of war; but by the "smoke, fire, and brimstone" that issued out of those horses' mouths. Evidently, the horsemen would not be equipped with the most recent body armor made of Kevlar or some other modern composite, but would rely on fanciful breastplates made of fire, jacinth, and yet more brimstone. Sounds expensive; and blisteringly hot! As a bonus, the horsemen that rode upon these mutant beasts would not even need any kind of weapon. They would just point their steeds in the right direction and the horses would do all the killing.

How could China (or any nation) handle the logistics of keeping these 200 million horses ready for military service? What country, or countries, could even stable that many animals? Think of all the pasture land that would be required, not to mention the land needed to grow the hay and oats to feed that number of horses. And what would they do with the enormous mountain of waste produced by this multitude of equines? I would sure hate to live downwind of that encampment.

Interpreting Scripture *literally* is the hallmark of Dispensationalism. Do Dispensationalists like Todd Strandberg actually take these verses from Revelation literally? Presumably they do! Since the Book of Revelation is full of symbolism, how do they know for sure John the Revelator meant a literal drying-up of the Euphrates River? Why would the Euphrates even need to dry up for a modern army to cross it? Military cargo aircraft, such as Lockheed Martin's C-5M Super Galaxy, can be used to transport virtually any type of equipment load at speeds exceeding 500 miles per hour. [7]

In addition, temporary bridges can be assembled with amazing rapidity and placed across rivers to allow military vehicles to pass over:

> Bailey bridges, named after their inventor, Donald Bailey, have been in use since the Second World War, when their light, modular design enabled soldiers to piece together bridges in a matter of hours without the need for cranes or specialist equipment. They are designed to hold the weight of a tank, and were credited by Field Marshal Bernard Montgomery as being one of the most important inventions of the war. [8]

Temporary bridges have been vastly improved since WWII, so modern armies can cross any river "lickety-split," dried-up or not.

Now let us examine another issue deemed so pivotal by Dispensationalists: the numeric 666—the Mark of the Beast. Just a short search on the Internet reveals a multitude of candidates for the Mark of the Beast. What would compel Strandberg and his fellow literalists to believe their explanation of the Mark—their one among the many—is the correct one?

Some scholars contend the number 666 is code for the Roman Emperor Nero. Others point to Emperor Domitian. Many Protestants and Reformers have equated the "beast" of Revelation with the papacy. One pope, Innocent III, went so far as to identify Muhammad as the beast of Revelation. Some of the preterist persuasion, such as Paul Spilsbury[9] and New Testament scholar Craig C. Hill,[10] identify the stamped image of the emperor's head on every coin of the Roman Empire as the Mark of the Beast.

Craig R. Koester offers a similar view:

> As sales were made, people used coins that bore the images of Rome's gods and emperors. Thus, each transaction that used such coins was a reminder that people were advancing themselves economically by relying on political powers that did not recognize the true God.[11]

The Seventh-day Adventists believe the Sunday Sabbath was imposed by the papacy and is a precursor to the future Mark of the Beast. They believe the Mark will accompany the eventual imposition of a universal, strictly enforced Sunday worship.

Those Dispensationalists who truly believe theirs is the only true interpretation of the Book of Revelation and the Olivet Discourse should at least take a peek at the four-volume set of books written by LeRoy Edwin Froom. In his scholarly and widely applauded work *The Prophetic Faith of Our Fathers,* Froom has painstakingly documented the prophetic interpretation of the Scriptures throughout the history of the Church. This valuable exegesis catalogs well-known beliefs along with lesser-known interpretations of prophecy and Biblical commentary. Through the years, it appears each new generation had its own take on the meaning of prophecy, which was inevitably replaced by a fresh crop of date setters with new light and more revelations to astound us.

Most Dispensational assertions (ludicrous as they are) would certainly not have been in vogue a century ago, two hundred years ago, or at any other time in Church history. And a hundred years from now, every bogus Dispensational interpretation of Scripture will have been quietly forgotten and aptly consigned to the dustbin of failed prophetic history. Nevertheless, ever eager to perpetuate the mythology they have so carefully crafted, subsequent generations of Dispensationalists will continue their longstanding tradition of false prophecy and false witness as they fervently attempt to justify their wrongheaded beliefs to anyone who will listen. The old proverb certainly applies to Strandberg, Lindsey, Camping, and all the other "last days" seers: "the only thing we learn from history is we don't learn from history."

MESSAGE WITH AN EXPIRATION DATE

For those who work for Irvin Baxter's ENDTIME MINISTRIES, there is no future beyond the next few years. Baxter's ministry joins with John Hagee and their fellow members of the elite club of Christian soothsayers who "know the times." They sincerely believe they are the only ones who have a special inside scoop on the timing of singular events they guarantee will occur within our generation.

On one of his videos Baxter states:

> Our message here at ENDTIME is that the "end time" is now. Jesus spoke of a generation that would be on the earth at the time of His second coming. We are that generation. One reason why all the people work here so diligently, and that is because we absolutely are sure from the prophecies in the Bible that the end time is now. We're not telling you that the end time is coming, we're telling you the end time is here right now, you're in it, I am in it. We are the generation that will see the second coming of Jesus Christ back to this earth as King of Kings and Lord of Lords.[12]

John Hagee's sermon titled, "10 Signs we are the Final Generation" echoes the same message:

> The 10 Bible signs that God has given to the generation that would be called the terminal generation, that is our generation … the third prophetic major sign that we're the terminal generation is the rebirth of Israel, on May the fifteenth 1948, that's the greatest miracle of the 20th century … we are looking at the soon appearing of Jesus Christ the Son of God …we are the terminal generation that's going to see the coming of the Lord Jesus Christ.… [13]

As Baxter clearly states, his organization exists for one purpose and one purpose only: to proclaim an "end time" message for this generation. His message has no validity for those generations who came before or for those who shall come. Never again, after this generation passes away, will Baxter's message be of any value. The message of the Gospel is timeless; it will never expire. But Baxter's organization does have an expiration date. After his message expires (when this generation ends), Baxter's ministry will be rendered moot, with no reason to continue.

Baxter says he is preaching the Gospel to the whole world. However, the Gospel is not a limited onetime offer given to just one generation. Its message spans the everlasting ages. It has been valid for all nations throughout all generations; and long after this generation has passed away, it will still be as valid as ever—forever. If Baxter was broadcasting just the Gospel, his message would continue to be relevant to our generation and all those to follow. But Baxter's ministry is presenting a message of strictly limited duration, after which it will have no validity whatsoever.

Baxter's premise could not have been preached a hundred years ago, two hundred years ago, or a thousand years ago. Nor can his message be preached fifty years from now, a hundred years from now, or a thousand years from now. Because according to Baxter, all those generations which came before us, and all those generations which shall arise after us, are not the terminal generation of which Baxter believes he is a member—the generation that shall see the second coming of Christ.

It cannot be clearer the ENDTIME MINISTRIES' message is just for a limited amount of time. That is right folks; it is indeed a onetime offer.

There is only a small window of opportunity to get in on their deal (a free flight to heaven via the Rapture). As Baxter declares, no other generation except this one could confirm the timing was right. No other generation except ours is permitted to witness the so-called "signs" of the second coming of Jesus. After their offer is discontinued and this generation has passed away, Baxter's deal will be withdrawn—never to be repeated. Baxter's message is akin to setting an hourglass. Once the sand runs out, his "end times" generation will be over, and another false prophet will be revealed.

Like the Gospel, the message of the preterist and postmillennialist is timeless. It has been valid since the Cross and Resurrection and will be valid for time immemorial. Yes, the postmillennialist does believe sometime in the distant future there is to be an end. But there is a time coming—no man knows when—where the sun shall never rise upon a nation, tribe, people, or kingdom that is not a disciple of the King of Kings and Lord of Lords, King Jesus!

CONQUERING WITH UNITY

Christian reformer Bojidar Marinov famously said, "Ideas have consequences, and bad ideas have bad consequences. And those who can tell bad ideas for what they are can take advantage of them."[14] History has provided the opportunity to clearly see the serial failures of Dispensationalism, which, at its core, is an anti-Biblical belief system that can never succeed. Regarding Dispensationalism, Bojidar Marinov is right. It has proven to be a bad idea with notably bad consequences.

Long before Dispensationalism emerged, a beastly, evil authority— the Holy See—held sway over many kingdoms and peoples. Countless bad consequences flowed from this unchecked and unrestrained tyranny. Henry H. Halley described this epoch well in his celebrated *Halley's Bible Handbook*. In the section titled "Summit of Papal Power" he writes:

Innocent III (1198–1216). Most Powerful of all the Popes. Claimed to be "Vicar of Christ," "Vicar of God," "Supreme Sovereign over the Church and the World." Claimed the right to

Depose Kings and Princes; and that "All things on earth and in heaven and in hell are subject to the Vicar of Christ."

He brought the Church into Supreme Control of the State. The kings of Germany, France, and practically all the Monarchs of Europe obeyed his will. He even brought the Byzantine Empire under his control. Never in history has any one man exerted more power.

He ordered two Crusades. Decreed Transubstantiation. Confirmed Auricular Confession. Declared that Peter's successor "can never in any way depart from the Catholic faith." Papal Infallibility. Condemned the Magna Carta. Forbade the reading of the Bible in vernacular. Ordered the extermination of Heretics. Instituted the Inquisition. Ordered Massacre of the Albigenses. More blood was shed under his direction, and that of his immediate successors, than in any other period of Church History, except in the Papacy's effort to crush the Reformation in the 16th and 17th centuries. One would think Nero, the beast, had come to life in the Name of the Lamb.[15]

Cotton Mather (1663–1728) was an American Congregational minister, author, and the most celebrated of all New England Puritans. In his book *Fall of Babylon*, he asks: "Is the Pope of Rome to be looked upon as The Antichrist, whose coming and reigning was foretold in the ancient oracles?" To which he answers: "The oracles of God foretold the rising of an Antichrist in the Christian church; and in the Pope of Rome, all the characteristics of that Antichrist are so marvelously answered that if any who read the scriptures do not see it, there is a marvelous blindness upon them."[16]

Even before the flames of reformation began to burn, there was a unifying theme among the faithful. And when heated arguments erupted among learned and notable men, that unity solidified their resolve and gave them the courage to face the beast that had control over much of Europe. What was the indestructible foundation those shining pillars of faith stood upon? With crystalline logic and voluminous proof, Froom concludes:

It therefore follows, from the evidence adduced, that for

the first two centuries of American history the Papacy, as the prophesied Antichrist, was the universally reiterated concept among Protestants.[17]

Froom also shows even in the centuries before the founding of America, many devout Christians believed the Scriptures pointed to the papacy as the prophesied agent of evil:

> In the centuries just preceding the Reformation an ever-increasing number of pious persons began openly to express the conviction that the dire prophecies concerning the Antichrist were even then in the process of fulfillment. They felt that the "falling away' had already taken place. They declared that Antichrist was already seated in the churchly temple of God, clothed in scarlet and purple. Numerous individuals of influence spoke mysterious things about the seven-hilled Rome, and solemnly pointed the finger at the Roman church as the predicted Man of Sin, which had now become a historical reality.[18]

In summing up his evidence, Froom states:

> We have seen the remarkable unanimity of belief of Reformation readers in every land that the Antichrist of prophecy is not to be a single individual – some sort of superman–who will wrack and well-nigh wreck the world just before the second advent of Christ. Instead, they found that it was a vast system of apostasy, or rather, an imposing counterfeit of truth which had developed within the jurisdiction of that divinely appointed custodian of truth, the Christian Church. Although ostensibly proclaiming the principles of Christianity, it denied the very essence of Christian faith–the apostolic spirit of truth, freedom, tolerance, and love–and perverted the very doctrine of Christ. Of this they were profoundly persuaded. This Antichristian system, which had developed within the inner precincts of the church, the Protestants declared to be the Papacy of history, in fulfillment of

prophecy. Such was the unanimous witness of the Reformation. That was the basic emphasis of the Reformation century.[19]

The Reformers' shared belief in the Scriptures, coupled with courageous action against an entrenched and implacable foe, became an unbeatable, unstoppable juggernaut that redefined the faith and greatly advanced the kingdom of Christ.

As we have already established, what many modern Christians believe concerning the Antichrist cannot be found in Scripture (see chapter 9). As Froom continues to show, many of our forefathers had a different prophetic view of the Antichrist than is currently popular among Dispensationalists:

> [The] "Reformation rests on a twofold testimony. (1) The just shall live by faith (not works of Romanism); and (2) the Papacy is the Antichrist of scripture."
>
> Luther discovered "Christ and His salvation" before 1517. And before 1520 he had discovered the identity of "Antichrist and his damnation." The entire Reformation rested on this twofold testimony. The reformers were unanimous in its acceptance. And it was this interpretation of prophecy that lent emphasis to their reformatory action. It led them to protest against Rome with extraordinary strength and undaunted courage. It nerved them to resist to the utmost the claims of the apostate church. It sustained them at the martyrs' stake. Verily, this was the rallying point and the battle cry that made the Reformation unconquerable.[20]

This testimony also shines through in the Epistle Dedicatory to the 1611 Authorized King James Version of the Holy Bible:

> ... that the zeal of Your Majesty toward the house of God doth not slack or go backward, but is more and more kindled, manifesting itself abroad in the farthest parts of Christendom, by writing in defence of the Truth, (which hath given such a blow unto the man of sin, as will not be healed....

I would essentially agree with those learned men of old, though not necessarily that the papacy was the "fulfillment" of John's antichrist or there would never be another organization—or individual—that fit the bill. However, the papacy, with its history of myriad depredations, seems to fit John's description to a remarkable degree.

I do question the Reformers application of time periods in the Apocalypse and their literal interpretations of Revelation, whereby they came to believe days were actually years in fulfillment of prophecies. In Addition, I do not believe those medieval saints erred in identifying the papacy as the Antichrist when viewed from the context of their sufferings under the Holy See.

The leaders of the Reformation—as well as those prominent churchmen (such as Cotton Mather) who so moved colonial America—similarly used Scripture as a mighty weapon to bring down apostate strongholds and put to flight the forces of evil.

Through their godly teaching, steadfastness, and courage, the Reformers brought the light of the Gospel to humankind once again. Moreover, in time, cities, nations, and the world were enlightened. The truth of the Gospel and belief in the Scripture were their weapons of choice, used to great advantage to harass and defeat the enemies of Christ and His kingdom.

Just as the Reformers had used Scripture to defeat a mighty foe and advance the kingdom of God, men like William Carey also wielded The Word to great effect against the powers of darkness.

Dr. Peter Hammond (see Appendix D) relates what inspired Carey's formidable and unconquerable faith—a faith so revelatory it transformed the nation of India. It was his eschatology of victory that proved so irresistible, for Carey was a Postmillennialist. Hammond writes:

> ... Carey was a Post-millennialist who believed that God who commanded His Church to "make disciples of all nations" would ensure that the Great Commission would ultimately be fulfilled. "The work, to which God has set His hands, will infallibly prosper ... He must reign until Satan has not an inch of territory!

During what Dr. Hammond calls the greatest century of Christian advancement, the 18th century, we find Scripture was once again used as a potent weapon to advance the cause of Christ. It was the belief in

Postmillennialism that inspired and motivated legions of missionaries to carry the teachings of Christ to the remotest regions of the world. Scripture, in the hands of righteous, knowledgeable, and undaunted Spirit-filled men and women, has changed the course of history. Christ's kingdom inevitably advanced. It was and is unstoppable.

There is a vast difference between today's teachers of the Dispensational doctrine and those heralded Reformers (such as Carey and Paton) from the past. The Reformation's ideals, staunchly maintained by the advocates of postmillennial eschatology, have changed the course of the world. The early followers of the Reformation overcame obstacles, trials, and ceaseless persecutions in ensuring the Word of God prevailed. In sharp contrast, Dispensationalism has not caused the kingdom of Christ to advance, nor has it helped take back ground lost to the enemy. It simply cannot!

Listen closely to John Hagee's sermons on YouTube or Baxter's messages on his ENDTIME website. You will soon realize Dispensationalists do not believe in a better future. In fact, they teach our children have no future on Earth, for in a few short years the Antichrist will lay waste, ravaging and demolishing everything the Church has accomplished over the last 1,900 years. According to Dispensational teaching, it is patently foolish to even consider reforming the world's societies; there is simply not enough time.

Let us for a moment imagine the end time soothsayers are correct. Soon it will all be over; the Lord will spirit us off this corrupt planet so the Antichrist can terrorize the Jews for the prescribed period of three and a half years. If time is really that short, can the end time beliefs of the postmillennialists and preterists somehow impede the advancement of the kingdom of God? Not at all! Those who believe in a victorious eschatology would continue to work hard—building, planting, doing everything in their power to lay a sure foundation and win souls for the kingdom that will be. All their actions and long-term goals would remain the same. Their disbelief in the end time eschatology would not hinder, restrain, or damage the Church of God in any way.

However, the pervasive belief in the Dispensational concept of end times has proven counter-productive and detrimental to God's kingdom. As history has shown, great devastation has and will continue to occur until the Spirit of God permeates the Dispensational segment and they repent of this negative and erroneous teaching.

Let me say at this point, I am not trying to be judgmental or presumptuous. I understand there are many who believe Christ's return is still to be looked for and because of that feel the urgency to be about the King's business and building His kingdom. I have used a broad-brush to outline the dispensational-teaching, and not everyone believes all the generalities as I have outlined. Hopefully, the reader may grasp some of the truths and points this book brings forward.

Many Christians believe we stand today on the very brink of the greatest advancement of the Gospel the world has ever seen. The technology and resources to spread the Gospel into every corner of this planet are available as never before. However, entrenched beliefs block the way for that great revival, especially the dire Dispensational eschatology that teaches evil will overcome the Church, requiring Christ's *ekklesia* to be spirited off this planet.

The fire of God blazed bright in the breasts of reformers like William Tyndale, Huldrych Zwingli, John Foxe, John Wycliffe, Martin Luther, John Knox, and John Wesley, as well as myriad other postmillennial believers who worked so ardently to establish God's kingdom. Those great men of Christ who believed in the eschatology of victory wielded the Word of God as a mighty weapon, not an escape manual.

Preterists are again using the Word of God to enlighten, build, and lay sure foundations so those Christian generations who come after us can achieve even greater triumphs for the kingdom of God.

We all believe the Scripture, which says, "*If my people, which are called by my name, shall humble themselves, and pray, and seek my face, and turn from their wicked ways; then will I hear from heaven, and will forgive their sin, and will heal their land*" (II Chron. 7:14).

Surely, by Dispensationalists maintaining their doctrine of the last days, would this verse not be in contradiction to that doctrine and their beliefs out of lockstep with the reformers? Yet, through their constancy in upholding the Scripture, the reformers of Luther's day and the great missionaries of Carey's day immeasurably contributed to God's kingdom. As our Lord Jesus taught, Dispensationalists should follow the reformers' example and "*Go and do likewise.*"

A TERMINAL EXPERIENCE

Beliefs and opinions are largely shaped by family traditions, historical events, and personal experience. When we write learned and serious articles, we also seek to use reliable sources. In seeking to understand a given subject, if we rely upon incomplete facts or incorrect information, our opinions and conclusions will be prone to error.

Many of today's Christians firmly believe prophecy teachers such as John Hagee, Irvin Baxter, and Hal Lindsey are stating the truth about the end times—despite the gaping lack of Scriptural evidence and the 100 percent failure rate of all those who have ever predicted "the end." Yet they still harbor hope that maybe *this* time those end time prophecies might be right because their favorite oracles state with such certainty we are the terminal generation that will see the second coming of Jesus.

A simple illustration will shine some light on this issue. Imagine all your planning and hard work have finally borne fruit. You have made it, and you now have the time and money to take that exotic vacation to the place that has always been your dream.

However, before you can be on your way, you must first select an airline to fly you to your Shangri-La. You are so excited to leave you do not call ahead to book a reservation; you just head right over to the nearest international airport to catch a flight you hope is leaving today. At the airport terminal, you discover there are only two airlines to choose from.

The first one is URPAPA—United Reformed Postmill And Preterist Airlines. You like its catchy slogan, "Guaranteed To Arrive At The Intended Destination"! Since you are a little nervous about flying, you ask about their "track record."

The agent replies, "The arrival of each flight is always punctual, and every URPAPA plane that has ever left this airport has always arrived at its intended destination." [The resurrection of Christ, the kingdom of God, and all its attendant prophecies were all fulfilled on time]

This answer steadies your nerves, and you prepare to purchase a ticket. However, their next flight will not be taking off for a few hours, so you decide to check out DPA—Dispensational Pathway Airlines—the second airline to choose from. Maybe their service is more to your liking.

The first thing you notice, as you follow the arrows to the DPA desk, is the cavernous waiting lounge. It's huge. In fact, you have never seen such a vast structure. Its glass-lined walls somehow stretch to the horizon, Buzz Lightyear-style—"to infinity and beyond." When you look up, the ceiling is not visible. The crystal-clear floors above appear to stretch through the clouds and into the heavens. You then notice steps leading to the lower levels. They seem to cascade unendingly downwards until they are lost in inky darkness.

Wait, what is that sound you hear? It is like the roar of Niagara Falls! You look around for the source of the clamor, which is getting louder with each step you take. As your eyes adjust to the gloom, you realize it is the collective droning of legions of people, talking as they sit in the vast lounge area, endlessly waiting.

Finally, after walking for what seems like hours, you see the sign for DPA. Moreover, there is its slogan, in gaudy, flashing red and gold lettering: "Always About To Depart For Your Heavenly Destination"!

As you question the smiling, smartly dressed, and very attractive ticket agent about specific departure times, she seems somewhat reluctant but finally insists that scheduled departures are always guaranteed. However, as you continue to question her, she becomes increasingly evasive and confused. At first, she seemed intelligent and well-informed—especially about coming events in the Middle East. However, after expending even more time trying to pinpoint the next flight, you begin to lose patience. All she will say is, "It's definitely soon." But she will not say how soon. So you ask how long the airline has been flying.

"We've been in business continually for 180 years … and counting," she says with that omnipresent smile.

You think to yourself, "*That's great! A long history of reliable service. Very reassuring.*" Moreover, when you inquire about DPA's safety standards, she insists the airline's Dispensational aircraft have a crash-free record.

She tries to persuade you to buy a ticket, reminding you that departure times are *always* guaranteed. She finally adds the clincher: "All our departures are prophetically-backed, which means your flight will be leaving very shortly. Our experts have total confidence in their timetabling."

You casually mention, on the way over, you noticed hordes of incredibly aged passengers idly sitting around, waiting in the departure lounge. They look as though they have been there for a very long time! Cobwebs are even hanging off the baggage of those long-suffering folks.

The agent replies, "Oh yes, they're waiting for the next flight. Bless them! It'll be leaving soon."

You respond. "Well, how soon is soon?"

"Soon! Real soon!" she says, with that indelible smile.

At this point, your suspicions take a quantum leap. "By any chance, are those passengers *all* waiting for the same flight?"

"Yes," she states. "Most of them have been sitting there, just waiting, for years and years. They're good Christian folk!"

"So what happened to all the earlier flights?," you ask.

She then reveals, somewhat hesitantly, every single passenger has been "upgraded" numerous times over the last century or so. There was the Miller October 22, 1844 upgrade; the Whisenant 1988, 1989, 1990, 1991, 1992, 1993, and 1994 upgrades; the Camping September 27, 1994, May 21, 2011, and October 21, 2011 upgrades; the Korean Mission for the Coming Days October 28, 1992 upgrade; the Marvin Byers Final Victory 2000 upgrade; the Jack Van Impe 2001 upgrade (and subsequent withdrawal); and countless other non-departures, all swiftly followed by more upgrades.

Perplexed and frustrated, you ask her, "Have any of your guaranteed flights ever actually departed from this airport?"

"Um … not exactly," she coyly admits. "So far—surprisingly—we've had to put everyone on a slightly later flight."

"And it's a real shame, too," she whispers under her breath. "Most of those passengers were booked on Mid-Air Rapture Class, with guaranteed glorified return tickets after seven years. We even included extra-bright, white linen robes for no extra charge."

"We also offered an all-inclusive excursion option with a shorter three-year return, for those who couldn't wait the full seven years. To us at DPA, it seemed like such a great value!"

~ ~ ~ ~ ~ ~ ~ ~

The sad reality is the Dispensational success rate for predicting the Rapture and end time events is a total, rock-solid, 100 percent—no margin for error—FAILURE. Indeed, *all* futurist eschatological persuasions can expect a surefire failure rate of—wait for it—100 percent! I will guarantee a full refund to every buyer of this book if/when "The Antichrist" sets up shop in Jerusalem—beastly marks negotiable!

Yes, purely by chance some prediction made by a lucky-Joe-Dispensationalist may come to pass. But without question, the whole end times plot they cling to has never—and will never—come anywhere close to being fulfilled.

It is also true that every week someone somewhere wins the lottery. Likewise, if you flip a coin and predict it will come up heads, you will be right about fifty percent of the time. Therefore, sooner or later, if someone makes enough nutty predictions, one of them might come to pass. Big deal! The problem is, such a lucky break might serve to convince and confirm the deluded in serious error.

Personally, such a consistent failure rate would not inspire, encourage, or incentivize me about anyone's capacity for foretelling, forecasting, or prophesying anything! Surely, after 1,900 years of failed predictions, is it not high time Christians stopped giving heed to these false prophets?

Neither preterists nor postmillennialists make declarations of future end time events. However, we do hold to the promise of victory and dominion made eons ago by Christ, by the prophet Daniel, and by others throughout the Holy Scriptures. We believe the revelation that was given by God to Daniel. We believe that Christ's promised kingdom, which is already established (Acts 2:30–33), will continue to grow until it fills the whole earth (Dan. 2:35, 44; Matt.13:24–33).

IT'S SIMPLY UNBELIEF

Now that we have laid out the anemic excuses for rejecting the veracity of a victorious eschatology, we will go right to the core reason the Church has been fighting over this for so long: simple unbelief.

Throughout the ages, God's people have been dogged by inconsistency in their walk with Him. Likewise, simple unbelief sometimes takes hold of all of us, to one degree or another.

Consider many of the kings of Israel; some were partly good and partly bad. The Bible shows how the good king of Judah, Jehoshaphat, was rebuked by the seer Jehu for his alliance with the wicked king of Israel,

Ahab: "*Shouldest thou help the ungodly, and love them that hate the LORD? Therefore is wrath upon thee from before the LORD. Nevertheless there are good things found in thee, in that thou hast taken away the groves out of the land, and hast prepared thine heart to seek God*" (II Chron. 19:2–3).

King Asa of Judah was a man whose trust in the LORD was unquestioned at the beginning of his reign. Nevertheless, with the passage of time, his ardent faith seemed to vanish. In the latter years of his reign he oppressed his people. As punishment, God caused an awful disease in the king's feet, an impetus for Asa to repent. However, "*he sought not to the LORD, but to the physicians*" (II Chron. 16:12).

Hezekiah was one of the best kings Judah ever had. Yet he sired a son by the name of Manasseh who became the worst ruler Judah had ever seen. Manasseh's reign of 55 years was also the longest of any king of Judah. The list of Manasseh's crimes against God and His people is a long one. Others in his kingdom also participated in the wickedness of their ruler. Sometime during Manasseh's reign of terror, "*the LORD brought upon them the captains of the host of the king of Assyria, which took Manasseh among the thorns, and bound him with fetters, and carried him to Babylon*" (II Chron. 33:11). It was during his time of affliction Manasseh turned to the God of his fathers. God heard Manasseh's supplication and answered the penitent king by allowing him to return to his homeland. For the rest of his life, Manasseh tried to make amends, to undo all the evil and suffering he had brought upon his kingdom.

Moses, King David, his son Solomon, and a host of others could be listed among those who at times compromised, lacked faith, or sinned deeply against the Lord. The truly faithful who sincerely repented were forgiven and restored to fellowship with the Lord.

All of us, in some ways, are like these kings of Israel. At times we have faith to the full; at times we lack discernment, trust, and faith. At times error takes hold and we cannot see the way. While it would not be right to suggest those who misunderstand or will not accept Jesus' clear-time statements are not true Christians, it is certainly clear Dispensational teaching has damaged and impeded the cause of the kingdom of Christ over the last century and a half. We should pray the Lord opens their eyes and they repent and believe the Scriptures—not the headlines or the prophecy experts—on this important issue.

The wind was boisterous that night on the Sea of Galilee as Jesus walked on the water toward the small fishing boat the disciples were in. When the disciples saw Jesus, they were afraid. However, Jesus spoke to them with words of assurance: *"Be of good cheer; it is I; be not afraid"* (Matt. 14:27–31). With some trepidation, Peter said, *"Lord, if it be thou, bid me come unto thee on the water."* Jesus said just one word: *"Come."* Then Peter stepped out of the boat and walked on the water to his Lord. However, as he looked around at the "current events"—the wind and the waves—he became afraid and began to sink.

All Dispensationalists seem to see are the current events. They seem to forget the power of the Holy Spirit that was bestowed upon the Church (Acts 1:8). They forget the mighty acts God has done for His people down through the ages. They ignore the works of Jesus *"which, if they should be written every one, I suppose that even the world itself could not contain the books that should be written"* (John 21:25). Preterists see through the eyes of faith and believe the words of Jesus, as when He said, *"Come."* Dispensationalists see through the eyes of Peter, noting only the "wind and the waves."

Todd Strandberg reinforced the Dispensationalist doctrine when he said, "I just cannot understand how anyone can follow a preterist line of thinking in light of current world events." Preterists have a similar reaction; we simply cannot understand how anyone can embrace the Dispensational argument, despite the clearly-stated, unambiguous language used by Jesus and the authors of the New Testament in regard to prescribed events.

Those statements concerning the last days and end times do not feature the obscure, symbolic, metaphorical, hyperbolic language found in the Book of Revelation or in Jesus' Olivet Discourse.

The 200-million-man army, the Mark of the Beast, the drying up of the Euphrates River, and many other such portions of Scripture have had their able defenders. Still, as already argued, the literalist interpretation used by Dispensationalists is nonsensical in the extreme.

As Froom has so eloquently shown, whatever the current generation of prophecy experts believes, the next generation will come along with a whole new set of meanings. They will deliver new insights (especially about geopolitics in the Middle East), while declaring their capacity to understand the mind and counsel of God. However, as you listen to their bombast, just remember the hopelessly false prophecies of William Miller, Edgar C. Whisenant, and Harold Camping, three of Dispensationalism's renowned useful idiots.[21]

The problem simply boils down to stubborn unbelief in the unequivocal time statements used by Jesus. It is also a sinful lack of faith in refusing to take Jesus at His word or the New Testament authors at their word. In the final analysis, Dispensationalism and futurism both reject the Biblical vision of victory and dominion here on earth—in time and eternity—for all God's saints.

It is beyond dispute that those who penned the New Testament clearly believed the end of the age was near, soon at hand, and shortly to come to pass. *"This generation shall not pass till all these things be fulfilled"* (Matt. 24:34). Jesus's words cannot be denied. He gave to John the Revelation to show *"His servants things which must shortly come to pass"* (Rev. 1:1). *"For the time is at hand"* (Rev. 1:3). Jesus indicated time and again (Rev. 22:7, 12, 20) His presence would be noted sooner than later. Dispensationalists and futurists should humbly accept and fully believe those emphatic statements, and then study the Scriptures as preterists have done to learn how all the elements of the last days most certainly came to pass within the prescribed time frame.

FOOTNOTES

1. D. James Kennedy and Jerry Newcombe, Thomas Nelson Publishers Nashville, Tennessee, 1994, p. 23.

2. Web page, *Rapture Ready,* article, *The Rapture–Answering the Critics* by Terry James.

3. Web page, *Rapture Ready*, article, *Preterism! I Can't Believe It* by Todd Strandberg.

4. Ibid.

5. Hal Lindsey, *Satan Is Alive and Well on Planet Earth,* Zondervan Publishing House, Grand Rapids, Michigan 49506, 1972, p. 129.

6. Irvin Baxter's EndTime Ministries tract: "Why I Believe Jesus Will Return in My Lifetime" China War—200-million-man army … the prophecy says that an army of 200 million will trigger a war that will kill one-third of the world's population—two billion people … No matter how we twist and turn its message, it still states that one-third of the world will be destroyed … The Bible describes an army of 200 million … The alarming news is that a nation has made the boast that it can field an army of 200 million. The late leader of China, Mao Tse Tung, bragged that he could field an army of 200 million soldiers. The 1999 World Factbook, put out by the CIA, stated that China had 198 million men of military age (15–49). That number went over the 200 million mark as of the year 2000.

7. Wikipedia, Cargo aircraft.

8. Web page, *The Telegraph*, Wednesday, August 24, 2011. "Floods in Cumbria: Army could build WW2 Bailey bridges."

9. Paul Spilsbury (2002), *The Throne, the Lamb & the Dragon: A Reader's Guide to the Book of Revelation*, InterVarsity Press; p. 99.

10. Craig C. Hill (2002), *In God's Time: The Bible and the Future*, Eerdmans; p. 124.

11. Craig R. Koester (2001), *Revelation and the End of All Things*, Eerdmans; p. 132.

12. Irvin Baxter *ENDTIME Ministries* website, About Us video. September 3, 2011.

13. John Hagee, at the Cornerstone Church San Antonio, TX, *10 Signs we are the Final Generation,* found on YouTube April 4, 2011. No date listed for the sermon.

14. American Vision website, September 14, 2011, by Bojidar Marinov, *The Swiss National Bank's Loss of Nerve Will Cost It Dearly,* Filed under Articles, Economic Edge, Economics.

15. *Halley's Bible Handbook* Zondervan Publishing House, Grand Rapids, Michigan 49506 1965, p. 776.

16. LeRoy Edwin Froom, *The Prophetic Faith of Our Fathers: The Historical Development of Prophetic Interpretation,* Washington, DC: Review and Herald, 1978, Vol. 3, p. 259.

17. Cotton Mather (1663–1728) *Great Prophecies of the Bible,* by Ralph Edward Woodrow, Riverside, CA: Ralph Woodrow Evangelistic Association, 1971, p. 170.

18. Froom, Vol. II, p. 66.

19. Froom, Vol. II, p. 793.

20. Froom, Vol. II, p. 243–244.

21. Useful Idiot: First used in Western media in 1948. It was a term used to describe Soviet sympathizers in Western countries. It has been used by commentators such as Amil Imani in his Internet article found on American Thinker, July 28, 2011, "Islam's Useful Idiots" to describe people whom the commentator believes are effectively supporting Islamic terrorism.

    The implication is that some naïvely think themselves an ally of a person (or a cause), but are actually held in contempt by their ally and are being cynically used. The phrase is applied to "those who are seen to unwittingly support a malignant cause through their naïve attempts to be a force for good." Wikipedia, the free encyclopedia, Useful Idiot.

CHAPTER TWELVE

THE KINGDOM OF GOD

—⦿—

THE KINGDOM OF GOD / A
NEGLECTED SUBJECT

In this final chapter, we will look at another fulfillment that was also at hand in Jesus' day: The kingdom of God. We will also learn, by example, what our roles, duties, and responsibilities as Christians should be during our lifetime.

> *All the ends of the world shall remember and turn unto the LORD: and all the kindreds of the nations shall worship before thee. For the kingdom is the LORD'S: and he is the governor among the nations* (Psalms 22:26–28).

The kingdom of God is a topic that is rarely preached in most churches. This being the case, it seems most preachers deem this doctrine is not of any real importance in the life of a Christian, therefore it does not warrant a closer look. But is that really the case?

The word "kingdom," referring to God's kingdom, is used 152 times by Jesus and the authors of the New Testament. Multitudinous other verses also relate to the kingdom of God. The teaching of the kingdom of God was foundational to, and the focus of, John the Baptist's ministry:

> *In those days came John the Baptist, preaching in the wilderness of Judaea. And saying, Repent ye: for the kingdom of heaven is at hand* (Matt. 3:1–2).

At the beginning, during, and at the end of Christ's earthly ministry, the teaching of the kingdom of God was crucial:

> *Now after that John was put in prison, Jesus came into Galilee, preaching the gospel of the kingdom of God, and saying, The time is fulfilled, and the kingdom of God is at hand: repent ye, and believe the gospel* (Mark 1:14–15).
>
> *Verily I say unto you, There be some standing here, which shall not taste of death, till they see the Son of man coming in his kingdom* (Matt. 16:28).
>
> *To whom also he shewed himself alive after his passion by many infallible proofs, being seen of them forty days, and speaking of the things pertaining to the kingdom of God* (Acts 1:3).

In the Book of Acts, the teaching of the kingdom was central to evangelist Philip's teaching:

> *But when they believed Philip preaching the things concerning the kingdom of God, and the name of Jesus Christ, they were baptized, both men and women* (Acts 8:12).

In the Book of Acts, chapter 28:30–31, we read that the kingdom was also essential to the Apostle Paul's teaching:

> *And Paul dwelt two whole years in his own hired house, and received all that came in unto him. Preaching the kingdom of God, and teaching those things which concern the Lord Jesus Christ, with all confidence, no man forbidding him.* (See also Acts 14:22; 19:8; 20:25; 28:23)

We also find this message scattered among the epistles of the New Testament:

Who hath delivered us from the power of darkness, and hath translated us into the kingdom of his dear Son (Col. 1:13).

That ye would walk worthy of God, who hath called you unto his kingdom and glory (I Thess. 2:12).

(See also I Cor. 4:20; 6:9–10; 15:24; 50; Gal. 5:21; Eph. 5:5; Col. 4:11; II Thess. 1:5; II Tim. 4:1; 18; Heb. 1:8; 12:28; James 2:5; II Peter 1:11; Rev. 1:9; 12:10)

Christ exhorted His disciples to *"Observe All Things"* He taught them (Matt. 28:20). Does it not make sense that the whole Gospel, the very essence of His worldview, should be scrupulously followed? Surely, the teaching of the kingdom should be paramount among the "things" we observe and heed!

WHAT IS THE KINGDOM OF GOD?

Before we continue to discuss this topic, it would be helpful to clarify the phrases "the kingdom of God" and "the kingdom of Heaven." These two terms, used interchangeably in Scripture, refer to the same kingdom. Nowhere in the New Testament does Scripture define what Jesus meant when He taught about the kingdom of God.

John Noē, Ph.D., in his book *Off Target*, delimits the kingdom of God as ...

The sphere of God's will, reign and rule. It is located throughout heaven and the cosmos, and wherever on earth the manifestation of his sovereignty, holiness, power, and kingly authority is acknowledged and obeyed. That means it is realized both internally and externally, within and among, to draw human hearts to Him, to bless and discipline his people, and to defeat his enemies. It is to be entered, exercised, and advanced by every Christian who follows Jesus, and experienced in every aspect of society. However, it is not universally recognized, is contested, opposed, and persecuted, and is greatly under-realized.[1]

"The earth is the Lord's and the fulness thereof; the world and they that dwell therein" (Psalm 24:1). We are agreed this is our Lord's world, His earth. Even so, the kingdom of Heaven does not yet occupy all of God's creation. Christ taught that the kingdom is as leaven (Matt.13:33) that would permeate and change the world as we know it until every aspect of our society, each culture and nation, will heartfully accept the will of God.

A marriage unites two separate individuals into "one." After the vows, each spouse shares every plan, hope, action, goal, and interest, for those are the things that affect and influence the health of the marriage. A marriage totally envelopes the life of those who bind themselves to it. It encompasses all until death releases the bond. Similarly, the kingdom of God should, in the life of a Christian, be an all-encompassing concept, principle, and ideology.

"Secular," as used in this book, means *without the true God and true religion*. For a true Christian, there is nothing that takes place outside the purview of our Lord and Savior—all things take place within the kingdom of Christ. That is why Christians can and should be involved in every social aspect to which they can contribute. Nothing is outside of His control, His domain, or His interest. There is no area of life that is off-limits to Christian involvement. Moreover, if something is intrinsically evil—such as slave-trading (or its modern equivalent, exploitation of human embryos)—it must be warred against or challenged.

DEMONSTRATING THE KINGDOM

Though the kingdom of God was never defined by Jesus or any writers of the New Testament, what it is, what it should look like, and how it should be exemplified in the life of a Christian is illustrated by the works of Jesus and His disciples.

The kingdom of God has been demonstrated through the centuries by thousands of men and women, in all walks of life, who changed history and the course of nations. These exemplars include eminent Christians like William Carey, missionary to India; and John Gibson Paton, missionary to the indigenous cannibals of the New Hebrides (Vanuatu) islands.[2]

Vanuatu is a chain of eighty islands about 450 miles long in the South Pacific, two-thirds of the way between Hawaii and Australia. The archipelago was discovered by Fernandes de Queirós of Spain in 1606 and explored by Captain James Cook in 1773. The population today is about 287,000.

Until John Williams and James Harris from the London Missionary Society landed on the island of Erromango in November 1839, there had been no Christian influence. Unfortunately, only minutes after going ashore, both missionaries were killed and eaten. Forty-eight years later, John Paton referenced this awful incident in his memoirs: "Thus were the New Hebrides baptized with the blood of martyrs; and Christ thereby told the whole Christian world that he claimed these islands as His own."[3]

In 1842, the London Missionary Society sent another team to the Island of Tanna, but they were forced to leave within seven months. However, by 1848 significant success was achieved on the Island of Aneityum, and by 1854 about 3,500 natives (more than half) had renounced their idols and heathen customs and given themselves up totally to the worship of the true God, Jehovah. By 1872, all of Aneityum was said to be Christian.

Paton, his wife, and his newborn son arrived on their appointed island of Tanna on November 5, 1858. However, in March of the following year, both his wife and son died of fever. He served alone for the next four years in constant danger and privation until he was driven off the island in February 1862. He then spent the next four years helping to promote the Presbyterian mission to New Hebrides while traveling around Great Britain and Australia. In 1864 he married again and took his wife, Margaret, back to the smaller island of Aniwa in November 1866. They labored together for 41 years until Margaret died in 1905, when Paton was 81.

In relating the success of his and other missions throughout New Hebrides and the South Pacific, Paton wrote:

> In Fiji, 79,000 Cannibals have been brought under the influence of the Gospel; and 13,000 members of the Churches are professing to live and work for Jesus. In Samoa, 34,000 Cannibals have professed Christianity; and in nineteen years, its College has sent forth 206 Native teachers and evangelists. On our New Hebrides, more than 12,000 Cannibals have been brought to sit at the feet of Christ, through (sic) I mean not to say that they are all

model Christians; and 133 of the Natives have been trained and sent forth as teachers and preachers of the Gospel. [3]

The decadence and debauchery of the native culture on most of the islands were horrendous and unsettling. Their entire way of life needed to be transformed, had to be leavened with the Word, so it would conform to the dictates and principles of the Gospel of Christ. When the Patons arrived on Aniwa in November 1866, the task before them was truly formidable:

> The natives were cannibals and occasionally ate the flesh of their defeated foes. They practiced infanticide and widow sacrifice, killing the widows of deceased men so that they could serve their husbands in the next world ...
>
> Their worship was entirely a service of fear, its aim being to propitiate this or that Evil spirit, to prevent calamity or to secure revenge. They deified their Chiefs . . . so that almost every village or tribe had its own Sacred Man. . . . They exercised an extraordinary influence for evil, these village or tribal priests, and were believed to have the disposal of life and death through their sacred ceremonies.... They also worshipped the spirits of departed ancestors and heroes, through their material idols of wood and stone ... They feared the spirits and sought their aid; especially seeking to propitiate those who presided over war and peace, famine and plenty, health and sickness, destruction and prosperity, life and death. Their whole worship was one of slavish fear; and, so far as ever I could learn, they had no idea of a God of mercy or grace. [3]

Paton learned the language and reduced it to writing. He created a dictionary. He translated hymns and catechisms and printed the Scriptures. They held worship services every Sunday and sent native teachers to all the villages to preach the Gospel. Paton built orphanages and trained the young people to be disciples of Christ. He ministered to the sick and dying, dispensed medicines, and taught the natives the use of tools. His wife taught the women singing, reading, and other life skills, such as sewing and plaiting hats.

Fifteen years after the Patons' arrival, the entire island of Aniwa had turned to Christ. Years later John wrote, "I claimed Aniwa for Jesus, and by the grace of God Aniwa now worships at the Savior's feet."[3] To put it another way, the Gospel turned murderous savages into noble Christians, transforming their cosmology from the slavery of superstition to one of true human dignity and liberty.

Today, over a hundred years later, the Patons' legacy remains, for most of the population of Vanuatu identify themselves as Christian. John Paton's great courage came from his abiding faith in God. He was a strong Calvinist who firmly believed in God's capacity to change the hearts of the most obdurate people. As John Piper states:

> His Reformed doctrine of regeneration was crucial here in maintaining his courage in the face of humanly impossible odds. Commenting on the conversion of one native, he said, "Regeneration is the sole work of the Holy Spirit in the human heart and soul, and is in every case one and the same. Conversion, on the other hand, bringing into play the action also of the human will, is never absolutely the same perhaps in even two souls."[3]

The staunch Calvinist doctrine that buttressed Paton inspired hundreds of other missionaries in their sacred tasks. Paton's source of courage, as John Piper relates, was "His confidence in the sovereignty of God controlling all adversities."[3]

Businessman John Wanamaker also demonstrated how the kingdom operates in the life of a Christian. His is the unlikely rags-to-riches story of a devoutly religious man whose exemplary Christian ideals forever changed how business is conducted in America and around the world.

In his biography of John Wanamaker, Joseph H. Appel writes:

> He was a merchant who believed (again in his own words) that "the Golden Rule of the New Testament has become the Golden Rule of business"; who in the face of cynical sneers—"Pious John" and "Honest John"—continued to shatter the old idea that religion

has no place in business, and business no place in religion; who testified, after living concurrently in both realms for more than sixty years: "The temptations of business are great, and unless a merchant has more than a creed or the ordinary ground-work of honesty and faithfulness he may be caught by the sudden wind of plausible opportunity and tumble over the precipice and be ruined"—and, in the other realm: " I am glad to stand up to say that religion is the only investment that pays the largest dividends possible to receive, both in this life and in that to come."[4]

Here is a list of some of John Wanamaker's most notable achievements:

- Inventor of the department store.
- Featured quality goods with a money-back guarantee on every item purchased.
- His concept of truth in advertising earned him the public's trust, which he never lost.
- Originated the price tag.
- Instituted a single price for all customers.
- Opened the first restaurant inside a general store.
- Installed the first electrical lighting in a store.
- Regularly sent buyers overseas to study foreign markets.
- Invented the "white sale."
- Named US Postmaster General, where he instituted technological advances like pneumatic tubes for the main post office, debuted the commemorative stamp, established 5,000 new rural mail routes, and greatly expanded the parcel-post delivery system, enabling the growth of mail orders.
- Founded the Sunday Breakfast Rescue Mission, which is still providing services to the homeless today.
- Founded Bethany Sunday School, the largest Sunday school in the country, along with the Bethany Brotherhood.
- The Bethany Church building had a lecture hall and classrooms, plus: a rescue mission, athletic teams, evening classes, organized visits to hospitals and prisons.

- Created the John Wanamaker Commercial Institute to instruct his workers in bookkeeping, finance, English, and math.
- Instituted Camp Wanamaker in Island Heights, New Jersey, which offered two weeks of summer camp for his stores' employees.
- Built housing for female employees.
- Opened a library branch in Philadelphia.

Wanamaker effectively reformed the world's business practices, not by demanding change or arguing for stifling government edicts, but by following the principles outlined in the Scriptures to establish the kingdom of God in the heart of every Christian.

When John the Baptist was in prison, he seemed to have some doubt whether Christ was truly The One. To ease his mind, John sent two of his disciples to the Lord with a question: *"Art thou he that should come, or do we look for another"* (Matt. 11:3)? *"Jesus answered and said unto them, Go and shew John again those things which ye do hear and see: The blind receive their sight, and the lame walk, the lepers are cleansed, and the deaf hear, the dead are raised up, and the poor have the gospel preached to them"* (Matt. 11:4). By performing the works of the kingdom, Jesus showed John's disciples He was the one Messiah to come—there would not be another. Christ demonstrated what the kingdom of God is, how it would operate, and how it would impact the people and the nations of the world.

The kingdom of God is definable as a kingdom because it has its own (universal) laws, its moral precepts (the Gospel), and subjects who are loyal to its ways. Most significantly, it has a king, the Sovereign of Heaven and Earth. And as Adam Clarke has pointed out, "Jesus Christ never saved a soul which he did not govern ..."[5]

What do builders do with a foundation once it has been laid, and what is its purpose? The answer is to build upon it. Moreover, the bigger the structure, the stronger the foundation must be to support it. The kingdom of Christ is worldwide in scope; only a firm and lasting foundation would be appropriate. Why do builders lay a cornerstone? What is its ultimate purpose? And what happens when it is set in place? Scripture frames it out:

> *For other foundation can no man lay than that is laid which is Jesus Christ. Now if any man build upon this foundation gold, silver,*

precious stones, wood, hay, stubble; Every man's work shall be made manifest: for the day shall declare it, because it shall be revealed by fire; and the fire shall try every man's work of what sort it is (I Cor. 3:11–14).

And are built upon the foundation of the apostles and prophets, Jesus Christ himself being the chief corner stone; In whom all the building fitly framed together growth unto an holy temple in the Lord: in whom ye also are builded together for an habitation of God through the Spirit (Eph. 2:20–22).

To whom coming as unto a living stone, disallowed indeed of men, but chosen of God, and precious, Ye also, as lively stones, are built up a spiritual house, an holy priesthood, to offer up spiritual sacrifices, acceptable to God by Jesus Christ. Wherefore also it is contained in the scripture; Behold, I lay in sion a chief corner stone, elect, precious: and he that believeth on him shall not be confounded (I Peter 2:4–6).

As we structure our lives, Christ is the chief cornerstone. And what was to be built upon the cornerstone, upon Christ the foundation, was His kingdom. *Everything* is built upon Him. To accept Christ and all He represents, we must be born again. Only after our new birth can we enter the kingdom of God (John 3:1–7)—the universal realm Christ came to establish.

To be born again is to rise and walk in newness of life. The kingdom of God is a present reality where Christ reigns. He is King of kings and Lord of lords. As such, He must have a kingdom to rule over. Where is that kingdom and who are its subjects? Because Christ was given *all* power and authority *"in heaven and on earth"* (Matt. 28:18), where does our Lord not have supremacy? Jesus came to establish His kingdom, which was built upon the firm foundation of His death, burial, and resurrection.

"We are lively stones built up a spiritual house" (I Peter 2:5). Christ's kingdom is a spiritual domain, composed of both spiritual and physical aspects. For those who fully embrace the kingdom, there is a life-changing power that works first within born-again Christians, to change and renew their minds and their lives. Through this power they can then challenge and change those around them. As the Savior's kingdom grows exponentially

(as it must), all who seek Him will inexorably be transformed by the Spirit that pulses through the Church of Christ.

WHAT YOU THINK REALLY DOES MATTER:
Examples of Culturally Ineffective Christian Mindsets

The early Christians had a tremendous effect on the world in which they lived. It was said of them, *"These that have turned the world upside down are come thither also"* (Acts 17:6). Can that still be said of today's Church?

Retreating from the world is not the Biblical answer—transforming it is. Many church organizations and religious factions have attempted to spread their own version of Christianity and reform God's kingdom here on earth. Others have helped themselves and their followers to prepare for the kingdom they believe will soon arrive. Some have been very successful, but not in a good way.

What Henry H. Halley wrote in his 1965 edition of *Halley's Bible Handbook* is still relevant today, though not as clear-cut:

> Hinduism has made India what it is.
> Confucianism and Buddhism have made China what it is.
> Mohammedanism has made southwest Asia and North Africa what they are.
> Roman Catholicism has made Italy, Spain and Latin America.
> Protestantism has made Britain, United States and Canada.
>
> THESE FACTS SPEAK FOR THEMSELVES, and SPEAK LOUDLY.[6] (emphasis his)

JEHOVAH'S WITNESSES

Has the Watchtower (Jehovah's Witnesses) organization ever established any charities, hospitals, schools, or public colleges rooted in their philosophy? Is there anything, apart from their meeting houses, which they have built that would benefit society at large?

I once asked a Jehovah's Witness why they don't do the types of things the Church does (or did!). She replied their calling was to send witnesses as missionaries to every country to preach their message. While it is true most Jehovah's Witnesses attempt to live godly and virtuous lives, they do not affect, to any appreciable degree, the greater community. If all Jehovah's Witnesses disappeared from the earth tomorrow, it would make no appreciable difference to any of the nations they now live in. Their presence on this planet has not made any significant difference in the culture of any nation since the founding of the organization. Moreover, to the reader, I would also ask; has your life on this Earth made any significant difference in your family, your community, or nation?

THE AMISH

The 2020 estimate of the number of Amish living in North America is 344,670. They are known for their simple living and plain dress. They are reluctant to adopt many conveniences of modern technology and strictly prohibit or limit the use of telephones, automobiles, and power line electricity.

The Amish are generally honest, hardworking people who place a heavy emphasis on church and family. They value rural life, manual labor, and humility. They also seek to maintain a degree of separation from the non-Amish world. Raising their children and socializing with friends, neighbors, and relatives are the greatest functions of the Amish family and are held in high esteem.

The Amish believe, *"Lo, children are an heritage of the Lord and the fruit of the womb is his reward ... Happy is the man that hath his quiver full of them"* (Psalm 127:3, 5). Large families are seen as blessings from the Lord. Thus, the Amish do not practice any form of birth control and are against abortion. Artificial insemination, eugenics, and embryonic stem cell research are also not consistent with their beliefs.

Because of their rural lifestyle, the Amish see no genuine need for "higher education"; thus, they do not educate their children past the eighth grade. (It is rare to find an Amish individual that has gone to high school or college.) Typically, the Amish operate their own one-room schoolhouses. The teachers are usually young, unmarried women from the Amish community.

Because of their disdain for higher learning, it is highly improbable the Amish culture will ever produce doctors, surgeons, great theologians, chemists, architects, researchers, engineers, mathematicians, scientists, politicians, lawyers (do we really need more lawyers?), economists, or any other discipline that takes years of study to master. In short, they are not apt to contribute to the pool of new discoveries so necessary for the advancement of civilization. Despite their wish to live outside of the mainstream, the Amish are occasionally compelled to seek help from those they consider ungodly and worldly to fill a medical or other need.

For the most part, Amish do not participate in any evangelistic endeavors. They partake of no outreach or ministry to the lost, nor do they send missionaries beyond their communities or to other nations.

From their arrival in this country, the Amish have successfully maintained their separate communities, living mostly virtuous and industrious lives. However, to most observers, their lifestyle is just a quaint, whimsical curiosity relegated to the fringes of society, with almost no effect or influence on the world around them.

EVANGELICAL CHURCHES

Most evangelical Christian churches, like their Jehovah's Witnesses counterparts, are no better at reforming or changing their surrounding communities. Both groups are so focused on the Armageddon ideology they cannot see past that supposed event. They thus lack any vision to instruct, train, or disciple the world and its institutions in the ways of the Lord.

The early revivals in the United States had an enormous impact on American culture. The revivals in England and other nations had a significant influence on their societies. The Reformation that took place in Europe in the 15th and 16th centuries shook the world and changed the whole course of history.

In our country's early days, churches founded hospitals, colleges, orphanages, schools, and many other institutions that helped change society for the good. The Church's influence was felt in its literature, arts, music, and every other area of life. Church members were inspired to do good works that benefited the entire nation and the world. Sadly, those days are gone.

No one will spend hours looking for a talented architect to design a skyscraper if they believe there will not be enough time to finish the project; nor if they believe they will not get a return on their investment once the project is complete. Why bother? No one will ever waste precious time, money, or resources on a venture that will never be completed—or, if finished, will never be used. So it is with God's people. They will not undertake any kind of project that takes years, decades, or even generations to complete if they believe they will run out of time. As a consequence, a once largely Christianized culture is now almost completely repaganized.

Recall, if you can, a bit of history; during the construction of castles and cathedrals, dating back to the 8th Century forward, the architects of those structures and even those who began and worked on them—first and second *generation* workers—never lived to see the completion of what they started. They did not see the world ending anytime soon.

For over one hundred years, at least in the United States, revivals have mostly failed to affect our society. Yes, millions of souls have been saved since the revivals of the 1950s. Nevertheless, the "soul" of the nation remains largely unaffected. For generations, the Church has steadily abandoned its mission, leaving much of society vulnerable to the prophets of humanism, evolution, and socialism. Can this dereliction of Christian duty be connected in any way to the Dispensational teaching that promises the kingdom of God—still yet to arrive—will appear with rapturous applause shortly?

CATHOLICISM

What the Roman Catholic Church has accomplished in the past far surpasses anything the current evangelical Church has achieved. Countless institutions have been built and are maintained by the Roman Catholic Church.

In the Philippines, for example, the majority of people are Roman Catholic. In most small towns and cities there, the largest, most ornate building is the local Catholic Church. Each Sunday scores of people attend services. Only a small portion of the Catholic population fails to attend a service each week.

However, despite this level of piety, most houses and public buildings have bars on the windows (not good in case of fire) and walls or fences around their property. This added security exists as a deterrent, for there are a lot of thieves who are good at their jobs. Life in much of the Philippines is like living in the inner city of any urban center in the United States, where, if you value what you own, you dare not leave your belongings unattended—even for a moment.

Ironically, as pointed out by Halley, the countries where the Catholic Church reigns supreme are also some of the poorest. In those benighted places, the Church has failed in improving living conditions, nor has it truly uplifted the spirit of those nations where it has taken hold. Moreover, the Church has not provided a moral compass (hence all the thieves) for those who adhere to its tenets. And the "kingdom" it preaches and teaches sadly lacks the firm foundation so necessary to elevate, inspire, and edify the impoverished communities that so ardently cleave to their faith.

As these examples show, a lack of Biblical teaching about the kingdom of God can affect the ethos of entire nations. (See Appendix D for the life of William Carey, and what a proper view of the kingdom of God can accomplish in the life of a righteous man.)

The early reformers and missionaries were consumed by a vision of victory to disciple the nations and expand the kingdom of God. They were not hindered by the misconception they were living in the end times or belonged to the terminal generation. Had that teaching been promulgated in their time, it would have killed their efforts and destroyed their passion. Worse still, their great accomplishments would have remained undone.

WHEN WAS GOD'S KINGDOM TO ARRIVE?

When a Jehovah's Witness knocks on someone's door, they have a message to present: the good news of the "kingdom of God." They have their message partly right, for it is based on what Jesus taught:

From that time Jesus began to preach, and to say, Repent: for the kingdom of heaven is at hand (Matt. 4:17).

> *And as ye go, preach, saying, The kingdom of heaven is at hand*
> (Matt. 10:7).
>
> *But if I cast out devils by the Spirit of God, then the kingdom of*
> *God is come unto you* (Matt. 12:28).
>
> *Jesus came into Galilee, preaching the gospel of the kingdom of*
> *God, And saying, The time is fulfilled, and the kingdom of God is at*
> *hand: repent ye, and believe the gospel* (Mark 1:14–15).
>
> *And he said unto them, I must preach the kingdom of God to*
> *other cities also: for therefore am I sent* (Luke 4:43; see also Matt.
> 4:23; 9:35; 12:28; 21:43; Mark 1:14; 15:43)

However, the kingdom the Witnesses present differs greatly from the Biblical one. They believe it was delayed for millennia and inaugurated just a century ago in 1914 in a manner discernable only to a Witness believer. The next event they are anticipating is the Battle of Armageddon. Nathan H. Knorr, their third president, has written:

> Jehovah God is now warning men and nations of this coming
> battle, through his witnesses on earth, that men of good-will
> toward God may heed and be preserved within the safety of God's
> organization.[7]

You will find similar teaching in their other books and pamphlets. For example:

> The time is now near when God's kingdom government will
> take action to destroy all the governments of the world.[8]

However, the Jehovah's Witnesses are not alone in believing the kingdom of God was delayed. They have an unlikely ally: Christians of the Dispensational persuasion, with whom they are in unity on this point. Dispensational believers also deny the clear teaching of Christ on this matter. And so they walk, the Witnesses and the Dispensationalists, doctrinally hand-in-hand.

The Dispensational doctrine teaches the kingdom Christ said was at hand—and had in fact arrived—is still pending. In amplifying this point, *Unger's Bible Dictionary* states:

John the Baptist, Christ and the Apostles announced the kingdom unto national Israel as "at hand." That offer was rejected. As a result the "kingdom of heaven" in its earthly manifested form was postponed until Christ's Second Advent. Widespread attempts to "bring in the kingdom" on the basis of Christ's First Advent are misplaced. According to the clear teaching of the Bible it will be realized only in connection with the Second Advent.[9]

Now then, when does this kingdom, Christ said was "at hand," actually start? Has Christ's kingdom not arrived yet? Has it been delayed, as Dispensationalists and Jehovah's Witnesses continue to teach?

Reading through the Epistles we find its authors seemed to believe they were already living within the kingdom of God, which was already established or about to happen:

> *Who hath delivered us from the power of darkness, and hath translated us into the kingdom of his dear Son* (Col. 1:13).
>
> *That ye would walk worthy of God, who hath called you unto his kingdom and glory* (I Thess. 2:11).
>
> *Wherefore we [are] receiving a kingdom which cannot be moved, let us have grace, whereby we may serve God acceptably with reverence and godly fear* (Heb. 12:28).
>
> *I John, who also am your brother, and companion in tribulation, and in the kingdom and patience of Jesus Christ, was in the isle that is called Patmos, for the word of God, and for the testimony of Jesus Christ* (Rev. 1:9).

Fulfilling the words of the prophet in the Book of Isaiah (9:1–2), Jesus began His ministry in Galilee. These were His first tidings, as recorded by Matthew:

> *Repent, for the kingdom of heaven is at hand* (Matt. 4:17).
>
> *The time is fulfilled, and the kingdom of God is at hand: repent ye, and believe the gospel* (Mark 1:15).

This kingdom, already at hand and amply fulfilled, was the long-promised and intensely awaited kingdom/dominion envisioned by Daniel (Daniel 2:44; 7:14, 18–27).

According to Daniel, there were five kingdoms that were to rule. The chronological fourth kingdom was the Roman Empire that controlled much of the known world in Jesus' day. This kingdom ended in AD 476. The fifth kingdom—the "kingdom of heaven"—was to start sometime during the previous kingdoms, for it was preordained to incrementally, but decidedly, break those other empires into pieces. Those four kingdoms have long since faded away; just remnants of their past glories remain.

The fifth kingdom (also referred to as the "stone kingdom") would destroy the four other kingdoms and would grow until it became a great mountain that filled the entire earth. This is the kingdom, the one and only, much longed for, much-anticipated empire Christ labored to usher in and said had arrived. This was the Gospel Jesus preached from the start of His ministry to the end.

Dispensationalists believe the kingdom Jesus was presenting was merely an "offer" that could be refused. And because the Jews rejected this offer, their opportunity to enter the kingdom was withdrawn.

Where is the Scriptural evidence for such a view? The kingdom Christ conveyed was a proposal He made to the Jews. However, its acceptance or rejection was a moot point, for it was coming regardless of what anyone decided. The kingdom of Heaven was a non-negotiable event because it was inevitable—and nothing could stop it.

The kingdom of God had been in process of fulfillment for hundreds of years. Three of Daniel's five kingdoms—the Babylonian, the Medo-Persian (under Cyrus the Great), and the Macedonian (under Alexander the Great)—had already fallen. The fourth, the Roman Empire, would soon feel the power and might of the stone kingdom, Christ's kingdom, and fall under its crushing weight.

Many Jews rejected Christ, but that did not stop His death, burial, and resurrection. In encompassing these events, the New Testament covers about 70 years. There are four gospels, a book dealing with the history of the first 35 years of the early Church (Acts), 21 epistles, and one book of prophecy. All proclaim the nearness of the kingdom of God. But no mention is ever made of Christ withdrawing the "offer" of His kingdom.

The Scripture presents the resurrection, the judgment, and the kingdom—as events about to happen within the lifetime of Christ's contemporaries. On this topic, the authors of the New Testament speak with a unified voice. As the Scripture (Greek text) puts it: "*Young children, a last hour it is, and as ye heard that antichrist is coming, even now antichrists many have arisen, whence we know that a last hour it is*" (I John 2:18).

Moreover, as Scripture (Gal. 4:4) further attests, Christ came at the "completion of time." Each world-changing event—the kingdom, the judgment, the resurrection—was part of the juggernaut that was promised to come and would not be delayed. "*For the vision is yet for an appointed time, but at the end it shall speak, and not lie: though it tarry, wait for it; because it will surely come, it will not tarry*" (Habakkuk 2:3). As the prophet Habakkuk saw so clearly, it was indeed the "appointed time." And Christ and the apostles affirmed it.

The death, burial, and resurrection of Christ started the chain of events that led to the judgment upon the wicked generation in AD 70. Nothing could hinder or delay what had long been written. And no decision by men or the rejection of Christ by any nation could thwart God's plan for the ages.

MANIFEST DESTINY

Clarence B. Carson is an author and lecturer on subjects pertaining mainly to history. In the first of his five-volume, *A Basic History of the United States,* he discusses how and why the European settlers, though at first greatly outnumbered by the Indians, could conquer and so quickly drive out this country's native people:

> Their sense and knowledge of history provided the European settlers with an edge over the Indians. It endued them with an awareness of their place in the scheme of things. It gave vitality to their belief that they had a special purpose, a mission, and even a destiny. The fullness of their awareness of the past gave vitality to their vision for the future.[10]

Native Americans, for the most part, had no written language. They had no real sense of the past, nor a vision for the future. They entertained no concept of "manifest destiny" for their people.

Manifest Destiny has always been an idea or a belief, not a specific policy. Its ideology continuously played a part in the reasonings of the Europeans who first stepped foot on the North American continent. Though the notion has fallen out of vogue today, it was an essential component in forming the United States and its expansion across the continent.

Webster's Dictionary defines "manifest destiny" this way:

> An ordering of human history as inevitable and obviously apparent that leads a people or race to expand to geographic limits held to be natural or to extend sovereignty over a usually indefinite area ... the doctrine or belief in such inevitable expansion (that peculiar type of historical mysticism that we in America call *manifest destiny*).[11]

The phrase was first coined by journalist John L. O'Sullivan in his *United States Magazine and Democratic Review* (July – August 1845).

The era from the end of the War of 1812 to the beginning of the American Civil War is even known as the "Age of Manifest Destiny." It was during that period the United States expanded to the Pacific Ocean, "from sea to shining sea." Manifest destiny was the providential notion behind the annexation of territories, such as Texas, Oregon, New Mexico, and California; and the justification for involvement in Cuba, Alaska, Hawaii, and the Philippines.

Early in the 19th century, John Quincy Adams helped codify the term "continentalism"—the fervent belief that, within his lifetime, the United States would eventually encompass all of North America. In a letter to his father in 1811, Adams wrote:

> The whole continent of North America appears to be destined by Divine Providence to be peopled by one *nation*, speaking one language, professing one general system of religious and political principles, and accustomed to one general tenor of social usages and customs. For the common happiness of them all, for their

peace and prosperity, I believe it is indispensable that they should be associated in one federal Union.[12]

Historian William E. Weeks denotes the three key themes usually adopted by advocates of manifest destiny:

1. the *virtue* of the American people and their institutions;
2. the *mission* to spread these institutions, thereby redeeming and remaking the world in the image of the US; and;
3. the *destiny* under God, to do this work.[13]

Over the years, the term "manifest destiny" has meant different things to different people. Not all their ideas were compatible, and many were open to dispute. Its various interpretations have occasionally led to ill-conceived policies and questionable actions implemented by an America that had seemingly lost its way.

The idea of a manifest destiny for the United States is founded upon a view of Scripture that has, at times, been distorted, misused, twisted, and exploited for political and personal ends. It has been applied to subjugate peoples and annex their lands. Its Biblical foundations have also been long forgotten or purposely ignored.

When we read about manifest destiny, its religious tones are unmistakable. Its early promoters frequently used phrases such as "Divine Providence," "moral ideal," "higher law," "divine destiny." Its advocates believed national expansion was not only wise and providential, but readily apparent (manifest) and inexorable (destiny).

Long before there was a nation called America, God had placed a manifest destiny within the hearts of willing vessels—those who were fortunate enough to hear that "still small voice of God." Christopher Columbus (his name means "Christ-bearer") was such a man. Columbus believed God had given him the special mission to carry the Light of Christ into the darkness of undiscovered, heathen lands. He wrote:

> It was the Lord who put into my mind (I could feel his hand upon me) the fact that it would be possible to sail from here to the Indies. All who heard of my project rejected it with laughter,

ridiculing me. There is no question that the inspiration was from the Holy Spirit, because He comforted me with rays of marvelous inspiration from the Holy Scriptures ...

I am a most unworthy sinner, but I have cried out to the Lord for grace and mercy, and they have covered me completely. I have found the sweetest consolation since I made it my whole purpose to enjoy His marvelous presence. For the execution of the journey to the Indies, I did not make use of intelligence, mathematics or maps. It is simply the fulfillment of what Isaiah had prophesied ...

No one should fear to undertake any task in the name of our Saviour, if it is just and if the intention is purely for His holy service. The working out of all things has been assigned to each person by our Lord, but it all happens according to His sovereign will, even though He gives advice. He lacks nothing that it is in the power of men to give Him. Oh, what a gracious Lord, who desires that people should perform for Him those things for which He holds Himself responsible! Day and night, moment by moment, everyone should express their most devoted gratitude to him.[14]

In *The Light and the Glory* Peter Marshall and David Manuel ask, "What if God had conceived a special plan for America?" In researching their book, Marshall and Manuel pored through dusty historical records, combed through dimly lit archives and libraries, located and read long-forgotten volumes—and found the answer they were looking for. Yes, God did have a special purpose for America. And that special plan, the belief in that special plan, was manifest in the sermons, books, and tracts written by men on fire and filled with the Spirit of God. Proclaimed from the pulpits of the colonies, the clarion call of manifest destiny filled those who heard it with the desire to build a "city on a hill" as a light for the whole world to see. Inspired and inspirited, the people who founded this nation moved heaven and earth to build that city on a hill.

In the early 5th century AD, Augustine of Hippo (Saint Augustine, considered by many the most influential Father of the Church), wrote a book titled *City of God*. The book, written in Latin, profoundly touched Christianity, which in turn shaped and influenced Western civilization for centuries. His influence is still felt through the doctrines and teachings of Dispensationalism/premillennialism and postmillennialism.

Augustine's book helped spawn numerous branches of millennialism. Its content describes two "cities" or kingdoms: The City of God and the City of Man. According to Augustine, the City of God (the New Jerusalem, or Christianity) should only be concerned with the "things of God," which are exclusively spiritual, rather than political or earthly. In contrast, the City of Man is entirely earthly and not concerned with spiritual concepts. According to Augustine, only these two kingdoms existed. Where one was immersed in the eternal truths of God, setting aside earthly pleasure and fully dedicated to serving the Lord and advancing the Christian faith, the other kingdom gave themselves over to the cares and pleasures of their godless, fleeting world.

These two cities, the City of Man and the City of God, were in constant conflict. But as time went on, the kingdom of God fulfilled its purpose to reign over the kingdom of Man. However, this victory came only after a great cataclysm. Augustine's book gave rise to at least three views about millennialism, but only two are relevant to our discussion: postmillennialism and premillennialism.

Premillennialism, sometimes called "Two Kingdom Theology," largely follows Augustine's thesis, so aptly conveyed in the *City of God*. It rejects earthly progress as a snare of the devil. Its advocates assert this world is so pervaded with evil, even with divine guidance, there is little we can do to redeem our humanity. Only after catastrophe and the direct intervention of Jesus (at the Rapture) will the eternal kingdom of God be ushered in.

Premillennialism and postmillennialism have coexisted through the centuries, with each vying for supremacy. During the 17th century, through the influence of Anglican Biblical scholar Joseph Mede, progressive millennialism (or postmillennialism) emerged as a new interpretation of millennial teaching. Mede believed the Book of Revelation held the promise of a literal kingdom of God, recording, as it does, the kingdom's historical progress through the ages. History, he thought, was the story of progress and victory, showing the continuously upward conquest of God's kingdom over evil and the vanquishing of Satan.

During the 18th century, progressive millennialists, such as commentator Daniel Whitby and the great revivalist Jonathan Edwards, positioned postmillennialism to become the dominant eschatology in many Protestant churches. This popular notion was also the ideology that helped fan the flames of manifest destiny. Right or wrong, as portrayed in the Encyclopaedia Britannica, it was a force to be reckoned with:

> The association of the millennium with the role of the United States proved to be a volatile 19th-century mixture in the hands of Protestant ministers, and for much of that period millennialism fed the fires of nationalism and Manifest Destiny. In a typical utterance, a leading Presbyterian minister of the 1840s, Samuel H. Cox, told an English audience that "in America, the state of society is without parallel in universal history ... I really believe that God has got America within anchorage, and that upon that arena, He intends to display his prodigies for the millennium." The late-19th-century movement known as the Social Gospel, dedicated as it was to establishing the Kingdom of God here and now, manifested most clearly the continuing influence of progressive millennialism.[15]

In the 19th century optimism was the mindset for the Church of God, for His kingdom was advancing rapidly on all fronts. Hope in victory abounded—but a victory grounded in reality, with all its attendant difficulties.

However, one of "the little foxes that spoil the vines" came along in the person of John Nelson Darby, the father of Dispensationalism. And his fellowship in the Plymouth Brethren quickly espoused his new doctrine. There were also the "Millerites," followers of William Miller, who posited the Second Advent of Jesus Christ would occur no later than 1844. Miller is notable as one of the most infamous false prophets in history—and there have been many.

Other cults sprang from Miller's deceptive teaching. The Seventh-day Adventist Church, along with the Jehovah's Witnesses, grew from the toxic seed Miller had sown. Miller's teachings were carried forward by the "prophetess" Ellen G. White, cofounder of the Seventh-day Adventist Church. White helped spawn the still-growing obsession with the end times, last days, and terminal generation—misguided notions that infect and cripple much of the modern evangelical Church. The oft-repeated idea that *"we are the generation that will see the second coming of the lord*" continues to render large swathes of the Church ineffective and irrelevant when it comes to winning this world and transforming its cultures. The pervasive belief in Premillennial Dispensationalism has almost extinguished the victorious eschatology which the Church has held for almost 2,000 years.[16] Some say ignorance is bliss. However, ignorance of church history can be a civilization-killer.

Yes, God had a plan for America. However, for God's people, the concept of manifest destiny is not limited to the United States alone, but foresees a kingdom that will evolve to fill the entire earth. Faith in the kingdom of God continues to this day, though it currently lies dormant while distorted and errant beliefs hold sway. Its trumpet call is often drowned by the noise of end time zealots who refuse to seriously search the Scriptures. Nevertheless, its embers still glow, awaiting a breeze, however slight, that will fan it once more into a roaring inferno no one can quench or resist.

CONCLUSION

One reviewer was disappointed I barely touched on the Book of Revelation in my text, although I did mention it throughout the book. She would have liked me to deal with questions such as: Who are the two witnesses of Revelation? Who is Babylon? When were these prophecies fulfilled historically, and how? These are good questions, and in tackling them I might have strengthened my arguments just a bit. However, expounding on that book was way beyond the scope of my consideration. Nevertheless, what is stated in this book will go a long way for those seeking answers to these and other analogous questions. Their search perimeters are narrow, the starting and ending point is given in the text, the "timeframe" of when those things were going to take place in history is really not open to debate, the time was near, for the text clearly states: *"the time is at hand"* (Rev.1:3). Those things would take place within the lifetime of those to whom the letter was written. So we know when those things took place, the years before and after AD 70, but not all the details, facts, and how those events were fulfilled.

We know from our study of the Scriptures *shortness of time* is key to the teachings concerning Christ's judgment upon unbelieving Israel; there was never to be a long delay before His coming, "return." The New Testament Church believed they would see Jesus's parousia in their lifetime. The soon presence of the Lord was their hope and expectation. Their faith in the Lord's imminent parousia and the Scriptural texts (*Surely I come quickly*; *the end of all things is at hand*; *the time is at hand*; *must shortly come to pass*; *these last days*; *the time is short*) cannot be stretched for 1,950 years and still retain any aspect of "soon." If Jesus had not returned within the anticipated time frame, so much of Scripture would be invalidated.

We have previously studied the Scriptural meaning of the words "soon," "shortly," and "quickly." We have amply defined these words according to *Strong's Concordance, Thayer's Greek-English Lexicon, Gesenius's Hebrew-Chaldee Lexicon, Bullinger's Lexicon, W. E. Vine's Expository Dictionary,* and *Webster's Dictionary of the American Language.* The usage and meaning of those three basic words do not differ from the way they are used today. Soon, shortly, and quickly have never meant "tarry," "delay," or "long period of time."

Dispensational teaching distorts the plain Scriptural meaning of those words by implying a long delay or passage of time was intended. By using their own private interpretation to determine what Jesus meant, Dispensationalists are guilty of perverting many passages of Scripture. By failing to interpret eschatology using the Scriptural method—comparing Scripture with Scripture—they are unable to comprehend what Jesus and the prophets truly said (II Peter 1:20, 3:16).

In sum, every time a Dispensational teacher, preacher, or TV evangelist expounds upon the end times or last days, they teach utter nonsense, not truth. They are also wasting precious time by pondering, theorizing, and speculating about momentous events that will never take place. And that is a serious mistake.

Instead of buttressing the expectation of Christ's Church overcoming this world, they have instilled in their believers a strange combination of hope, apathy, and fear. They cling to a false hope of exiting this planet alive, via the Rapture, instead of the grave (Heb. 9:27). Because of their belief in a soon departure, they are profoundly indifferent to the idea of a future society. This has caused many Dispensationalists to withdraw from society without even trying to effect any Gospel-inspired changes that would benefit mankind. Fearing the trouble and tribulation to come has had a paralyzing influence on those who cling to the Dispensational doctrine.

To review, the Scriptural phrase "*it was at hand*" always means "nigh," "imminent," "soon," "impending," or "soon to come to pass." The New Testament believers expected the Lord to return in their lifetime. And Scripture shows how Christ's return was fulfilled (His coming to judge Israel in AD 70). Jesus did come quickly, as He promised He would—within the generation of the first Christians.

This inescapable conclusion is very easily arrived at because it is based on the fact Jesus told His disciples He would return in their lifetime!

Dispensationalists have a lot of explaining to do, for if Jesus did not return as the Scriptures teach—when the first Christians expected Him to—Jesus is guilty of giving false hope to the first believers.

In one sense, Dispensationalists have become last-days scoffers for they do not believe what Jesus and the authors of the New Testament believed concerning end times eschatology. In their unbelief, they choose to ignore Jude's solemn instruction to *"earnestly contend for the faith which was once delivered unto the saints"* (Jude 3).

We have also explored the plague of date-setting that has infected the Church for many centuries, and why this series of misjudgments and miscalculations have continued for so long.[17] Dispensationalist thinkers have long taught the seventy weeks of Daniel, the regathering of the nation of Israel, the return of Jesus, and the entire Olivet Discourse—all the prophecies that are long fulfilled—still have not come to pass. This is the reason every date-setter has been wrong for nineteen centuries and never will be correct on any end time or last days events. This is the reason why the modern-day regathering of Israel and any other "signs of the times" do not—and never will—have anything to do with Bible prophecy. This truth will never falter: once a prophecy is fulfilled, it can never be fulfilled again.

I have stated this before and hopefully made it clear. I do not believe futurists or Dispensationalists are heretics, although some may be. And, because of their heretical doctrine, they should be assigned to the deepest pool in the lake of fire, "come the judgment day." However, their error *is* very serious and does have detrimental and far-reaching consequences for the advancement of the kingdom of God. For this reason, and for the sake of truth, the Dispensational doctrine needs to be abandoned.

The preterist and the postmillennialist do not deny any teaching of Jesus or the prophets. The disagreement between the Dispensationalist and the preterist is not the inerrancy of the Scripture, but the nature of the fulfillment of Jesus's return, of which the seventy weeks of Daniel, the Book of Revelation, and the Olivet Discourse all play an integral part.

Dispensational doctrine is a horse of a very different color. Within the Dispensational camp, there are many opinions about last day's events and how they will unfold. However, on one point there is general agreement: the Church of Christ will be defeated by the rising tide of evil and will be "raptured" off this planet.

Those in the same Dispensational camp as MacArthur, Baxter, Camping, and Whisenant are completely out of sync with the historic beliefs of the Church. Consequently, although they pay lip-service to winning souls, gaining disciples, fighting against sin and corruption, etc., there is no long-term or strategic commitment to Christ's kingdom being established here on Earth—or even around the corner—because they expect to be whisked away in the very near future.

While there are some minor (and a few major) differences of opinion in the preterist and postmillennial camps, there is unity on one theme: victory *and* dominion for the Church of Christ.

The difference between the two factions is plain; there is no middle ground, just two sides to choose from: The preterists/postmillennials, who believe the Church will reign supreme; or the Dispensationalists, who believe in defeat, retreat, and escape in the face of evil. On which side does Christ reside? On which side does Scripture repose? And with which side shall we choose to cast our lot? Victory (Preterist) or Defeat (Dispensationalist)?

In this book, we have weighed Dispensationalism on the scales of Scripture and found it wanting. We have scrupulously tested Dispensational thought against the Word of God (Acts 17:11; Rom. 12:2; I Cor. 2:14; Eph. 5:10; Phil. 1:10; I Thess. 5:21; II Tim. 2:15; I John 4:1; Rev. 2:2) and Dispensationalism has failed.

The resolution shared by members of the early Church, the medieval Reformers, and Preterists past and present can be summed up thus:

> Men and women of flesh, with an eschatology of victory that produced an iron will, fortified with determination set in stone and anchored in the foundation of the Rock of Ages—the Word of God—changed the whole course of history!

If only all those who claim to believe in Christ would heed the words of this old hymn:

'Tis So Sweet to Trust in Jesus

'Tis so sweet to trust in Jesus,
Just to take Him at His word;
Just to rest upon His promise,
Just to know, "Thus saith the Lord."

I'm so glad I learned to trust Thee,
Precious Jesus, Savior, Friend;
And I know that Thou art with me,
Wilt be with me to the end.

Chorus:

Jesus, Jesus, how I trust Him,
How I've proved Him o'er and o'er,
Jesus, Jesus, Precious Jesus!
O for grace to trust Him more.

FOOTNOTES

1. John Noë, *Off Target* (East2West Press; Publishing arm of the Prophecy Reformation Institute, 5236 East 72nd Street Indianapolis IN 46250 USA 2012) p. 51.

2. Much of the information about Paton comes from the desiring God website: *You Will Be Eaten by Cannibals! Lessons from the Life of John G. Paton/* Courage in the Cause of Missions/ 2000 Bethlehem Conference for Pastors/Message by John Piper.

3. Ibid.

4. *THE BUSINESS BIOGRAPHY OF JOHN WANAMAKER FOUNDER AND BUILDER/Americas Merchant Pioneer* from 1861 to 1922, Joseph H. Appel, p. xv.

5. Clarke, *Clarke's Commentary*, Matthew—Revelation vol. III, p. 51.

6. *Halley's Bible Handbook* Zondervan Publishing House, Grand Rapids, Michigan 49506 1965, p. 802.

7. *Encyclopaedia Britannica Macropaedia*, (William Benton, publisher 1943–1973, 1977) vol. 10, p. 132.

8. *You Can Live Forever in Paradise on Earth*, (Watch Tower Bible and Tract Society of Pennsylvania 1982, 1989) p. 119.

9. Merrill F. Unger, *Unger's Bible Dictionary* (Chicago: Moody Press, 1966) p. 632.

10. Clarence B. Carson (1983), *A Basic History of the United States Volume 1*, American Textbook Committee, PO Box 8, Wadley, Alabama 36276, p. 3.

11. *Webster's Third New International Dictionary and Seven Language Dictionary*, 1976 G. & C. MERRIAM CO.

12. Adams quoted in McDougall 1997, p. 78.

13. Internet-Manifest Destiny, *New World Encyclopedia*, #2 Themes and influences.

14. Peter Marshall & David Manuel, *The Light and the Glory*, Power Books, Fleming H. Revell Company Old Tappan, New Jersey, 1977, p. 17.

15. *Encyclopaedia Britannica Macropaedia*, (William Benton, Publisher, 1943-1973, 1977) vol. 12, p. 202.

16. The "Apocalypse/Frontline" website features the article, A Pictorial Chronology: The apocalyptic worldview through the ages. Adventist movement. The type of eschatology espoused by the Millerites is called premillennialism, which holds that the world will grow more and more sinful until Christ returns to usher in the Millennial Kingdom—in other words, man can't save himself. Although their failure would serve as a great caution against hard date-setting, historians view them as a harbinger of the type of apocalyptic thinking so prevalent in the 20th century.

17. Harold Camping (after three of his predicted Rapture dates came and went) finally acknowledged his faulty projections and issued an apology to his followers.

On October 28, 2011, the transcript of the audio apology was published on Family Radio's website. The 90-year-old broadcaster told his listeners that the Rapture did not occur on October 21, 2011, because it was ultimately God's will. "He could have stopped everything if He had wanted to," he said. He also admitted that his calculations were wrong and told his followers that "we should be very patient about this matter. At least in a minimal way we are learning to walk more and more humble before God."

What is conspicuously missing from Camping's entire apology is any recantation of his belief in end times theology that led to his error. He claimed to have cracked a code in the Bible that allowed him to calculate the date of the Rapture, yet he still miscalculated the date three times! Ever hopeful, Camping remained undaunted because he "knew" without question his theology of the end times was right.

EPILOGUE

It can be argued fundamentalist Christians have not maintained nor even promoted a culture of victory. For the last one hundred years, Fundamentalism has taught defeat and retreat and has reaped exactly what it has preached. It is this author's prayer this book will persuade many fundamentalists to re-examine the pessimistic Dispensational doctrine, seize afresh the torch of hope and victory, and plant it in their homes, churches, and communities. The Church once again needs visionaries like the Apostle Paul, William Carey, and those others whose devotion to Lord Jesus Christ illuminated the darkness and changed the course of the world.

We are most certainly not the last generation; there will be many more generations after we pass from this life. The reader owes it to his/her children, family, church, and country to work toward a better tomorrow and build a future where Christ's kingdom stretches from east to west and pole to pole.

After more than a century of pessimism, retreat, and defeat, the Dispensational doctrine has debased the Church and impeded its mission. It has reversed the cause of the Gospel not only here in the USA, but in other parts of the world.

This book has pointed out the reasons for the wreckage caused by a defeatist doctrine and worldview. It is now each reader's responsibility to put all the pieces together, learn from earlier errors, and build anew toward a victorious future. Christ's omnipresent kingdom knows no bounds. May we all, as one, advance with it!

APPENDIX A

Who Are God's People?

⸻

The disobedient Israelites (Jews) were not God's people under the Old Covenant; neither are they God's people under the New Covenant Christ instituted on the cross with His shed blood.

God did not replace Israel with the Church. However, He did replace the Old Covenant with the New Covenant. Both the Old and New Covenants required faith and obedience to become a "son" of God—the same faith that resided in Abraham, the father of all the faithful.

The New Testament Church is not a different entity, organization, or group of people from Israel. All believers, whether they lived under the Law of Moses or live this side of Calvary, are part of the same body of people—those who believe in the one true God and live by His teachings.

The Church did not, as some mistakenly think, start with the New Testament on the day of Pentecost. God's Church, His "called out ones," has existed ever since *"Abel offered unto God a more excellent Sacrifice than Cain"* (Heb. 11:4). Enoch, who walked with God, was part of the Church of God (His one body of believers). Noah, who *"found grace in the eyes of the LORD"* (Gen. 6:8) was a member of God's Church. Abraham, Isaac, and Jacob were included within the Church of God. All Jacob's faithful descendants, including those under the care of Moses, were described as *"the church in the wilderness"* (Acts 7:38).

The Book of Romans, alluding to an olive tree, stresses that the body, the one people of God, comprises Jew and Gentile. The tree is the saving faith in the one true God. Unbelieving Jews were the branches that were broken off. Gentiles were once unbelievers in the one true God, but now, because of their faith in Christ, they are grafted into the tree of true faith and are one with those Jewish believers who lived under the Law of Moses. Likewise, through faith in Christ, Jewish believers became Christians. Today, as in the days of the early Church, unbelieving Jews can be brought into fellowship with God. They can be grafted into the olive tree with those who embrace Christ and live as Christians upholding the one true faith—the Church of God.

The Book of Ephesians states, whereas there was a distinction between Israel and the Gentiles, now, through Christ, God has made *"of twain one new man ... that he might reconcile both unto God in one body by the cross"* (Eph. 2:15–16). There has always been only one way to God—the path forged through faith and obedience. There has always been only one people of God—those who believe in and walk in obedience to Him. The following two illustrations, *One Faith - One Body - One People*, and the comparison of Scriptures adapted from Charles D. Provan's book *The Church Is Israel Now*, will bring that truth home in an eye-opening way.

ISRAEL/JEWS		CHRISTIANS/CHURCH
Israelites are the Chosen People	T	**Christians are the Chosen People**
Deut. 7:7, 10:15, 14:2; Isa. 43:20, 21	H	Eph. 1:4; Col. 3:12; I Pet. 2:9
Israel is the House of God	E	**Christians are the House of God**
Num. 12:7		I Tim. 3:15; Heb. 3:2, 5-6,
	C	10:21; I Pet. 4:17
Israel is Beloved of God	H	**Christians are Beloved of God**
Ex. 15:13; Deut. 33:12;	U	Rom. 9:25; Eph. 1:6; Col.
Isa. 5:1; Jer. 11:15	R	3:12; I John 3:2
Israelites are the Children of God	C	**Christians are the Children of God**
Ex. 4:22; Deut. 14:1; Isa. 1:2,	H	John 1:12, 11:52; Rom. 8:14,
4, 63:8; Jer. 31:9; Hos. 11:1		16; II Cor. 6:18; Gal. 3:26, 4:5-
	I	7; Phil. 2:15; I John 3:1
Israelites are the People of God	S	**Christians are the People of God**
Ex. 6:7; Deut. 27:9; II		Rom. 9:25; Eph. 4:12, 5:3; II Thess.
Sam. 7:23; Jer. 11:4	I	1:10; II Cor. 6:16; Titus 2:14
Israel is the Flock of God	S	**Christians are the Flock of God**
Ps. 77:20, 78:52, 80:1; Isa. 40:11;	R	John 10:14, 16; Heb. 13:20;
Jer.23:1-3, 31:10; Ezek. 34:12,15-		I Pet. 2:25, 5:2-3
16, 31; Mic.5:4; Zach. 10:3	A	
Israel is the Field of God	E	**Christians are the Field of God**
Jer. 12:10	L	I Cor. 3:9
Israel is the Kingdom of God		**Christians are the Kingdom of God**
Ex. 19:6; I Chron. 17:14, 28:5	N	Rom. 14:17; I Cor. 4:20;
	O	Col.1:13, 4:11; Rev. 1:6
Israel, the Priests of God	W	**Christians are the Priests of God**
Ex. 19:6		I Pet. 2:5, 9; Rev. 1:6, 5:10

Israel, the Wife/Bride of God		Christians are the Wife/ Bride of Christ
Isa. 54:5-6; Jer. 2:2, 31:32; Ezek. 16:22; Hos. 1:2	**T** **H** **E**	II Cor. 11:2; Eph. 5:31-32; Rev. 21:9
Israelites are the Children of Abraham	**C**	Christians are the Children of Abraham
II Chron. 20:7; Ps. 105:6; Isa. 41:8	**H** **U**	Rom. 4:11, 16; Gal. 3:7, 29, 4:23, 28, 31
New Covenant with Israel	**R**	New Covenant with Christians
Jer. 31:31, 33; Ezek. 11:19-20	**C**	Luke 22: 20; I Cor. 11:25; II Cor. 3:6; Heb. 8:6, 8, 10
Israel is an Olive Tree	**H**	Christians are the Olive Tree
Ps. 52:8; Jer. 11:16; Hos. 14:6		Rom. 11:24
Israel, the Circumcised	**I**	Christians are the Circumcised
Gen. 17:10; Judges 15:18; Rom. 4:9-12	**S**	Rom. 2:29; Phil. 3:3; Col. 2:11
Israel is the Vineyard of God	**I**	Christians are the Vineyard of God
Isa. 5:3-7; Jer. 12:10	**S**	Matt. 21:33-44; Luke 20:16
Jerusalem is the City & Mother of Israel	**R** **A**	Jerusalem is the City & Mother of Christians
Ps. 149:2; Isa. 12:6, 49:18,20,22, 51:18; Lam.4:2	**E** **L**	Gal. 4:26; Heb. 12:22
Israelites are Jews		Christians are Jews
Jer. 34:8-9; Zech. 8:22-23	**N**	Rom. 2:29; Phil. 3:3
Israel is Israel	**O**	Christians are Israel
Gen. 32:28	**W**	Eph. 2:11-16, 19; I Cor. 10:1; Gal.

ONE FAITH — ONE BODY — ONE PEOPLE

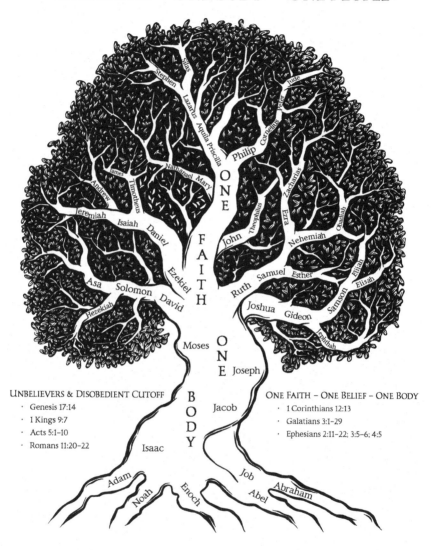

UNBELIEVERS & DISOBEDIENT CUTOFF
- Genesis 17:14
- 1 Kings 9:7
- Acts 5:1–10
- Romans 11:20–22

ONE FAITH – ONE BELIEF – ONE BODY
- 1 Corinthians 12:13
- Galatians 3:1–29
- Ephesians 2:11–22; 3:5–6; 4:5

APPENDIX B

A Tale of Two Eschatologies
By Bojidar Marinov | Published: May 26, 2010

———⸙———

Politically correct historical myths to the contrary, the myth of the efficiency of the German *Blitzkrieg* in WWII died not in the winter of 1942 in the plains west of Moscow but in the mild comfortable spring of 1940 in central Belgium, a few miles from the town of Gembloux. On May 12–14 there the French Cavalry Corps (the name for the French armor division) met two (the 3rd and the 4th) Panzer division in an open field. A relatively small force of only 239 French tanks without tactical air cover engaged 674 German Panzers supported by 500 tactical bombers and 500 Messerschmitt fighters. The French objective was simple: Slow down the German offensive until the French infantry divisions marching into Belgium take and fortify positions at the Gap of Gembloux, according to the Dyle Plan. The Dyle Plan turned out to be a strategic failure: It did not expect that the main force of the German invasion will attack through the Ardennes in the South to reach Sedan. That may have been the reason for the quick defeat of France.

But what happened at Gembloux wasn't expected at all by the German High Command. And it could have been France's chance.

Within several hours on May 12th, the French Cavalry Corps, vastly outnumbered and pounded from the air, was able to stop the German advance. Fewer than 100 French tanks were destroyed versus 160 German Panzers. The Germans soon discovered that their best tank, the Panzer IV, was no match for the French Somua S35. At the beginning of the war

311

S35 was in fact the best tank on all battlefields of the war, with superior armor and armament. The effective range of the German Panzers against the French was less than 200 meters, while a French S35 could destroy a Panzer III or IV at 600–700 meters. Besides, even from a very close distance the German guns couldn't produce more than a few dents in the strong armor of the Somua; by the end of the day on May 13 most of the surviving Somuas were hit 15–20 times, some more than 40 times, without any serious damage to the tanks or the crews. In the first all tank battle of the war, the German confidence in the Panzers was shattered badly.

The Panzers were stopped, and they had to wait for the arrival of the German infantry. Two days later, when the attack against the French positions at the Gap of Gembloux was launched, there were even more surprises for the Germans. The French infantry, far from being dispirited and unprepared, proved to be a serious obstacle to the German advance. Outnumbered three to one on the ground, and bombed around the clock from the air, the Moroccan Division held its ground for several more days. Of the attacking German regiments some were completely wiped out, most of the rest lost about 30% of their officers. So serious was the French victory that the Germans expected the French to move south and cut off the main German advance. The time the heroic French won at Gembloux allowed for the regrouping of the Belgian forces in the north, and the British Expeditionary Force in the rear. The significance of this French victory is underestimated today but at the time it was serious enough to make Hitler give orders to move his headquarters close to the front lines, something he would only do when he expected the war to last longer than expected.

We in America like to think of the French military as an ill-equipped, low-morale, incompetent, cowardly bunch. Such an assessment is very far from the truth. To the contrary, the French were excellent soldiers on the battlefield. Heinz Guderian who fought the French in two world wars, characterizes the French soldier as "tough and brave," and holds him in great esteem. At Gembloux, the soldiers and the officers of the Cavalry Corps and the Moroccan Division confirmed Guderian's assessment of them. In May 1940, despite the German successes in the first couple of weeks, the Germans were still very far from their victory.

It was the French government and the French General Staff that saved the day for the Germans. On that same May 13, while the Cavalry Corps were beating back the German advance, the mood in the French General Staff was "fear, tears, and panic," according to a witness. The French generals on that day were not debating how to organize their forces more effectively; they were discussing how to convince their own government to capitulate. In the next several days the French government – to a large degree influenced by the German propaganda communiqués – was entirely pessimistic of the outcome of the war. That pessimism spread, and soon Winston Churchill was giving his own generals orders to evacuate. The Netherlands, whose territory was only partially invaded – more than 80 per cent of the Dutch troops, those in Fortress Holland – never saw battle – capitulated after a few bombs dropped on Rotterdam. Belgium capitulated soon thereafter. Large numbers of British and French troops evacuated through Dunkirk. And the Germans were unopposed.

France, Belgium, and the Netherlands together had a population of 56 million. Together with Britain, they could have stopped the German invasion, and the history of the World War II would have been different. But they didn't.

The French leadership had an operational eschatology – expectations of the future – about the coming war. According to that eschatology, the last days of France would start when the Germans invade. Not much could be done, except for a few troops to escape through Dunkirk, and hopefully expect help from the United States, three and a half – or maybe four – years later.

That operational eschatology trumped the heroism and the skill of the French soldiers and officers. France, Belgium, and the Netherlands lost the war, and it brought unspeakable misery to whole populations for the next four years.

The best summary of the eschatology of the Swiss political and military leaders was given by a Swiss army captain to the Kaiser of Germany when the latter asked him what the quarter of a million Swiss citizens' militia would do if invaded by a half million German regular army.

"Shoot twice and go home," was the laconic reply of the highlander.

Both men knew what that meant. The German army at the time trained its soldiers to shoot at 100 meters. Any target practice beyond 100 meters was considered exceptional marksmanship. The Swiss routinely practiced at their shooting festivals at 300 meters, with their army rifles, which the Swiss men kept in their homes, clean and loaded and ready to use. In case of an attack, in order to take position to open fire, the German soldiers would have to cross the zone between 300 meters distance and 100 meters distance from the Swiss positions: enough time for the Swiss comfortably to shoot, reload, and shoot again. And go home. The Swiss knew their own strengths, and they couldn't be intimidated by the enemy's numbers. Any invader would be defeated, and that was as inevitable as the sunrise the next day.

That unshakable faith in their superiority, the optimism about the future of Switzerland was cultivated over the centuries after in 1291 representatives of the three mountain cantons Uri, Schweiz, and Unterwalden met on the Rütli Meadow to create the free confederation of people who refuse to live under any dictatorship. Since then, the Swiss peasants have invariably defeated much stronger armies of knights and professional soldiers sent against then. In remarkable feats of courage and tenacity, sometimes outnumbered 15 or 20 to one, the Swiss proved to the world that there was no way their land would fall in foreign hands. Over the years, tyrants and dictators learned the lesson: Don't touch Switzerland. The Kaiser's bluff was empty, and he knew it, and the Swiss captain knew it too. When the Great War started, all the participants – more populous than Switzerland – preferred to honor her neutrality.

The expectations of the future, the eschatology of the Swiss, were always positive, optimistic. The land was theirs, given by God, and they were obligated to dress it and keep it. It wasn't the most fertile land in the world, it didn't boast numberless resources, it had rugged mountains and precipices and narrow valleys . . . but it was theirs and theirs it would remain. For centuries Switzerland would remain the poorest of its neighbors because of the hardness of its terrain. As late as 1940, most Swiss citizens were living in much poorer conditions than their neighbors in France or Germany. But poor or not, they would remain free.

In 1940, after France fell to the Wehrmacht, the Chief Commander of the Swiss army, General Henri Guisan, assembled his officers on the same Rütli Meadow where 650 years earlier the Swiss Confederation was founded. His address told the Swiss officers what they already knew in their very being as Swiss citizens and soldiers: *Switzerland would never surrender*. In case of invasion, all announcements of surrender must be considered enemy propaganda, and every Swiss soldier must continue the fight to the last cartridge, and then use the bayonet.

In 1940 the whole population of the small Alpine republic numbered a little over 4 million, with an army of about 400,000, armed mainly with rifles and mountain artillery, and limited number of fighter planes. The Wehrmacht had 6.6 million men, thousands of heavy artillery, tanks, and tactical and strategic bombers in the air. Between 1939 and 1944 the German High Command developed six plans for invasion of Switzerland, that "stinking little state" as Josef Göbbels called it. Hitler never dared take action. He knew that unlike France, Poland, Czechoslovakia, Yugoslavia and others who believed in inevitable defeat, the Swiss believed in victory against all odds. Hitler knew that *you don't conquer a people who don't believe in being conquered.*

As a result, Switzerland remained an island of freedom during the war. Hundreds of thousands of Jews were saved, and hundreds of American pilots whose planes were shot over Germany. Hitler never got control of the mountain passes and this impeded the movement of German troops when Italy was invaded by the Allies. In France, the belief in inevitable defeat produced defeat; in Switzerland, the belief in inevitable victory kept evil at bay.

Like my friend Ben House says in his book, *Punic Wars and Culture Wars*, "Victory is often a matter of not having a culture of defeat."

In other words, eschatology matters.

* * * * * * *

For this article, I am grateful for the work of two men and great historians who worked hard and had the courage to bust modern politically correct myths in the name of preserving historical truth for the future generations: John Mosier (The Blitzkrieg Myth: How Hitler and the Allies Misread the Strategic Realities of World War II), and Stephen Halbrook (Target Switzerland: Swiss Armed Neutrality in World War II).

Author: Bojidar Marinov

Bojidar Marinov is a well-respected author who has written over

87 articles, generally focused on religious matters. In his capacity as a Reformed missionary, he has served his native Bulgaria for over 10 years. Bojidar preaches and teaches doctrines of the Reformation while promoting a comprehensive Biblical worldview. Having founded Bulgarian Reformation Ministries in 2001, he and his team have translated over 30,000 pages of Christian literature on the application of the Law of God in every area of society, and have published those translations online for free. Bojidar was a prime mover in the formation of the Libertarian movement in Bulgaria and is a co-founder and first chairman of the Bulgarian Society for Individual Liberty. If you would like Bojidar to speak at your church, homeschool group, or other organization, contact him through his email at:

info@bulgarianreformation.com.

Or

Bulgarian Reformation Ministries
P.O. Box 234
Willis, VA 24380
United States of America

APPENDIX C

What Difference Can One Person Make?
(William Carey)
Article by Dr. Peter Hammond from Frontline Fellowship.

———— ∞ ————

It's impossible! It can't be done! Don't be ridiculous – what difference can one person make? Have you ever encountered those kinds of reactions? Anyone who embarks on a challenging enterprise – especially those determined to end legal abortions, eradicate pornography, establish a Christian school or Christian Teacher Training College, stop the ongoing slave trade in Sudan or work for national Reformation and Revival – will encounter those people who seem to believe that they have "the gift of criticism" and "a ministry of discouragement!"

Should Christians be Involved in Politics?

Then of course there are those who maintain that Christians shouldn't even be involved in social issues at all! When you tell them of the abortion holocaust or the pornography plague they mutter that *"all we can do is pray"*, *"just preach the Gospel"* and *"it's a sign of the last days!"*

We often suspect that such attitudes are motivated more by laziness and cowardice or a selfish desire to shirk responsibility and hard work than anything else. Certainly those people who resort to such superficial excuses are being disobedient to the clear commands of Scripture: *"Love your neighbour as yourself"* (Luke 10:27); *"Go and do likewise"* (Luke 10:37); *"Speak up for those who cannot speak for themselves"* (Prov. 31:8); *"Rescue those being led away to death"* (Prov. 24:11); *"Make disciples of all nations"* (Matt 28:19); *"Anyone, then, who knows the good he ought to do and doesn't do it, sins"* (James 4:17).

Those who maintain that Christians shouldn't be involved in social or political issues display their ignorance of both the Bible and church history.

If you sometimes feel overwhelmed by the immensity of the task before you or discouraged by a seemingly never-ending series of obstacles and opposition, frustrations and failures – take heart! The man whom God used to launch the modern missionary movement faced all this and much, much more.

Launching a Reformation

Undereducated, underfunded and underestimated, William Carey seemed to have everything against him. He was brought up in abject poverty and never had the benefit of high school. Carey's formal education ended in junior school. Yet, at age 12 Carey taught himself Latin. Then he went on to master – on his own – Greek, Hebrew, French and Dutch! He became professor of Bengali, Sanskrit and Marathi at the prestigious Fort William College in Calcutta (where the civil servants were trained). Carey and his co-workers started over 100 Christian schools for over 8,000 Indian children of all castes and he launched the first Christian College in Asia – at Serampore, which continues to this day! Carey finally succeeded in translating the Bible into 6 languages and New Testaments and Gospels into 29 other languages!

Mission Impossible

Carey's achievements are all the more astounding when you consider that his bold project to plant the Gospel among the Hindus in India was completely illegal! By an act of the British Parliament it was illegal for any missionary to work in India. For the first 20 years, Carey's mission to India had to be carried out with ingenuity and circumspection, until at last the British Parliament – under pressure from evangelical Members of Parliament such as William Wilberforce – reversed its policy and compelled the British East India Company to allow missionaries in India.

Carey was considered a radical in his day. He boycotted sugar because he was so intensely opposed to slavery and sugar from the West Indies was produced with slave labour. Carey also took the extremely unpopular stand of supporting the American War of Independence against Britain.

He was also subjected to vicious criticism and gossip. Under the extreme heat and in abject poverty, initially with daily dangers from snakes, crocodiles and tigers in a remote and mosquito ridden jungle house, Carey's wife, Dorothy, went insane. She would rant and rave about the imaginary unfaithfulness of her husband and on several occasions attacked him with a knife. She was diagnosed insane and had to be physically restrained with chains for the last 12 years of her life. The Carey's also lost their 5-year-old son, Peter, who died of dysentery in 1794. Every family member suffered from malaria, dysentery and other tropical diseases – frequently.

Carey's first co-worker squandered all their money and bankrupted the mission forcing William to work on a plantation to provide for his malnourished family. In their first seven months in India the Careys had to move home five times! And although Carey wrote home, to family and mission society, frequently – it was 17 months before they received their first letters! One of these first letters from the Society criticized Carey for being "swallowed up in the pursuits of a merchant!"

Somehow, while often sick, holding down a full time secular job surrounded by domestic turmoil, with an insane wife screaming from the next room, Carey mastered Bengali and Sanskrit and by 1797 the New Testament was translated into Bengali and ready for printing. Carey had also established several schools and was preaching regularly in Bengali. However, after seven years of tireless toil in India Carey still did not have a single convert!

How did William Carey manage to maintain such a productive schedule while having to endure all these crushing disappointments, the endless distractions, the undeserved criticisms, the physical ailments and the heartbreaking tragedies? How did he manage to persevere and to keep on keeping on without even the encouragement of a single convert to justify all his effort and sacrifice? To understand what motivated this most remarkable man we need to look back at what inspired him in the first place.

One of the most influential sermons in world history was preached on 31 May 1792 by William Carey in Northampton, England. Carey's sermon literally sparked the greatest century of Christian advance. It marked the entry of the English-speaking world into missions. Since that time English speakers have made up 80% of the Protestant missionary work force.

The text of this historic sermon was Isaiah 54:2–3:

"Enlarge the place of your tent and let them stretch out the curtains of your dwellings. Do not spare, lengthen your cords and strengthen your stakes! For you shall expand to the right and to the left and your descendants will inherit the nations, and make desolate cities inhabited."

The theme of his sermon was summarized as:

"Expect great things from God! Attempt great things for God!"

Yet, riveting as the sermon was, the result was initially indecision. Carey was considered *"an enthusiast"* (a fanatic) and an embarrassment – because *"he had a bee in his bonnet about missions."* But Carey persisted until, five months later, 12 Reformed Baptist ministers formed the *"Particular (Calvinist) Baptist Society for Propagating the Gospel among the Heathens."*

What inspired Carey's landmark book *"An Enquiry into the Obligation of Christians to use Means for the Conversion of the Heathens"* and this prototype pioneer missionary society was his eschatology of victory. William Carey was a Post-millennialist who believed that God who commanded His Church to "make disciples of all nations" would ensure that the Great Commission would ultimately be fulfilled.

"The work, to which God has set His hands, will infallibly prosper . . . We only want men and money to fill this country with the knowledge of Christ. We are neither working at uncertainty nor afraid for the result . . . He must reign until Satan has not an inch of territory!"

Time and again, in the face of crushing defeats, disappointments, diseases and disasters, Carey reiterated his unwavering optimistic eschatology:

"Though the superstitions of the heathen were a thousand times stronger than they are, and the example of the Europeans a thousand times worse; though I were deserted by all and persecuted by all, yet my faith, fixed on that sure Word, would rise above all obstructions and overcome every trial. God's cause will triumph!"

And Carey's faith was most certainly vindicated. The years of hard work and wholehearted sacrifice were graciously rewarded by God. Carey's ministry literally transformed India.

Transforming a Nation

When Carey stepped ashore at Calcutta in 1793, India was in a terribly degraded state. If an infant was sick, it was assumed that he was under the influence of an evil spirit. The custom was to expose sick infants to the elements – perhaps hanging them up in a basket. Near Malda Carey found the remains of a baby that had been offered as a sacrifice to be eaten alive by white ants. At the Sagar Mela where the Ganges River flows into the sea, Carey witnessed how mothers threw their babies into the sea to drown, or to be devoured by crocodiles. This the Hindus regarded as a holy sacrifice to the Mother Ganges!

Carey undertook a thorough research into the numbers, nature and reasons for the infanticide and published his reports. He presented several petitions to the government until, in 1802, infanticide was outlawed. This marked the first time that the British government interfered directly with religious practice in India. It set a precedent for the abolition of other practices.

Hinduism had an extremely low view of women. It was often stated *"In Hinduism there is no salvation for women until she be reborn a man."* Her only hope lay in serving men in complete subjection. Many female babies were smothered at birth. Girls were married as young as 4 years old! Widows were perceived as bad omens who had brought about the deaths of their husbands. Widows were also seen as an economic liability. Bereaved widows had to shave off all their hair, remove all jewellery and were forbidden to remarry – but were required to cohabit (niyogo) with her deceased husband's nearest male relative. Tremendous pressure was exerted on the widow to submit to Sati or immolation – to be burned alive on the funeral pyre of her husband. Amongst the Weaver (Kories) caste, widows were buried alive.

So, because of the Hindu practice of Sati, children who had lost their father would also lose their mother and be orphaned at the same time.

The Hindu practice of polygamy compounded the problem. On one occasion Carey documented 33 wives of one man burned alive at his funeral. On another occasion an 11-year-old widow was burned on the funeral pyre of her husband!

Lepers were rejected by their families and society and burned alive. Hinduism taught that only a violent and fiery end could purify the body and ensure transmitigation into a healthy new existence. Euthanasia was also widely practiced with those afflicted by other sicknesses. The infirmed were regularly carried out to be left exposed to cold and heat, crocodiles or insects, by the riverside.

Carey fought against these and many other evils – including child prostitution, slavery and the caste system. He publicly criticized the government for inaction and passivity in the face of murder. He organized public debates and spoke out and wrote often on these atrocities. At first he met with official indifference. The Indian Supreme Court in 1805 ruled that Sati had religious sanction and could not be questioned.

A Pioneer for Freedom

Carey established the first newspaper ever printed in an oriental language, the Samachar Darpan and the English language newspaper Friends of India. Carey pioneered mass communications in India, launching the social reform movement, because he believed that *"Above all forms of truth and faith, Christianity seeks free discussion,"*

Carey was the first man to stand up against the brutal murders and widespread oppression of women through female infanticide, child marriage, polygamy, enforced female illiteracy, widow burning and forced euthanasia. He conducted systematic research and published his writings to raise public protest in both Bengal and England. He educated and influenced a whole generation of civil servants through his lectures at Fort

William College. Carey fought against the idea that a woman's life ceases to be valuable after her husband's death. He undermined the oppression and exploitation of women by providing women with education. He opened the first schools for girls.

It was Carey's relentless battle against *Sati* – for 25 years – which finally led to the famous Edict in 1829 banning widow burning.

Carey was also the first man who led the campaign for a humane treatment for leprosy and ended the practice of burning them alive.

Carey certainly had a comprehensive view of the Great Commission. He ministered to body, mind and spirit. Carey introduced the idea of Savings Banks to India and made investment, industry, commerce and economic development possible. He founded the Agric – Horticultural Society in the 1820's (30 years before the Royal Agricultural Society was established in England). He introduced the steam engine to India. He pioneered the idea of lending libraries in India. He persuaded his friends in England to ship out tons of books to regenerate and reform India.

Carey also introduced the study of Astronomy into India. He saw that the prevalent astrology with its fatalism, superstitious fears and inability to manage time had terribly destructive consequences. Hinduism's astrology makes us subjects – with our lives determined by the stars. However, the Christian science of astronomy sets us free to be rulers – to devise calendars, identify directions, to study geography and to better plan our lives and work.

Carey was the first man in India to write essays on forestry. Fifty years before the government made its first attempts at forest conservation, Carey was already practicing conservation, planting and cultivating timber. He understood that God had made man responsible for the earth. Carey was also a botanist who cultivated beautiful gardens and frequently lectured on science, because he believed *"all Thy works praise Thee, O Lord."* He knew that nature is worthy of study. Carey pointed out that even the insects are worthy of attention – they are not souls in bondage but creatures with a God given purpose.

William Carey was also the father of print technology in India. He introduced the modern science of printing, built what was then the largest printing press in India and devised the fonts. In 1812 a devastating fire destroyed Carey's warehouse with his printing presses, paper stock and manuscripts representing many years of work. Even in the face of this catastrophe Carey praised God that no lives had been lost and quoted Psalm 46: *"Be still and know that the Lord is God."* He resolved to do better translations than the ones that were now ashes and consoled himself *"Every branch that beareth fruit, He purgeth it, that it may bring forth more fruit."*

"However vexing it may be, a road the second time traveled is usually taken with more confidence and ease than at the first," declared Carey, He quoted Isaiah 61:1–4 and trusted God for better printing presses and more accurate translations – a "phoenix rising out of the ashes."

Not only was Carey hit by the fire, but deaths in each of the seven missionary families at Serampore. Carey himself had just buried a grandson. Carey also had to endure unjust and unbalanced criticisms from young new missionaries who actually split from the Serampore Mission; and slanderous accusations from the Mission Society in England, as well as an earthquake and a flood. One of his sons Felix, also caused much embarrassment when he backslid, adopted a lavish lifestyle and began drinking heavily. Ultimately Felix came back to the Lord and became fully committed to the mission.

Yet, despite the controversies, calamities and conflicts, William Carey's monumental achievements outshine all his critics. He was a dedicated Christian whom God used in extraordinary ways to launch the greatest century of missionary advance, to translate the Scriptures into more languages than any other translator in history and to save literally millions of lives by his compassionate social action and tireless labours.

We need to follow his example by ministering to body, mind and spirit and persevering through all disappointments and opposition with an unshakeable faith in God's sovereign power.

Dr. Peter Hammond

Dr. Peter Hammond is the Founder and Director of *Frontline Fellowship* and cofounder of over 100 Christian schools and Bible Colleges throughout war-torn Africa. He is the author of many influential books and articles.

Frontline Fellowship is a Bible-based African mission that has pioneered ministerial work in many isolated areas notably resistant to the Gospel.

Since 1982, Frontline missionaries have travelled hundreds of thousands of kilometers by foot, motorbike, dugout canoe, car, truck, and aircraft to boldly proclaim the Gospel of repentance and everlasting faith in Christ to soldiers, guerrillas, resistance fighters, and civilians on all sides of Africa's many conflicts.

Dr. Hammond has carried out over 100 missions in dangerous war zones and presented over 12,000 sermons, Bible studies, and lectures in 33 countries. In the course of their missionary activities Frontline missionaries have been ambushed, come under artillery bombardment, been stabbed, shot at, beaten by mobs, arrested, and imprisoned. The Frontline mission base and high school in Sudan repeatedly came under aerial bombardment by the Sudan Air Force (10 times in 18 months). Over the years, 20 missionaries from Frontline Fellowship have been imprisoned in Marxist or Muslim countries. Yet, by the grace of God, every Frontline missionary was freed in response to persistent prayer and pressure (Luke 18:1–5).

Frontline Fellowship
P.O. Box 74
Newlands 7725
Cape Town
South Africa
admin@frontline.org.za
www.frontline.org.za

Frontline Fellowship USA
P.O. Box 728
Manitou Springs
CO 80829
Tel: 719-685-2899
Fax: 719-685-9330
Web:www.frontlinefellowship.net

Email: info@frontlinefellowship.net

APPENDIX D

9.5 Theses for the Next Reformation

———— ∞∞∞ ————

We the undersigned, out of love for the truth and a desire to see all Christians honor and acknowledge all that God has revealed in his Word, submit these 9.5 Theses for your prayerful evaluation and participation with us in calling for further reform. May these theses be the spark that ignites the next Reformation of Christianity.

1. ***Everything*** Jesus said would happen ***happened*** exactly ***as*** and ***when*** He said it would—within the lifetime of his contemporaries.

2. ***Everything*** every New Testament writer expected to happen ***happened*** exactly ***as*** and ***when*** they expected it would—within their lifetimes—as they were guided into all truth and told the things that were to come by the Holy Spirit (Jn. 16:13).

3. Scholars across a broad spectrum are in general agreement that this is ***exactly how*** every NT writer and the early Church ***understood*** Jesus's words. If they were wrong on something this important, how can we trust them to have conveyed other aspects of the faith accurately, such as the requirements for salvation?

4. ***No*** inspired NT writer, writing twenty or more years later, ***ever corrected*** their Holy Spirit-guided understanding and fulfillment expectations (Jn. 16:13). Neither should we. Instead, they intensified their language as the "appointed time of the end" (Dan.12:4; Hab. 2:3) drew near—from Jesus's "this generation" (Mat. 24:34) to Peter's "the end of all things is at hand" and "for

it is time for judgment to begin" (1 Pet. 4:7, 17) to John's "this is the last hour . . . it is the last hour" (1 Jn. 2:18).

5. Partial fulfillment is *not satisfactory*. 3 out of 5, 7 out of 10, etc., won't work. Partial does not pass the test of a true prophet (Deut. 18:18–22). Again, Jesus time-restricted *all* of his end-time predictions to occur within the 1st-century time frame.

6. God is faithful (2 Pet. 3:9) and "not a man that he should lie" (Num. 23:19). Faithfulness means not only doing *what* was promised, but also doing it *when* it was promised.

7. First century fulfillment expectations were the *correct ones* and everything happened, right on time—no gaps, no gimmicks, no interruptions, no postponements, no delays, no exegetical gymnastics, and no changing the meaning of commonly used and normally understood words. Such manipulative devices have only given liberals and skeptics a foothold to discredit Christ's Deity and the inerrancy of Scripture.

8. What needs adjusting is our understanding of both the *time* and *nature* of fulfillment, not manipulation of the time factor to conform to our popular, futuristic, and delay expectations.

9. The *Kingdom of God* was the *central teaching* of our Lord Jesus Christ; it is a present but greatly under-realized reality, and must again become the central teaching of his Church.

9.5. We have been guilty of proclaiming a *half-truth*—a partially delivered faith to the world and to fellow Christians. We must repent and earnestly "contend for the faith that was once for all delivered to the saints" (Jude 3). If Christianity has been as effective as it has by proclaiming that Jesus Christ, the Messiah, came, died for our sins, bodily arose from the dead, and ascended to Heaven "at just the right time" (Rom. 5:6; Dan. 9:24–27), how much more effective might it be if we started preaching, teaching, and practicing the *whole truth*—i.e., a faith in which everything else also happened "at just the right time," exactly *as* and *when* Jesus said it would and every NT writer expected (Jn. 16:13). Dare we continue to settle for less? Surely today, the words of Martin Luther, as he stood in defense before the Diet of Worms in 1521, are still applicable and compelling for the "always reforming" Church:

"Unless I am convinced by the testimony of the Scriptures or by clear reason (for I do not trust either in the pope or in councils alone, since it is well known that they have often erred and contradicted themselves), I am bound by the Scriptures . . . and my conscience is captive to the Word of God . . . I cannot do otherwise."

* Based on Martin Luther's famous "95 Theses" that were posted on the door of the Castle Church in Wittenberg, Germany on October 31, 1517. Luther's document empowered and propelled the Protestant Reformation.

Published by the Prophecy Reformation Institute: a conservative, evangelical ministry dedicated to continuing the Reformation into the field of eschatology-end-time Bible prophecy, and the International Preterist Association.

John Noē
Prophecy Reformation Institute
5236 E 72nd St.
Indianapolis, IN 46250
E-mail: jnoe@prophecyrefi.org
Ph.# 317-842-3411

Edward E. Stevens
International Preterist Association
122 Seaward Ave.
Bradford, PA 16701
E-mail: Preterist1@aol.com
Ph.# 1-814-368-6578
Fax# 1-814-368-6030

What others are saying:

I look forward to your publication of *Israel*–it's audacious, thought-provoking, and genuinely deserving of a wide readership.

– Freelance editor Bruce Victor Zatkow

A must read for any Person who wants a closer walk with God/Yahuah! The majority of Christians today, have been blinded, & or deceived, into a non-Biblical way of looking into the near future for Scriptural things that have long past. This book gives Scriptural proof, that is relevant & a blessing to all who dare to read.

– Johnny E. Lester

Printed in the United States
by Baker & Taylor Publisher Services